Distressed
SECURITIES

Analyzing and
Evaluating Market
Potential and
Investment Risk

Distressed SECURITIES

Analyzing and Evaluating Market Potential and Investment Risk

By Edward I. Altman

BeardBooks

Washington, DC

Library of Congress Cataloging-in-Publication Data

Altman, Edward I., 1941–
   Distressed securities : analyzing and evaluating market potential
and investment risk / Edward I. Altman.
      p.   cm.
   Originally published: Chicago, Ill. : Probus Pub. Co., 1991.
   Includes bibliographical references and index.
   ISBN 1-893122-04-2 (pbk.)
   1. Securities—United States.   2. Investments—United States.
I. Title
HG4910.A67   1999
332.63'2—dc21   99-12364
                                      CIP

Printed in the United States of America

Contents

5 The Market for Defaulted Private Trade and Bank Debt   37

6 The Performance of Distressed Securities   55

7 An Index of Defaulted Straight Debt Securities   83

Preface

In today's uncertain, vulnerable and volatile business climate, the market for distressed companies' debt and equity securities has captured the interest and imagination of the investment, legal, banking and advisory communities like never before. Record numbers of bond defaults and Chapter 11 bankruptcy filings provide a continuing supply of highly distressed securities, and investors are awakening in large numbers to this new "growth" area.

Once an esoteric and unpopular sector of financial investments and markets, the distressed and defaulted debt securities "market" has grown to an approximate size of $350 billion at the end of 1990. The $350 billion number includes both public and privately placed debt that has either defaulted or is selling at such distressed levels so as to be considered part of the new arena.

Parallel growth and interest has exploded in the bankruptcy legal community with scores of lawyers forming bankruptcy and restructuring groups at major law firms. Investment banking restructuring units are taking up some of the slack created by the demise of the mergers and acquisitions business and the new issue "junk bond" business. The latter has been reduced to a trickle in 1990. Specialized consulting and advisory firms and divisions have been formed to service management of distressed firms, attempting to salvage any productive assets. Since a good deal of the large firm defaults have been caused by the leverage excesses of the late 1980s, the likelihood that tangible assets remain under the smothering burden of huge layers of debt is high. In the last two years alone, about 20 firms with liabilities of at least $1 billion have filed for protection under the Bankruptcy Code.

This book attempts to analyze the "new" market for distressed securities. I will draw upon the experience of a relatively small number of astute investors over several decades. Indeed, one of the most astute of this "old bunch" was the late Max L. Heine, a man whom I knew and respected and whose friends and relatives endowed a chair in his name at the Stern School of Business at New York University. I am proud to be associated with Max Heine's legacy.

The impetus for the research that went into writing this book came from my own research interests in the bankruptcy areas spanning over two decades and the generous support and encouragement of the Foothill Group of Los Angeles, California. I would like to thank that organization, especially Donald Gevirtz, John C. Nickoll and Karen Sandler for their wonderful support and for sponsoring the original Altman/Foothill report, completed in April 1990. This book builds on the findings of that report.

I would also like to thank the many investors who assisted my efforts by supplying data and completing a questionnaire that was used to document the distressed investor profile. A list of these respondents can be found in Appendix B. In addition, the folks at Merrill Lynch Capital markets, particularly Brian Barefoot and Martin Fridson, have provided me with a continuing access to real-world problems and issues.

Finally, to the assistants and typists at the Stern School of Business, NYU, who worked many, many hours providing me with the necessary data to carry out this work. Empiricists are at the mercy of capable assistants, and the talents of David Chin, Thierry Genoyer, Thomas Ng, Eric Katzman and Robert Kissel were indispensable. The work of Eric Katzman and Thierry Genoyer on the Defaulted Debt Index (Chapter 7) was particularly helpful, as was the research by John Beiter on trade debt (Chapter 5). Gina de Simone and Lourdes Tanglao round out the group at NYU who helped to put my writings into readable form.

Having written about bankruptcy and corporate distress for many years, I am constantly amazed at the richness of the issues and materials waiting to be analyzed. I hope that this book can assist in that analysis in some small way and stimulate future work.

Edward I. Altman
Max L. Heine Professor of Finance
Stern School of Business, NYU

Background of the Distressed Securities Market and Summary of Major Findings

The purpose of this book is to document and analyze the unique asset class of distressed debt and equity securities. We refer to distressed securities as a market and as an asset class. These labels, however, are premature due to the field's developing condition and the fact that there has been a lack of rigorous research. It is a securities market of problem firms that affords opportunities if their problems are resolved and if current prices are over discounted. A descriptive anatomy of the major characteristics, participants and an analytical treatment of the market's pricing dynamics and performance attributes will be addressed. This market has captured the interest and imagination of the investment community. The diversity of bankrupt and near bankrupt companies and the perceived sizeable upside potential of securities selling at deeply discounted prices fueled this interest. Investors consider this area one of the growth opportunities of the 1990s. In addition, analysts, lawyers, traders, and researchers are finding the distressed securities "market" one of the few "boom" areas in the 1990s.

Size of the Market

Distressed securities can be narrowly defined as publicly held debt or equity of firms defaulting on their debt obligations or filing for protection under Chapter 11 of the Bankruptcy Code. An estimate of these securities market value in the beginning of 1990 was approximately $13 billion ($11.5 billion in debt). These comprised 178 different issuing firms. Estimates as of June 1, 1990 increased the market value to about $13.2 billion, with a book value of $29.5 billion. And, during the period June–November 1990, an additional $00 billions (book value) of publicly traded debt securities defaulted.

A more comprehensive definition would include those publicly held debt securities selling at sufficiently discounted prices, yielding a minimum of 10 percent over comparable maturity U.S. Treasury bonds (about 18.6 percent in 1990). This amount is estimated to be slightly above $50 billion in par value. Using this more liberal definition, at least $80 billion in par value of distressed and defaulted securities are outstanding. They are made up of several hundred issuers with over 600 issues. These public defaulted and distressed securities have a probable market value of $45 billion. If one also added the private debt with public registration rights, bank debt and trade claims, the relevant population for investor consideration increases substantially. Private defaulted claims add about another $90 billion in book value. An additional $150 billion in distressed debt brings this total book value of defaulted and distressed securities and claims to about $320 billion. The market value, both public and private, was estimated to be about $210 billion. Estimates for the end of 1990 put the entire market at over $350 billion (book value).

We will analyze the performance attributes of investing in distressed securities following a descriptive and analytical treatment of investors and current developments. Our focus will be on the performance of debt securities. We also will use information derived from a survey. It was sent to about 80 investors in distressed securities. Our response rate was excellent, with 56 returns. Insights into the size and age of these entities, their investment focus, required and minimum rates of return criteria, and their outlook for opportunities in this area were ascertained.

Supply of Distressed Securities

Over the last 20 years, the American bankrupt company profile has been transformed. Once a small, undercapitalized distressed firm, it now increasingly involves large enterprises with complex asset and liability structures. Penn Central, Dolly Madison and other large companies filing for bankruptcy protection made 1970 a watershed year. There have been more than 100 enterprises, with over $120 million in liabilities, that have filed for bankruptcy in the last twenty years. In the 1970s we increasingly experienced sizeable business reversals. The severe inflationary-recession in the early 1980s caused a consistent increase of failures. Included were manufacturers, airlines, farmers and service firms of all types followed by the energy industry collapse. The *Dun & Bradstreet* failure rate rose to a high of 120 per 10,000 in 1986. Although we experienced numerous years of positive expansion in the GNP in the 1980s, that same period has seen an increased vulnerability to firms of all sizes. This is due to severe and chronic problems across a number of industry categories, slow response to global market demands by established firms, and a record number of new company startups. Technological advances have lowered costs of products and services by those who utilize them. Finally, deregulation has increased competition and leverage excesses have weakened corporate structures.

The investment market in distressed debt and equity securities has been growing dramatically. There was an outstanding market value of defaulted securities of $13 billion as of February 1990 and over $16 billion as of the end of 1990. This compares with $4 billion in market value in 1984. The supply of defaulted debt has been swelled (about $40 billion par value of publicly traded straight debt) in the past five years. Defaulted debt was $7.9 billion in 1989 and over $16.0 billion in the first eleven months of 1990. Several billion dollars of defaulted convertible debt and equities add to the total. The par-value of such issues has increased substantially. The near-term looks for even greater "growth."

Tempering this market value increase is the noticeable reduction in recovery rates on the sale of debt just after default. This is especially true amongst the senior subordinated and subordinated debt issues. Recovery decline on recent defaults of junior debt is probably due to the increased layers of debt. There is also a general increase in the amount of indebtedness compared to asset values.

For several decades there has been investor curiosity and interest in bankrupt securities. Media stories of huge gains (e.g., bankrupt railroads,

REIT securities and Toys-R-Us) have fueled this attention. Besides the interest caused by sizeable increases in this market, some emphasis is being given to deeply discounted but not yet defaulted debt issues. Even more intriguing is the attention given to bank and trade debt claims of defaulted companies. Often, these issues have significant intrinsic value and profit potential.

To estimate the ratio of private to public debt, we have examined the capital structures of 103 bankrupt firms. The ratio was just under four to one for the entire sample and a bit over three to one for those firms (68) that had public debt outstanding. Amongst the large LBO defaults and those expected to fail in the next few years, the ratio of bank debt to public debt is about 1.5 to 1. This suggests that these defaults were caused mainly by leverage excesses. They relied on public debt to a greater extent than did the traditional business failures of the 1970s to mid 1980s. With several layers of senior and subordinated debt, the default recovery rates on the most junior issues have declined—i.e., prices just after default have fallen.

Distressed Security Investor Profile

New investors' capital have been attracted by distressed securities and the likely continued growth in the size of this "market." Our survey results show there was (in late 1989) at least $5 billion under active management by investment firms dedicated to the distressed securities field. Assorted other investors also trade these securities, many times involuntarily. The majority of the responding companies indicated their commitment to distressed securities investing was between $20 and $100 million. Many of these institutions are specialized groups of larger money management firms. While 12 invested less than $20 million, 13 are investing $100–300 million. There were just two with over $300 million dedicated to this area. Since the start of 1990, however, at least three additional investment firms have been formed, each with over $200 million in capital dedicated to distressed companies. A fairly complete list of investors is available in Appendix A. The actual questionnaire is contained in Appendix B. These were the primary respondents to our survey as discussed in Chapters 3, 6, and 10.

The investors represent many types of organizations. These include private partnerships (the most common type), open-end mutual funds, closed-end funds, special groups within larger fund operations and broker-dealer pools of funds. Departments of commercial and investment banks, arbitrageurs and other firms are also looking to take over distressed companies at bargain prices. There are always funds available from other investment vehicles that can be shifted to distressed securities purchases when opportunities present themselves. Some LBO funds now seek out other vehicles as the highly leveraged restructuring movement is reduced in scope and relegated to smaller, privately financed deals. In early 1990 a new crop of "White Squire" investors have raised sizeable amounts of investment funds to participate in and, sometimes, precipitate corporate restructurings.

These investors are serviced by firms specializing in bankrupt security analysis (Appendix C). Increasingly, the distressed firms themselves are working with the restructuring departments of large securities firms and boutique operations (Appendix D). Several specialized publications have emerged in the last three years to report and comment on bankruptcies and the related securities.

Most distressed investors specialize in debt securities, rather than equity, placing between 85 and 100 percent of their assets in them. Often, the initial debt purchase evolves into an equity interest in the firm after reorganization. A list of Trade Debt purchasers, discussed in Chapter 5, is given in Appendix G.

Investors have become more active while also continuing to operate under the traditional passive investment strategy. This indicates that they are inclined to seek either control of the restructuring process or the company itself. An example of this is the newly formed Japonica Partners, which acquired control of the bankrupt Allegheny-International Corporation. This movement toward active investing is one of the emerging trends. A creditor-owner pre-packaged Chapter 11 (e.g., Resorts International, Trump Taj Mahal, and Coleco Industries) is a different example of this active strategy.

A number of investment firms are beginners in this field. New entities with inexperienced portfolio managers are troubling to some investors. Of 56 respondents, 8 were in business for less than 1 year and 19 for less than 2 years. Most of the newer portfolio managers had considerable experience, however, with established institutions before entering these companies. There are 22 firms who have been in business more than 5 years; 7 of these more than 20 years.

Anyone who has analyzed the distressed security market concludes that this is not a market for amateurs. It is necessary to earn extraordinary returns in order to attract new investment dollars. The risky nature, the relatively poor liquidity and the necessary costly skills lead to the high required rates of return. We queried our sample on their rates of return. As expected, the target rates of return were, on average, higher than the minimum. Many respondents gave identical answers to the questions. The most common response was a target return of 30 percent and a minimum return of 20–25 percent. One-third had a 30-percent target return while the other two-thirds split evenly below and above 30 percent. Two-thirds of the investors required a minimum return of 20 or 25 percent. The remainder sought higher returns.

Returns on Distressed Securities Investment Strategies

There has been an impressive increase in the market's size and diversity. The major interest has developed from the reports of attractive returns earned by a small number of astute investors. Successful investing formulas will continue to require a difficult set of fundamental valuation and technical legal-economic skills. It demands a patient and disciplined approach to asset management. These basics are also important in the less efficient private bank and trade debt markets. Negotiating skills also will be rewarded. Extraordinary gains over relevant alternative investments can be earned by careful credit and asset valuation strategies. Concentration should be on firms where the probability of successful reorganization is high.

Bankrupt equity studies have shown that returns were exceptionally high from firms successfully reorganized. The overall return was about equal to the relevant equity opportunity costs. Often, the equity is wiped-out when the old creditors become the new equity holders. Sample variability of these equity returns was extremely high.

Our new tests concentrated on distressed, not defaulted, debt. Distressed is defined as a security with a current yield of 10 percent above comparable U.S. Treasury bonds. Over an 11-year sample period (1978–1989), 310 issues so qualified. Over one-half of these eventually defaulted. The key to successful investing is to avoid as many defaults as possible or to invest in those that do default but are successfully reorganized. A "blind" naive strategy of investing in all distressed bonds yields very poor returns. Avoiding the minefield brings substantial reward. If one avoided all defaults, returns averaged over 90 percent for the three-year post-distress period.

When we used the ZETA® credit evaluation system (Hoboken, N.J.), the results were impressive, revealing positive absolute and relative returns. These tests show that a prudent credit approach can be successfully used in distressed securities. Techniques like ZETA® can be combined with other security selection approaches. These include in-depth financial and legal analysis.

We also constructed an index using a market weighted basis. It was based on an initial sample of 43 defaulted debt securities in January 1987 and increased to 118 in late 1989, then to 128 in May 1990. Investors in this market index received a compound annual return of 10 percent per year over the period 1987-1990 (July), despite very poor years in 1989 and 1990. This was about equal to our respondents' most frequent answer regarding required rates of return on investments in these securities. Within this four-year period, the large issues did considerably worse than the small ones.

The distressed securities index had relatively low correlations with other debt and equity returns indices. Investors who combine distressed security investing with other asset classes have attractive diversification choices.

While no data exists for investment returns on private debt and trade claims, it is reasonable to suppose that even higher returns are possible because the market is less efficient than in the public security arena.

Our analysis includes a segment of the junk bond market that has received virtually no attention in literature. I refer to the so-called "fallen angel" market. These are publicly traded bonds originally issued with the rating agencies' "seal of approval" (i.e., one of the top four ratings). Then they have fallen from the credit community's graces becoming non-investment-grade "junk" bonds.

This fallen angel research analyzes the pre- and post-downrating performance of those bonds during the period 1984-1988. "Fallen angels" are examined as a class of debt. Additionally, they are separated into event risk vs. credit deterioration downgrades, utility vs. non-utility bonds and those that fall to BB vs. B-rated debt. We also examine the change in price involved with dramatic restructurings (i.e., event risk situations) for the period of the downrating.

The results show that fallen angels represent a decreasing but sizeable proportion of the junk bond market. For periods of up to two years after the downrating, fallen angels total performance is similar to that of high-yield junk bonds. We found that utilities outperformed non-utilities. The latter perform significantly worse than junk bonds for the two-year period. For shorter post-downrating periods of up to one-year, there appears to be significant negative performance of fallen angels in general.

Bonds falling to BB significantly outperform those falling to B. Finally, we do not find much evidence of bond price decreases in event risk financial restructurings for the six-month period before the downrating.

Market Importance and Outlook

The bankruptcy-reorganization system in the United States is a unique process. It affords rehabilitative opportunities to distressed, yet productive, entities. The market for distressed firm securities reflects this process and, in a sense, monitors the system's performance. Continuous feedback about the distressed company's progress actually facilitates the allocation of new capital to the most promising assets. Investors operate in their own best interest and unwittingly contribute to this process.

The future outlook is mixed in the short run. The supply of new opportunities will likely exceed the amount of new capital allocated to distressed issues. This supply-demand situation has contributed to the recent softening of prices. Some investors have the impression that the number of promising new reorganizations is small and too much money is chasing these situations. This phenomenon may exist for a time, but the vast majority of our respondents expressed optimistic enthusiasm about profit potential in the future. In addition, the private bank and trade debt claims market promises excellent prospects. The key, as always, is to be able to select the successful reorganizations and undervalued securities.

## 2

Supply of Distressed Securities

One dramatic change in the fixed income debt markets is the enormous increase of distressed securities. These securities include those companies that have filed for protection under Chapter 11 of the Bankruptcy Code, have defaulted on interest payments, were involved in a distressed exchange issue, or are selling at a significant yield spread (e.g., 10 percent over U.S. Treasury bonds). These definitions can be overlapping.

In mid-1990, the market value of defaulted debt and equity securities was tabulated at $13.2 billion, with about 90 percent comprised of debt (Exhibit 2.1). This was up from a $12.8 billion total just four months earlier (Exhibit 2.2). The par value of these securities as of June 1, 1990, was $29.5 billion and over $40 billion as of December 1990.

The market value of distressed debt was estimated at about $50 billion. These securities were selling at a yield-to-maturity (YTM) of 10 percent above comparable U.S. Treasury securities, about 18.6 percent as of June 1, 1990. The market value is near $33 billion, i.e., selling at approximately 66 percent of par value. The market value of both defaulted and distressed securities was about $45 billion with an $80 billion par value (Exhibit 2.3).

The analysis of private distressed and defaulted markets is discussed in this chapter. These estimates are less precise than actual tabu-

Exhibit 2.1

Market Value of Securities
Companies in Chapter 11 Reorganization and in Default*
June 1, 1990

AMEX

Bonds	$3,153,814,000
Convertible Bonds	$0
Common Stock	$257,650,313
Preferred Stock	$0
Warrants	$892,125
Total	$3,412,356,438

NASDAQ

Bonds	$5,501,783,250
Convertible Bonds	$0
Common Stock	$245,849,063
Preferred Stock	$0
Total	$5,747,632,313

NYSE

Bonds	$2,631,317,7 75
Convertible Bonds	$64,844,938
Common Stock	$2,147,773,719
Preferred Stock	$337,302,875
Warrants	$42,862,500
Total	$5,224,10 1,806

*Total All Exchanges***

Bonds	$11,286,915,025
Convertible Bonds	$64,844,938
Common Stock	$2,651,273,094
Preferred Stock	$337,302,875
Warrants	$43,754,625
Total	$14,384,0 90,556

*Includes coupon bonds of distressed securities trading flat.
**Total par value of bonds. $29,324,130,000

Exhibit 2.2

Market Value of Securities
Companies in Chapter XI Reorganization and in Default*
August 31, 1989

AMEX

Bonds (21)	$4,609,652,130
Convertible Bonds (8)	$208,347,450
Common Stock (3)	$14,882,750
Preferred Stock (1)	$1,233,960,375
Total (33)	$6,066,842,705

NASDAQ

Bonds (34)	$615,947,700
Convertible Bonds (17)	$62,475,500
Common Stock (6)	$26,067,000
Total (57)	$704,490,200

NYSE

Bonds (42)	$4,877,579,640
Convertible Bonds (12)	$185,250,100
Common Stock (17)	$1,270,387,016
Preferred stock (7)	$221,127,750
Total (78)	$6,554,344,506

Total All Exchanges (168)	$13,325,677,411

*Includes bonds trading flat and making no interest payments. (number of companies).

Exhibit 2.3   Market and Par Values of Defaulted and
Distressed Debt (Public & Private Markets—June
1, 1990)

	Market Value ($ Billions)	Par Value ($ Billions)	Market/Par Ratio (%)
Publicly Traded			
Defaulted Debt	$ 11.4	$ 29.5	0.39
Distressed Debt	33.0	50.0	0.66
Privately Traded			
Defaulted Debt	53.1	88.5	0.60
Distressed Debt	112.5	150.0	0.75
Total Public & Private	$210.0	$318.0	0.66

lations. They indicate a ratio of three to four times private to public debt. Using three as the more conservative figure, the par value of private defaulted debt is then estimated to be $88.5 billion with another $150 billion of distressed debt. Since most private debt is senior to the public debt, it is approximated that the defaulted debt sells at 60 percent of par value and the distressed debt at 75 percent of par. The market values become $53 billion for defaulted and $112.5 billion for distressed private debt. The grand total of public and private, defaulted and distressed debt was $318 billion in book value and $210 billion in market value. Exhibit 2.3 shows this data. As noted earlier, this figure was probably $350 billion or more by the end of 1990.

Bankrupt Companies and Business Failures

Over the last 20 years, the American bankruptcy scene has been transformed. Once a small, undercapitalized distressed company situation, it now involves larger enterprises with complex asset and liability structures. During this time, there have been nearly 100 enterprises, with over $120 million in liabilities, that have filed for bankruptcy (Exhibit 2.4). In the 1970s we experienced sizeable failures in retailing, REITs, and railroads. The severe inflationary-recession pressures of the early 1980s caused more of the same. Manufacturers, airlines, farmers and service firms of all types were included. The *Dun & Bradstreet* Business Failure Rate rose, from a low of 24 per 10,000 firms in 1978, to 110 in 1983 and a high of 120 in 1986 (Exhibits 2.5 and 2.6). One would have to go back to 1932 when the failure rate last exceeded 100 per 10,000. In the last eight years, our economy has enjoyed an unprecedented consecutive number of positive GNP growth years. It has also seen an increased vulnerability to firms of all size categories, due to persisting difficulties. These include the oil industry collapse, increasing global competition, deregulation and the leverage excesses of numerous liability restructurings in the last few years.

Those business failures involve long- and short-term marketable and privately placed debt. Estimated short-term obligations, not included before, were about $36 billion in 1988 (Exhibit 2.5), decreasing by about 10 percent in 1989. Long-term indebtedness, however, has increased substantially in 1989 and 1990. Preliminary estimates show that business failures are higher in 1990 than in 1985 and 1989.

The coming recession of 1991 was pre-dated by a sizeable increase in bankruptcy filings. Over 55,000 companies declared bankruptcy over the first 11 months, listing $64 billion in liabilities. In 1989 and 1990 alone, 14 companies with liabilities of over $1 billions filed for protection under Chapter 11 of the Code.

Junk Bond Defaults

From 1985 through December 1990, almost $40 billion of long-term, publicly traded securities defaulted. Additionally, several billion dollars of distressed exchange issue debt has been involved. $8.1 billion of par value failures took place in 1989 and over $16 billion so far in 1990, the largest corporate bond amounts ever (Exhibit 2.7). The default level on *all* publicly traded corporate debt was slightly over one percent in 1987 and 1989. These rates exceeded one percent in every year but four from 1912 through 1940 (Vanderhoof, et. al, 1989).

Exhibit 2.8 shows the market value recovery rates on junk bond defaults during the last five years. These are based on bond prices just after default (month end prices). This is an increase in the value of newly defaulted paper of $14 billion. Some portions are no longer distressed, primarily the Texaco $5.5 billion. Most is still outstanding, though at different market values now. A comprehensive discussion of default rates is in Chapter 9. A list of junk bond defaults, for the period

Exhibit 2.4

Largest U.S. Bankruptcies*
As of July 1, 1990

Company	Liabilities ($ millions)	Bankruptcy Date	Company	Liabilities ($ millions)	Bankruptcy Date
Texaco, Inc. (incl. Capital subs.)	21603	Apr-87	Saxon Industries	461	Apr-82
Campeau Corp. (Allied & Federated)	9947	Jan-90	Commonwealth Oil Refining Co.	421	Mar-78
Lomas Financial Corp.	6127	Sep-89	W. Judd Kassaba	420	Dec-73
LTV Corp. (incl. LTV Int'l NV)	4700	Jul-86	Erie Lackawanna Railroad	404	Jun-72
Penn Central Transportation Co.	3300	Jun-70	White Motor Corp.	399	Sep-80
Eastern Airlines	3196	Mar-89	Sambo's Restaurants	370	Jun-81
Drexel Burnham Lambert	3000	Feb-90	Investors Funding corp.	370	Oct-74
Wickes	2000	Apr-82	Todd Shipyards	350	Aug-87
Global Marine Inc.	1800	Jan-86	Amarex	348	Dec-82
Itel	1700	Jan-81	Food Fair Corp.	347	Oct-78
Public Service, New Hampshire	1700	Jan-88	Buttes Oil & Gas	337	Nov-85
Baldwin-United*****	1600	Sep-83	Great American Mortgage & Trust	326	Mar-77
Integrated Resources	1600	Feb-90	Mclouth Steel	323	Dec-81
Revco Corp.	1500	Jul-88	World of Wonder	312	Dec-87
Placid Oil***	1488	Apr-85	MGF Oil	304	Dec-84
Ames Department Stores Inc.	1440	Apr-90	U.S. Financial Services	300	Jul-73
McLean Industries	1270	Nov-86	Hunt International	295	Apr-85
Hillsborough Holdings (Jim Walter)	1204	Dec-89	Radice	291	Feb-88
Bell National	1203	Aug-85	Chase Manhattan Mort. & Realty Tr.	290	Feb-79
GHR Energy Corp.***	1200	Jan-83	Doskocil Co.	265	Mar-90
L. J. Hooker	1200	Aug-89	Daylin, Inc.	250	Feb-75
Manville Corp.	1116	Aug-82	Guardian Mortgage Investors	247	Mar-78

Braniff Airlines (1)	1100	May-82	Waterman Steamship Corp.	242	Dec-83
Continental Airlines****	1100	Sep-83	Revere Copper & Brass	237	Oct-82
Circle K	1100	May-90	Air Florida System	221	Jul-84
W.T. Grant	1000	Oct-75	Chicago, Rock Island & Pacific	221	Mar-75
Charter Co.	967	Apr-85	Hellenic Lines, Ltd	216	Dec-83
Allegheny International	845	Feb-88	Wilson Foods	213	Apr-83
North American Car Corp	841	Dec-84	Lion Capital Group	212	Apr-84
Seatrain Lines	785	Feb-81	KDT Industries	203	Aug-82
A.H. Robins	775	Aug-85	Equity Funding Corp. of America	200	Apr-73
Penrod Drilling***	764	Apr-85	De Laurentis Entertainment	198	Aug-88
Storage Technologies	695	Oct-84	Triad America Corporation	198	Jan-87
General Development	695	Apr-90	Interstate Stores, Inc.	190	May-74
Coral Petroleum***	682	May-83	Fidelity Mortgage Investors	187	Jan-75
Nucorp Energy	615	Jul-82	HRT Industries	183	Nov-82
Continental Mortgage Investors	607	Mar-76	Technical Equities Corp.	180	Feb-85
Evans	600	Mar-85	Braniff Airlines (2)	178	Sep-89
Allis Chalmers	570	Jun-87	Terex Corp.	176	Mar-83
United Merchants & Manufacturing	552	Jul-77	Lionel Corp.	175	Feb-82
Greyhound Lines	540	Jun-90	Omega, Alpha Corp.	175	Sep-74
Coleco Corp.	536	Jul-88	Marion Corp.	175	Mar-83
Maxicare Health Plans	535	Mar-89	Michigan General	170	Apr-87
AM International	510	Apr-82	Dart Drug Stores	169	Aug-89
OPM Leasing***	505	Mar-81	U.N.R. Industries	165	Jul-82
Bevill Bresler Schullman	498	Apr-85	Thatcher Glass	165	Dec-84
Smith International Inc.	484	Mar-86	Towner Petroleum	163	Sep-84

*Does not include commercial banking entities.
***Privately held firm.
****Subsidiary of Texas Air Corp. estimate of long term debt only.
*****Not including annuities.

Exhibit 2.5

Number of Failures

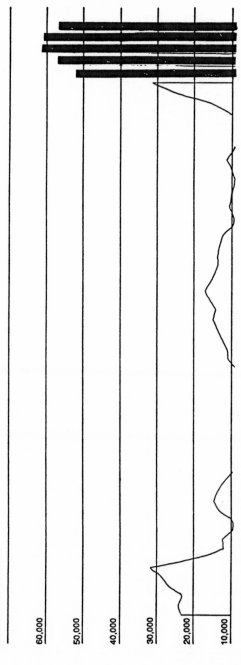

60,000

50,000

40,000

30,000

20,000

10,000

Source: Failure Record, Dun & Bradstreet, New York, 1989.

Exhibit 2.6 Historical Default Rate: Low Rated, Straight Debt
Only, 1978–1990 ($ millions)

Year	Par Value Outstanding	Par Value Default	Default Rate
1990	$210,000	$18,354.00	8.740%
1989	201,000	8,110.30	4.035
1988	159,223	3,944.20	2.477
1987	136,952	7,485.50*	5.466*
1986	92,985	3,155.76	3.394
1985	59,078	992.10	1.679
1984	41,700	344.16	0.825
1983	28,233	301.08	1.066
1982	18,536	577.34	3.115
1981	17,362	27.00	0.156
1980	15,126	224.11	1.482
1979	10,675	20.00	0.187
1978	9,401	118.90	1.265

Arithmetic Average Default Rate 1970 to 1990   2.783%
Arithmetic Average Default Rate 1978 to 1990   2.607%
Arithmetic Average Default Rate 1983 to 1990   3.460%

Weighted Average Default Rate 1970 to 1990   4.276%
Weighted Average Default Rate 1978 to 1990   4.364%
Weighted Average Default Rate 1983 to 1990   4.594%

* $1,841.7 million without Texaco, Inc., Texaco Capital, and Texaco Capital N.V. The default rate without these is 1.345%.

1985–1989, is provided in Appendix E. Appendix F lists those firms either on listed exchanges or over-the-counter as of June 1, 1990.

Exhibit 2.7   Market Value of Defaults, High Yield Debt Market, 1985–1990

Year	Par Amount of Default ($ Billions)	Weighted Price After Default (% of Par Value)	Market Value of Defaults ($ Billions)
1990[*]	16,480.0	26.5	4,367.2
1989	8,110.3	38.3	3,106.2
1988	3,944.2	43.6	1,719.7
1987	7,485.7	75.9	5,681.6
1986	3,115.8	34.5	1,075.0
1985	992.1	45.9	445.4
Total	$40,128.1		$16,405.1
Yearly Average	$6,688.0	44.1	$2,734.2

[*] Through December 1, 1990

Distressed Securities by Yield

A more "liberal" definition of distressed securities involves those selling at significant discounts from par value, resulting in high-yield spreads over Treasuries. A recent "Bottomfishers" study (Shearson Lehman Hutton, January 10, 1990) estimated over $45 billion of corporate, publicly traded debt is selling at a yield-to-maturity of at least 20 percent. Included were non-interest paying issuers. This survey involved 512 issues and 258 issuers. Yield criterion was slightly more than 10 percent above Treasury Bonds. First Boston (1989) estimated there was $22.5 billion of straight corporate debt (not including defaults or convertibles) yielding 20 percent or higher at the end of October 1989. A recent (December 29, 1989) Drexel Burnham Lambert assessment indicated $78 billion of high-yield debt was trading over a 17 percent yield. This was a spread of almost 10 percent over 10-year Treasuries. Some experts estimated that more than one half of the $200-billion junk bond market was distressed at the end of 1990.

Publicly Traded Debt Securities

The number and market values of firms with defaulted securities in May 1990 are listed in Exhibit 2.1. They trade on bond and stock exchanges or over-the-counter markets. This data shows the extent of the market and the interest in these securities. The majority are straight debt with over $11.3 billion (par value) encompassing more than 100 issuers. Convertible bonds accounted for $0.64 billion with preferred stock $0.34 billion and common stock $2.7 billion. Many defaulted firms still trade their outstanding common equity. Market values for these are relatively small, reflecting their low priority in a bankruptcy reorganization or liquidation plan.

The market value of new defaulted obligations increased by $1.8 billion from September 1989 through January 1990. This was a par value increase of $5.9 billion. During the same period, the market value of all outstanding debt and equity *decreased* by $496 million. This was caused by a significant dollar drop in the existing securities and by firms emerging from reorganization.

Private Debt

We estimate that the market value of private long-term and supplier debt of defaulted companies is at least four times their outstanding public debt. This amounts to about $50 billion of additional "securities" that are traded in confidential transactions. A more complete discussion of the private debt market, particularly trade debt, can be found in Chapter 5.

We compared the total liabilities of over 100 bankruptcies to the par value of public debt outstanding to derive estimates of private debt outstanding. If we subtract public debt from the total, the result is our estimate of private debt (including trade debt purchases). Our sample was derived from those firms listed in Exhibit 2.4 (supplemented by several from Appendix E). Sixty-six percent had public debt outstanding. The proportion is much higher than the total population of bankrupt companies. Most of the 60,000 business bankrupts each year do not have publicly traded debt. For example, in 1989, there were only about 40 firms that defaulted on their public debt or were involved in a distressed-exchange issue. Still, this book is concerned with distressed security investors and it is the larger firms that have the most relevant

Exhibit 2.8 Default Rates and Losses High Yield Debt Market 1985-1989

Year	Par Amount of Default	Default Rate	Weighted Price After Default	Weighted Coupon	Weighted Default Loss
	($MM)	(%)		(%)	(%)
1989	8110.3	4.03	38.3	13.40	2.76
1988	3944.2	2.48	43.6	11.91	1.54
1987	7485.7	5.47*	75.9	12.07	1.65*
1986	3115.8	3.39	34.5	10.61	2.40
1985	992.1	1. 68	45.9	13.69	1.02
Average	4,729.6	3.41*	47.6	12.34	1.87*

*Including Texaco. Without Texaco, default rate and default loss for 1987 would have been 1.34% and 0.89% respectively. The average default rate and average default loss for the years 1985-1989 would have been 2.58% and 1.72% respectively.

investment opportunities. The private debt of smaller concerns, however, can be a potentially fruitful arena for attractive investment returns.

Exhibit 2.9 lists our results for the 103 bankrupt companies. We found that the ratio of private to public debt was just under four to one overall and just over three to one for those with public debt outstanding. The average is derived by summing all private vs. all public debt in the relevant sample. The distribution of private/public debt for the 68 enterprises with public debt outstanding is shown in Exhibit 2.9. No central tendency emerges. The largest number of businesses had ratios between either 0–1.99 or 2.0–3.9 times. The frequency distribution was rectangular (constant) up to an eight times ratio. The median ratio for the 68 samples was five times.

Our estimate of privately placed defaulted debt was derived by multiplying a ratio of three times the $29.5 billion publicly held debt outstanding as of June 1, 1990 (an $88 billion book value).

Another way of estimating the ratio of private to public debt is to examine the recent corporate restructurings. LBOs are a good example. Exhibit 2.10 shows the average LBO had 60 percent of the new capital structure in the form of senior debt (mostly private). The ratio of private/public debt for those large restructurings was about 2.3 to 1. This lower estimate is for large firm restructurings; however, it does not represent the majority of defaults.

Trade Debt Claims

Trade debt is a part of the private debt total. The market for dealing in trade debt claims is unstructured. It is inefficient without knowledge of comparable transactions and "market" quotes. This subject is discussed in depth in Chapter 5. A partial list of active trade claim buyers is in Appendix G.

The trade claim process in a formal Chapter 11 reorganization must be described as cumbersome, awkward and time consuming. The buyer of the trade claim must seek out, or be sought out by, the existing claimant to establish an exchange price. The primary source of information is the A-4 Schedule of claims and liabilities filed in the Bankruptcy court. The purchaser determines if the claim is undisputed by the bankrupt debtor. Only then should a motion for a transfer of claim be filed with the court. The judge may require an affidavit be filed by the purchaser on how the transaction was initiated and the price established. The price of the exchange may have to be filed with the court. This is

Exhibit 2.9   Ratio of Private to Public Debt of Large Bankrupt
Companies

For 103 Bankrupt Companies:
Private Debt/Public Debt = 3.82

For 68 Companies With Both Private & Public Debt:
Private Debt/Public Debt = 3.11

Distribution

Ratio	Number of Companies	Percentage of Total
0-1.99	14	21
2.0-3.99	16	24
4.00-5.99	9	13
6.00-7.99	10	15
8.00-9.97	5	7
10.00-11.99	4	6
12.00-13.99	2	3
14.00-15.99	2	3
16.00-17.99	1	1
18.00-19.99	0	0
> = 20.00	5	7
	68	100

especially true in the Southern District Court of New York. Most judges permit the price to be "whited-out" in the "transfer of claim form."

This type of transaction is increasing, especially in the larger, more complex reorganizations. The process could take more than six months before final approval, after the transfer and affidavits are filed. This leads to a large backlog of claims, appeals and decisions. The transfer is finally officially recorded. It is then communicated to all interested parties on a "service form."

The objective function of the sophisticated distressed security investor will almost certainly be different from that of the original supplier. When the supplier is no longer holding the debtors' paper, the

Exhibit 2.10 Selected Capital Structures

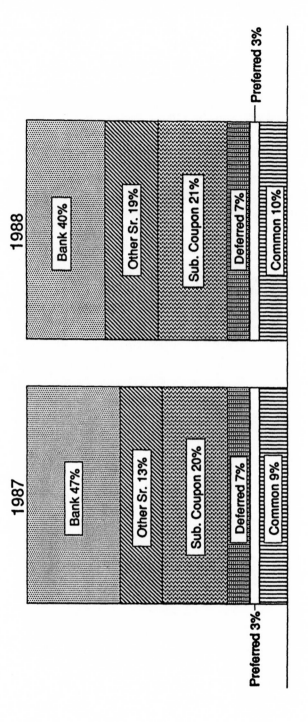

future relationship between them becomes irrelevant. The sophisticated investor, who has bought up a significant proportion of trade debt claims, will be in a better negotiating position against the debtor and other creditors than the smaller supplier would have been. While this probably will result in higher recoveries for the new trade claimant, it will also mean lower recoveries for other general creditors. The trade claim, often equal with senior debt holders, can be a prized asset. We would not be surprised if a "market-maker" in trade debt claims emerges. The amount and significance of trade claims will certainly increase, even though there is no data available now.

Conclusion

The distressed securities market is "booming." There has been an enormous increase in the last few years. It has created both an increased supply and heightened demand. The distressed securities market is clearly attracting new money and people. We now turn to the demand side of the equation.

## 3

Demand for Distressed Securities

Coincident with the massive supply increase of distressed securities has been a significant interest upswing of investor's specializing in this analysis and trading. These investors represent firms, or subsidiaries, that specialize in distressed securities. A portion of their total investment resources is dedicated to this growing area. They represent both existing and new players. A large number of these firms have been formed within the last two years.

Questionnaire Results

A survey-questionnaire was sent to 80 distressed securities investors in the fall of 1989. We received 55 responses. Representatives from 50 of these institutions indicated a specific amount of funds invested in distressed securities, five did not. The list is given in Appendix A. The respondents total invested dollars was about $5.3 billion. The distribution of amounts is shown in Exhibit 3.1. The majority invest either in the $21–50 million range or the $51–100 million range. Eleven of the 50 invest less than $20 million. However, two have $300–500 million under management in this area. This is not a complete list as some firms did not respond to the questionnaire. All of the more important investors,

Exhibit 3.1   Distribution of Invested Dollars Among Distressed
                   Investor Institutions

Amount Under Management In Distressed Securities (in $ millions)	Number of Firms	Percentage of Firms
$0-20	11	22.0
21-50	13	26.0
51-100	13	26.0
101-300	11	22.0
301-500	2	4.0
Total	50	100.0

with the exception of the arbitrageur segment, are included in the respondent data. Since our survey, at least three new investment partnerships have raised a total of $2.0 billion for active investment in distressed companies.

The investors represent various types of organizations. Many are private partnerships (the most common), open-end mutual funds, closed-end funds and special groups within larger fund operations. There are broker-dealer pools of funds, departments of commercial and investment banks, arbitrageurs and other firms looking for bargains. In addition, there are funds available from other investment vehicles. These can be shifted to distressed securities when opportunities present themselves. For instance, LBO funds may seek out other vehicles as the highly leveraged restructuring movement comes to a halt.

The majority of these investors specialize in debt securities, investing 85–100 percent of their assets in this class. Often, the initial purchase will evolve into an equity interest. Over 80 percent of the respondents indicated that they analyze or invest in the *private* debt of distressed companies.

Most investors have become more aggressive while continuing to also operate under the traditional passive investment strategies. This indicates that they are more inclined to seek either control of the restructuring process or the company itself. They will have an influence on the choice of management and the terms of the reorganization. This movement toward vigorous investing is one of the emerging trends in the distressed securities markets. For example, a pre-packaged Chapter 11 negotiated prior to the filing between a majority in number and two-thirds in dollars of the various creditors and the existing owners has become a viable alternative to the less certain typical reorganization process.

A number of distressed investment firms are newcomers to the field. Of the 55 respondents, eight were in business for less than one year and 18 for less than two years (Exhibit 3-2). Most newer portfolio managers had considerable former experience with established institutions before entering the new companies. The number of new entities with inexperienced portfolio mangers are troubling to some established investors. However, there are 22 firms who have been in business more than five years; seven of these for over twenty years.

I will return to our investor-respondent profile when discussing investment performance (Chapter 6) and the outlook for the future (Chapter 10).

Involuntary Investors

A $5 billion total of actively managed distressed securities funds is impressive. The largest amounts of distressed securities, however, are held by investors who bought them when they weren't distressed. These include investment-grade and high-yield "junk" bond mutual funds, insurance companies, pension funds and other financial institutions (including the original underwriter in some cases). These enthusiastic investors became involuntary holders of distressed paper. The growing awareness of the potential for increased prices has motivated these participants to become more knowledgeable and active. This will influence transactions, making it more difficult to purchase debt and equity at bargain prices.

Providers of New Capital-DIP Financing

A critical ingredient of a successful restructuring is the ability to raise capital after the distressed condition is apparent to all. In a Chapter 11 bankruptcy, this form of funding is called debtor-in-possession (DIP) financing. Traditionally, commercial banks have provided post-default financing. They have the opportunity to lend at attractive spreads and receive priority status in the repayment hierarchy (sections 364 (b) and (c) of the Bankruptcy Code).

Exhibit 3.2   Distribution of Years in Business of Distressed
Investor Firms or Groups (as of December 1989)

Years in Business	Number of Investors	Percentage of Investors
<1	8	15
1-2	10	18
3	7	13
4	2	4
5	6	11
6-10	6	11
11-15	9	16
16-20	0	0

A typical DIP loan is an oversecured, revolving credit facility with a maturity up to two years. A new development in 1990 has been secondary sales in smaller denominations than the original syndicated loan. For instance, the Federated Stores ($400 million) and Allied Stores ($300 million) DIP financings have been sold off in pieces as small as $10 million. Front-end fees average 2.0–2.5 percent of the loan amount with an additional 0.5 percent on the undrawn-down portion. The interest rate on DIP loans is typical of at least 1.5 percent above the prime rate.

Our respondent group did not represent these traditional lenders but over one-half stated that they do lend, or intend to lend, to distressed companies. The basis for this lending was unspecified. It could include significant ownership options as well as priority status for repayment. Some investors (the Foothill Group in Los Angeles, for instance) have funds that specialize in investing in distressed bank debt and, at the same time, provide DIP financing in selected situations.

While few institutions participate in post-petition DIP financing, competition between banks and a few experienced non-bank investors has been increasing. Some of the larger DIP providers are Chemical Bank, Marine Midland Bank, Continental Bank, and Mellon Bank as well as a few banks that have been in the business for decades. In addition, some foreign banks like Societe Generale and Canadian Imperial Bank have become involved. Foreign banks have a competitive advantage because they do no need to put away special reserves for DIPs.

Margins have eroded a bit. Nevertheless, those institutions with experience in this area have probably built up a competitive advantage. One venerable competitor is Sterling National Bank. Other non-banks, such as the CIT Group, GE Capital, and Heller Financial, are also active. DIP financers are not usually among the original bankers holding the distressed debt, but choose to enter after the bankruptcy petition is filed.

During the first nine months of 1990, almost $43 billion of DIP financing for bankrupt firms has been arranged. This is as much as 2 percent of the entire bank loan activity—an unprecedented proportion. The outlook is for even a greater portion of the loan market in DIP financings.

The acquisition of DIP financing is an important indicator of a successful reorganization. It permits the firm to engage in its normal business activities. One of the keys to successful returns on investment is the likelihood of a timely reorganization plan and its acceptance. The distressed securities investment performance will be discussed later.

## 4

Price Levels and Recovery Rates on Defaulted Securities

The enormous increase in the supply of distressed debt has contributed to a general fall in the average price level of newly defaulted securities. Poor investor rates of return in 1989 and 1990 can partly be attributed to this increase (see our discussion on performance in Chapters 6 and 7).

Adding to the recent mismatch of supply and demand have been the many types of defaults occurring in bankruptcies. The basic earning power of a firm's assets, including distressed firms, will determine its ultimate survival. The amount and layers of debt will determine the restructured firm's value to the old debt-holders. Equity holders will receive little or no return if the absolute priority doctrine is strictly followed. The old creditors will certainly become the primary equity-owners in the most "successfully" restructured company.

Exhibit 4.1 illustrates our analysis of the recent supply-demand relationship for these securities. At the initial point A, the historical recovery value, just after default, is depicted at the intersection of supply and demand. Over the last few years, the greater increase in supply from S_1 to S_2 results in a lower recovery value at B (the new equilibrium). This is despite a heightened demand from D_1 to D_2. The increasing supply has put pressure on the existing securities, causing a general decline in values. The classic supply-demand relationship, depicted in Exhibit 4.1, normally refers to the same commodity in both periods. In distressed issues, each security is unique and the new equilibrium point is based on a more complex analysis.

Capital Structures

In Chapter 2, we examined the typical capital structure of the heavily leveraged restructuring that took place with increasing frequency in 1987 and 1988. Several of these, such as Campeau's Federated and Allied Stores, Revco, Southmark, and Southland, have either defaulted or are selling at distressed levels today. While the underlying assets of many firms are still earning excellent returns, the amount of debt is suffocating, with debt-equity ratios going from 1:1 to 8:1 "overnight." The excesses of some restructurings have increased defaults to new record levels of over $16 billion in 1990, while others have worked well. The lower layers of subordinated and junior subordinated debt are selling at deeply discounted prices. Some are in the single digits. Subordinated interest and non-interest paying debt accounted for 25–30 percent of the total financing of the typical LBO in 1987 and 1988. This firm-specific capital structure has recently led to a significant lowering of recovery rates.

Recovery Rates

Exhibit 4.2 shows the recovery rate trends over the period 1985-1989. For the first time, we break down the rates of recovery by the seniority level of each type of debt. Remember that the weighted average return has come down only slightly (to about 38 percent in 1989) from a historical average of about 40 percent (Altman and Nammacher, 1987 and Hickman, 1958). Note that the average recovery rate on senior-subordinated and subordinated debt has decreased significantly (from 30 to 40 percent in 1985–1988 to around 23 percent in 1989). Many market observers expect that recovery rates will continue to decrease as long as defaults involve these heavily leveraged firms and the supply of new defaults continue to increase. Indeed, in 1990, the average recovery rate just after default fell to 25 percent of par value.

Exhibit 4.1   Price-Quantity Relationship
                  Distressed Securities Market

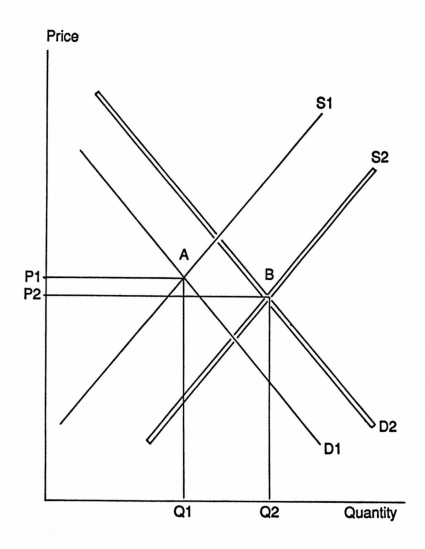

Exhibit 4.2 Recovery Prices* on Defaulted Debt by Seniority (1985-1990)

Year	Secured		Senior		Senior Subordinated		Subordinated	
							Cash Pay	Non-Cash Pay
1990	$35.04	(7)	$32.02	(27)	$24.04	(28)	$17.93 (17)	18.99 (12)
1989	82.69	(9)	53.70	(16)	19.60	(21)	23.95 (30)	—
1988	67.96	(13)	41.99	(19)	30.70	(10)	35.27 (20)	—
1987	12.00	(1)	70.52**	(29)	53.50	(10)	40.54 (7)	—
1986	48.32	(7)	37.09	(8)	37.74	(10)	31.58 (34)	—
1985	74.25	(2)	34.81	(3)	36.18	(7)	41.45 (15)	—
Average **Total:**	$53.38	(39)	$45.02	(102)	$33.63	(86)	$31.79 (123)	$18.99 (12)

Simple
Average: $35.16

( ) Number of issues
* Price at end of default month
** Without Texaco,
    1987 recovery rate = $29.77;
    Average senior recovery = $38.23

The impression is that the relative number of promising reorganizations or distressed exchange issues is very small with too much money chasing them. This results in inflated values for these attractive securities. It has made it difficult to sustain the high rates of return common in the past. While this circumstance may persist for some time, many observers still feel very optimistic about the long-term opportunities (see Chapter 10).

## 5

The Market for Defaulted Private Trade and Bank Debt *

Interest in "distressed" securities and debt claims has been stimulated by the dramatic rise in the number of bankruptcy filings. The sheer size of this debt has attracted much notice. The market value of distressed public securities rose to approximately $16 billion in late 1990. Various investors have different objectives. Some are interested in the accumulation of large positions of publicly traded securities. The intent is to control the company through the plan of reorganization. These investors are referred to as "Active." A recent example of this aggressive investment behavior can be seen in Alleghany International. A tender

---

* This chapter was jointly written with John Beiter. He is an attorney and advanced MBA student at NYU Stern School of Business and a distressed claims analyst with Bear Stearns.

offer for the company's public bonds was made by Japonica Partners, a firm interested in control after reorganization. Typically, the old bond-holders became major shareholders after a plan is executed.

On the other hand, many investors prefer to be "Passive." The Passive investor acquires public or private debt with the intention of holding the debt for the duration of the bankruptcy. The hope is a rate of return commensurate with the risks associated with distressed securities.

The following comparative discussion will describe and analyze the passive approach to bankruptcy investing, primarily in the area of private debt claims. Most other published material has concentrated on public securities alone. For a comprehensive discussion of active investment strategies involving trade claims, see Fortgang and Mayer (1990). These authors describe, among other current items, the first hostile take-over of Allegheny International.

Public and Private Debt

Public debt and equity comprise all debt and equity issued pursuant to a Registration Statement filed in accordance with the 1933 Securities Act. Straight debt, convertible bonds, preferred and common stock make up the various categories.

Private debt is bank loan claims (e.g., term loan agreements and revolving credit lines), commercial paper, privately placed securities (notes), personal injury and property damage claims. Also claims for breach of contract, rejection of executory contracts and "trade claims" are included. A trade claim arises from the delivery of goods or services that remain unpaid on the filing date of bankruptcy. Allied/Federated, a large department store Chapter 11 case, is an example. Trade creditors included garment manufacturers who sold on credit to debtor stores. They were owed money at the time the company filed their bankruptcy petition.

Private claims are not usually "traded" on a regular basis, but a widening group of investors are being attracted to these opportunities. The Wheeling-Pittsburgh and LTV Corporation bankruptcies are other examples. Almost every conceivable type of debtor claim has been traded following the filing of the Chapter 11 petitions ("post-petition"). Among the claims and interest traded were privately placed notes, secured notes and bonds, secured bank claims (under both revolver and standby letters of credit), trade claims and damage claims for rejection of executory contracts.

Markets for Public Debt

The filing of a petition in bankruptcy does not freeze trading in the debtor's public securities. It may result in a temporary state of illiquidity until the market thoroughly digests the impact of the filing. More often, the market has anticipated the filing and the claims have responded accordingly. Sometimes securities and claims may "trade-up" immediately following the filing, especially when ample security is involved.

The post-petition public securities markets function essentially the same as the pre-petition (or non-default) markets. The markets consist of trading on exchanges or over-the-counter. Under Bankruptcy Rule 3001 (e) (2), the buyer and seller of bonds and debentures are not required to file notice of transfer for approval by the bankruptcy court.

Profit opportunities abound for the prudent investor. These markets can provide a great degree of liquidity. Investors can trade freely in these securities throughout the bankruptcy. Liquidity is considered very important in the uncertain world of bankruptcy.

The public securities markets are covered by the 1933 and 1934 Securities Acts. They are subject to the Securities and Exchange Commission regulatory oversight. The bankruptcy court does not exercise much supervision over the trading of public securities. However, the courts will intervene in this area when large amounts of public securities are purchased for the expressed or implied purpose of controlling the debtor and its plan of reorganization. Strategies associated with acquiring control of the debtor are beyond the scope of this inquiry.

Bankruptcy Rules

Bankruptcy Rule 3001 (e)(2) sets forth the requirements governing the transfer of claims. The Rule states:

(e) Transfer Claim

(1) Unconditional Transfer Before Proof Filed. If a claim other than one based on a bond or debenture has been unconditionally transferred before the claim has been filed, the proof of claim may be filed only by the transferee. If the claim has been transferred after the filing of the petition, the proof of claim shall be supported by (A) a statement of the transferor acknowledging the transfer and stating the consideration therefor or (B) a statement of the transferee setting forth the consideration for the

transfer and why the transferee is unable to obtain the statement from the transferor.

(2) Unconditional Transfer After Proof Filed. If a claim other than one based on a bond or debenture has been unconditionally transferred after the proof of claim has been filed, evidence of the terms of the transfer shall be filed by the original claimant by mail. The filing of the evidence of transfer and objection thereto, if any, must be filed with the clerk within 20 days of the mailing of the notice or within any additional time allowed by the court. If the court finds, after a hearing on notice, that the claim has been unconditionally transferred, it shall enter an order substituting the transferee for the original claimant, otherwise the court shall enter such order as may be appropriate.

As pointed out, Rule 3001 (e) (2) exempts claims based on a "bond or debenture" from court regulation. The courts have construed this language to include trading in other private securities (e.g., notes or equipment trust certificates). In such cases the Trustee usually requires the preparation of written agreements and the rendering of legal opinions. This is unnecessary in the case of public bonds or debentures. It is generally required, in the case of unregistered securities, to preserve the exemption from the registration requirements under the 1933 Securities Act.

The Rule imposes trading requirements on private claims. It requires that the transferee file a statement of transfer of the claim "stating the consideration therefore." This is necessary if a claim is transferred after the petition has been filed but before a "proof of claim" has been submitted. A "Proof of Claim" is filed with the bankruptcy court, on a form provided by the clerk of the court. The claimant sets forth the amount and the basis of the claim. See Exhibit 5.1 for a Proof of Claim form. The Rule does not require notice, a hearing, or judicial approval. While this appears straight forward; this type of transfer is quite rare.

These transfers are limited for several reasons. First, the timing would have to occur early in the bankruptcy. Creditors must file proofs of claim before the "Bar Date," ordinarily within the first three months after filing. At this point, both creditors and investors are analyzing the values of the securities and reorganization scenarios. Second, investors might hesitate to purchase claims (particularly from the trade) before the creditor files the Proof of Claim. The "proof" is sworn testimony, under criminal and civil liability, as to the existence and amount of the claims.

Exhibit 5.1

B-19 (3-88) United States Bankruptcy Court _____ DISTRICT OF _____	PROOF OF CLAIM	
Name of Debtor	Bankruptcy Case No.	

A. CREDITOR INFORMATION

(The creditor is the person or other entity to whom the debtor owes money or property)

Name and Address of Creditor	☐ Check box if you never received any notices from the bankruptcy court in this case. ☐ Check box if this address differs from the address on the envelope sent to you by the court. ☐ Check box and attach copy of assignment if claim has been assigned to you.	THIS SPACE IS FOR COURT USE ONLY
Number by which creditor identifies debtor:	Check here if this claim ☐ replaces ☐ amends a previously filed claim dated: _____ ☐ supplements	

B. CLAIM INFORMATION

1. BASIS FOR CLAIM:
- ☐ Goods purchased
- ☐ Services performed
- ☐ Monies loaned
- ☐ Other forms of contract (Identify)
- ☐ Personal Injury/Wrongful death/Property damage
- ☐ Other (Describe briefly)

☐ Wages, Salaries and Commissions (Fill out below)
Your social security number _____
Unpaid services performed from _____ to _____
Nature of services (Describe briefly)

2. DATE DEBT WAS INCURRED:

3. CLASSIFICATION OF CLAIM: Under the Bankruptcy Code all claims are classified as one or more of the following:(1) Unsecured nonpriority, (2) Priority, (3) Secured. It is possible for a claim to be partly in one category and partly in another - such as wage claim which may be a priority claim for the first $2,000 and an unsecured nonpriority claim for the balance. Clarify the nature of the claim by CHECKING THE APPROPRIATE BOX OR BOXES which you believe best describe the claim. STATE THE AMOUNT OF THE CLAIM.

☐ UNSECURED NONPRIORITY CLAIM $ _____
For the purposes of this form, a claim is unsecured if there is no collateral or to the extent the value of collateral is less than the amount of the debt.

☐ SECURED CLAIM $ _____
Attach evidence of perfection of security
Brief Description of Collateral:
Real Estate   Motor Vehicle   Other

PRIORITY CLAIM $ _____
Specify the priority of the claim by checking the appropriate box(es)
- ☐ Wages, salaries or commissions (up to $2,000, earned not more than 90 days before filing of the bankruptcy petition or cessation of the debtor's business, whichever is earlier) - 11 U.S.C. § 507(a)(3)
- ☐ Contributions to an employee benefit plan- 11 U.S.C. § 507 (a)(4)
- ☐ Up to $900 of deposits toward purchase, lease, or rental of property or services for personal, family or household use - 11 U.S.C. § 507 (a)(5)
- ☐ Taxes or penalties of governmental units - 11 U.S.C. § 507 (a)(7)
- ☐ Other specify:

4. TOTAL AMOUNT OF CLAIM: $ _____ + $ _____ + $ _____ = $ _____
(Unsecured)   (Secured)   (Priority)   (Total)

5. Attach copies of documents in support of this claim, such as purchase orders, invoices, itemized statements of running accounts, contracts, court judgements, or evidence of security interests. If the documents are not available, explain. If the documents are voluminous, attach a summary.

THIS SPACE IS FOR COURT USE ONLY

6. This form should not be used to make a claim for expenses incurred after the filing of the bankruptcy petition. Such expenses may be paid only upon proper application and notice pursuant to 11 U.S.C. § 503.

7. CREDITS AND SETOFFS: Attach an itemization of all amounts and dates of payments which have been credited against the debt. Set forth any setoff or counterclaim which the debtor may have against your claim.

8. To receive an acknowledgment of the receipt of your claim, enclose a stamped, self-addressed envelope and a copy of your claim.

C. CERTIFICATION

The undersigned certifies under penalty of perjury that the debtor named above is indebted to the claimant in the amount shown, that there is no security for the debt other than that stated above or in an attachment to this form, that no unmatured interest is included, and that the undersigned is authorized to make this claim.

Date	Sign and Print the Name and Title, if any, of the Creditor or Other Person Authorized to File this Claim (attach copy of power of attorney, if any)

Penalty for Presenting Fraudulent Claim: Fine of up to $500,000 or imprisonment for up to 5 years, or both. Title 18, U.S.C. § 152 & § 3623.

Another issue associated with investor hesitation is the debtor's unknown reaction to the claim. Until the Schedule A-3 (trade claimants) is filed with the court, the investor is unable to assess the validity or contestability of the claim. Normally the debtor files the A-3 schedule with the Chapter 11 Petition. The debtor may contest any claim until confirmation. Investors should be relieved when the debtor has recognized the existence and amount of such claims. This is accomplished by listing the claim as "liquidated" and "not contingent" on the Schedule A-3. Most investors require a Proof of Claim to be on file, although it is not compulsory.

The second section of the Rule deals with transfers of claims after a Proof of Claim has been filed. The Rule requires the transferee to file "evidence of the terms of transfer" with the court. It requires the clerk to notify the transferor (original claimant) that any objection to such transfer must be filed within 20 days. The bankruptcy court's local rules generally require the transferee to serve notice of the "evidence of the terms of transfer" on all other interested parties (which appear on the "Service List").

The Rule then requires the court to make a determination that the claim has been "unconditionally transferred." This is almost a pro-forma task. It is rare for an objection to be filed. Therefore, the determination process is reduced to "confirming" that objections have not been filed and signing an order approving transfer. Although the rule is fairly straightforward, in several cases, e.g., *In re Revere Copper and Brass, Inc.* and *In re Allegheny International, Inc., the court restricted or halted claims transfers. In the latter case, the judge ruled that the purchase of private debt was to gain control prior to a vote.*

While the process is straight-forward, several practical problems might arise. Courts are generally slow in making the "determination" that the transfer was "unconditional." In our view, it is through no fault of the court. The sheer size of recent bankruptcy filings, and the immense volume of everyday business, has crowded already overburdened dockets. It is surprising that judges and clerks can sort through the unending morass. Consequently, Notice of Transfer of Claims are assigned low priority and a wait of between three and six months is not uncommon. In one recent case, a Notice filed on October 13th of one year was not approved until May 31st of the next.

One practical problem is associated with such delays. The status of the case, and value of the claim, may change dramatically during pendency of the "determination" of approval process. Thus, the agreement under which the claim is transferred or "assigned" must be explicitly worded. Whether the parties can or cannot later undo the transaction must be established. One reason for nullifying the transaction might be that the claims' value has dramatically appreciated or depreciated.

The transferee may ask for particular language that permits claims, disallowed for any reason by the court, to be "put" back to the transferor (seller). There is a practical problem with putting back portions of claims. By the time the court has determined that some, or all, of the claim should be disallowed, months or years may have elapsed. The investor may be unable to locate the original claimant to honor its legal obligation. As a result, the investors only recourse may be costly litigation. Due diligence is required before attempting investments in this forum.

Judge Lifland's Court

Chief Bankruptcy Judge of the Southern District of New York, Judge Burton Lifland, requires a somewhat novel local procedure that expands the requirements found under Rule 3001. In addition to the "evidence of the transfer," Judge Lifland mandates two further documents. A memorandum issued by the Judge to "interested parties" on May 1, 1989, stated:

> SUPPLEMENT TO THE REQUIREMENTS
> OF THE FED. R. BANKR. P. 3001 (e) (2)

> In connection with requests for claimant substitution pursuant to Fed. R. Bankr. P. 3001 (e) (2), the following shall be included in the application accompanying each claim assignment order:

> 1) A statement of the consideration paid for each assigned claim.

> 2) A representation that the assignee of the claim did not solicit the assignor via the use of misinformation. This requirement may be satisfied by either:

>> (a) providing a copy of the letter from the assignee to the assignor which solicited the claim assignment; or if the claim was not solicited, by letter,

>> (b) a statement that the claim assignment was not solicited by letter, accompanied by a certification that in

soliciting the claim, no misleading information was disseminated to the assignor.

Requirement (a) is a declaration of the amount paid by the transferee for the claim. The second requirement is an affidavit from the transferee. It is to set forth the circumstances under which the transferee came into contact with the transferor (e.g., letter or telephone solicitation, attorney reference, etc.). It also is to describe the content of the negotiation. Included are any representations made by the transferee to the transferor concerning the bankruptcy case and values of the claims. Rule 3001 (e) (2), followed exactly by courts, does not require any such disclosures, representations or certifications. Judges, such as Lifland, are probably concerned with the small or unsophisticated creditor's interest. Small creditors and the need for liquidity will be discussed later. It is our view that the best way to protect the little creditor is through an efficient market.

Proposed Changes to Rule 3001 (e) (2)

Significant changes to Bankruptcy Rule 3001 (e) (2) have been proposed. They are pending adoption by the Judicial Conference in the Fall of 1990. Approval by the United States Supreme Court is expected sometime in the Spring of 1991. The changes eliminate the requirement of judicial approval for the transfer of private claims when no challenges to the transfer are filed. (Objections must be filed within 20 days of the filing of the Notice of Transfer.) This will result in a more streamlined process and will be useful to both bankruptcy court judges and investment claimants. The lack of review, and the corresponding minimization of judicial interest, may operate to increase the potential abuse of smaller creditors unfamiliar with the process.

Direct Assignments

When a company files a Petition for Protection under Chapter 11 of the Bankruptcy Code, it is required to include several schedules. One of the schedules is the A-3. As noted, this schedule lists all trade claimants by name and amount. Many firms and investors find this schedule useful in identifying and contacting original trade claimants. Another way is to contact major investment houses directly. These claimants hear of major houses' interest in the claim by word-of-mouth from other claimants.

Once an original claimant has been located, the process of negotiating a sale price begins. The claimant may have heard what others have received and will use that price level as a starting point. In the event the claimant does not have this information, then it is vulnerable to the investor's "analysis." However, investors must be careful not to make representations about the value of the claim. Most contracts include language to the effect that the claimant has made its own determination of value and has not relied on any statements of the investor. As referred to earlier, Judge Lifland requires the filing of an affidavit by the transferee. It sets forth the circumstances and content of negotiations between the original claimant and the transferee.

Recently, a trade journal called *Turnarounds & Workouts* has begun publishing a limited table of trade claim price levels in its "Supplement." Exhibit 5.2 is a listing of the price levels reported in a recent issue.

The journal compiles the list by sending bi-weekly inquiries to approximately 15 active trade claim buyers. The prices are based on quotes for transactions of $30,000 of trade debt (face value). These "quotes" are not actual transaction values. The publishing of trade claim price levels described above (although from limited sources and with narrow

---

Exhibit 5.2   Trade Claim Bid Prices

Company	Bid Range; Cents/$
Abraham & Strauss	.08–.10
Allied Federated	.30
American Freight Systems	.30–.40
Chicago South Shore South Bend	.30
Duckwald-Alco Stores	.10
Eastern Airlines	.10–.15
Lazarus	.08–.10
LTV Aerospace	.50
LTV Steel	.20
Public Service New Hampshire	.75–.85
Revco	.20
Sharon Steel	.15
Sunbeam	.85
Wheeling Pittsburgh	.52

Source: Turnarounds and Workouts, Supplement, Summer 1990.

dissemination), is a positive step in the direction of establishing a more efficient private market.

After a price has been agreed upon, an agreement in principle is usually executed by the parties. This agreement sets out the price, and other terms, to be included in the formal written contract. Thereafter, a written contract is prepared (usually by the transferee) and executed. This contract is then attached to a Motion for Transfer of Claim. This is filed with the Bankruptcy Court and included on the Service List. Any other documents required under the local rules of the Bankruptcy Court are also filed.

Some of the larger bankruptcy "players" take a more global approach to identifying and purchasing original trade claims. This is accomplished by a "mass mailing" to some, or all, claimants listed on the Schedule A-3. Some large bankruptcies have more than one thousand individual trade claimants. Included in the mailing is a transmittal letter identifying the purchaser. It sets forth the price offered and the procedure to be followed if the claimant is interest in selling. Also included is a form of contract to be used. This method offers the purchaser certain economies of scale associated with wide exposure at little cost. The claimant also benefits because this procedure is the first step toward the development of an efficient market for private debt in bankruptcy. It presents tangible information that can be utilized by claimants. They can make an informed decision about the market belief of its' claims.

Participations

An alternative method to a total purchase is to buy a "participation" interest in a pool of claims assembled by another investor or broker. This is similar to purchasing a participation or consortium interest in bank debt. For trade claims, it is simpler, with no need to review complicated loan and related agreements. One avoids legal and administrative fees associated with the administration of a bank loan participation agreement.

Trading Pre- and Post-Petition Bank Debt

Bank debt, whether pre-petition or post-petition, is actively traded among banks and investors. This market, while harder to enter, also presents attractive potentials. Just as banks "syndicate" regular loans to other banks, bankrupt bank loans are also traded. Entry is difficult, largely because banks have their "regular" customers and brokers. If the investor is not one of these, then it might not "see" any of the bank debt. Thus, this market is less developed than the trade claim market. It is not only more difficult to enter, but also more complex to operate in.

When bank debt is traded, Rule 3001 (e) (2) also requires a Notice of Transfer be filed. Bank debt is more difficult to deal with because of two factors: (1) the underlying loan and participation agreements and (2) the potential legal problems associated with bank (and Leveraged Buy Out - "LBO") loans. The underlying loan, participation and related agreements are voluminous and complicated. A thorough understanding of the terms, conditions, rights and obligations is necessary before the purchase of bank debt can prudently be undertaken. This is apart from the financial analysis.

The potential legal problems inherent in bank, and particularly LBO debt, are more troubling. Here the investor must take care to avoid purchases that may later be subject to fraudulent conveyance or other lender liability claims. The investor should be concerned whether the debtor received "value" for commitments undertaken with respect to the bank loan being purchased and whether the bank had exercised such a degree of control over the debtor's business as to subject the loan to equitable subordination. Did the bank receive preferential payments during the 90 days, or in some cases one year, preceding the filing of the petition? These concerns account for the significance investors place on representations and warranties in the sale or participation of bank debt. These skills and information sources are substantial impediments to the average investor. Those who can effectively deal with these issues can reap substantial rewards.

Unregistered Securities

Unregistered securities include private placement instruments such as Notes and Equipment Trust Certificates. These securities are originally issued pursuant to an exemption from the registration requirements set forth in the 1933 Securities Act. After the issuer files a petition in bankruptcy, these securities continue to trade in a manner similar to the procedures before bankruptcy. These securities are held and traded by the same investors who hold and trade bonds and debentures. The filing of a bankruptcy petition does not substantially alter the process. The Bankruptcy Code remains silent on the issue of unregistered securities. It becomes a matter for the trustee to determine the procedure and filings, if any, required by the Bankruptcy Court to transfer ownership (post-petition). Eastern Air Lines 17 3/4 Secured Equipment Trust Notes is an example. The Trustee required the same procedures to trade the unregistered notes post-petition than pre-petition. The parties must comply with the requirements for transfer of unregistered securities set out under the exemption to registration contained in the 1933 Securities Act. This includes legal opinions, investor accreditation and related representation and warranties.

On the other hand, the trustee or counsel in the bankruptcy may require a more involved procedure. This may be in addition to the 1933 Act requirements, including comprehensive filings with the Bankruptcy Court. In the Public Service of New Hampshire bankruptcy case, the debtor and the trustee established a procedure for trading the unregistered Notes. This involved three separate filings with the court, entered specifically to deal with the matter. Unregistered securities may require the same, or a potentially more complex, trading process in such proceedings.

Representations and Warranties

Most prudent post-petition investors in trade claims and bank claims attempt to protect themselves. They do this with representations, warranties and covenants from the selling claimants. The investor is seeking information about the causes that give rise to the underlying claim. This information ranges from the form content and amount of value advanced by the claimant to the behavior of the selling claimant toward the debtor. The former concern is of more importance, ordinarily to the buyer of trade claims (and possibly bank/LBO debt). This investor is concerned about effects (e.g., from merchandise returns or defective goods) to the value of the claim. The latter aspect is usually paramount to the buyer of bank debt. The investor is concerned with potential debtor claims of equitable subordination or lender liability.

In trade claim transfers, the seller (or original claimant) usually agrees to refund any portion of the claim disallowed by the court. Some trade claim contracts give the buyer the right to "put" the claim being purchased back to the seller. This is conditioned upon the bankruptcy court failing to enter an order approving transfer of the claim within a specified time period. Delays, which trigger these type of clauses, are not uncommon.

Opportunities for Profit

Inefficient private markets presents opportunities as well as difficulties. Profitable investments are associated with this inefficiency. Higher than average returns are very possible for the investor in distressed securities, more so than those traded in more efficient public markets (see Chapters 6 and 7). The inefficiencies stem from the absence of information and informed claimant/investor groups. They are also the source of considerable risk for the average investor unfamiliar with bankruptcy processes, rules and nuances.

Empirical evidence suggests that trade claims are usually priced at levels below other public debentures and bonds. This is true even though trade claims are equal in priority with such other securities.

Trade claims are generally unsecured debt. As such, these claims rank equally with all forms of unsecured debt. Under a reorganization plan, or other distribution pursuant to the Bankruptcy Code, trade claimants are treated the same as unsecured senior bank claims and bonds or debentures. Importantly, if an issue of bonds or debentures is subordinated to bank debt (by the terms of the indenture), then the trade claimant is preferred over the subordinated holder.

Other Regulation

Trade claims are equal with senior debentures and entitled to similar treatment under the plan of reorganization. The securities laws treat these claims quite differently. This phenomenon has to do with the definition of a "security." In effect, securities laws do not, either on their face, or as interpreted by courts, define trade claims as "securities." Debentures and bonds are clearly securities and entitled to the rights given them under the Securities Act of 1933 and the Securities and Exchange Act of 1934. Trade claims are not so affected.

The reading of relevant cases interpreting the securities laws shows that bankruptcy trade claims do not fall within the definition of "security." One might argue that the legislature should intervene to amend pertinent securities laws (or the Bankruptcy Code). A compelling discussion can be made that the filing of a petition in a Chapter 11 bankruptcy transforms trade claims into instruments that have all the equitable ownership characteristics of other debt in bankruptcy. This view is discussed in detail later in this chapter.

Heightened Bankruptcy Court Supervision

Bankruptcy Court Judges have demonstrated a willingness to intervene in the normally routine area of claim transfers when unusual circumstances (e.g., foul play) are present. They also will intervene when the buyer's motivation is the pursuit of control of the debtor or its plan of reorganization. In these cases, the court will exercise its discretion under the Bankruptcy Code to disallow transfers made without appropriate "disclosure." In a landmark case, Revere Copper and Brass, Inc., 58 Bankr. 1 (Bankr. S.D.N.Y., 1985), a company called Phoenix Capital Corp. purchased a number of unsecured claims against Revere for approximately twenty-eight cents on the dollar. Phoenix acquired the claims by sending letters to original claimants between November 5 and December 6, 1984. Although Revere had not filed a plan of reorganization and disclosure statement, *The Wall Street Journal* reported on November 30, 1984 that Revere was planning to offer unsecured creditors between sixty-five cents and par.

When Phoenix sought Bankruptcy Court approval for the transfer of the claims, Judge Prudence Abram refused, holding in part:

One of the evils upon a solicitation of assignment of claims for a cash payment such as is being made by Phoenix Capital is that solicited creditors may be unaware of their rights and options and fall prey to the belief that bankruptcy inevitably will result in their receiving the proverbial 10 cents on the dollar or worse. Creditors may not be aware of the difference between a straight bankruptcy case under Chapter 7 and a reorganization case under Chapter 11 of the Bankruptcy Code. Bankruptcy Code Section 1125 prohibits solicitation of acceptances or rejections of a filed plan unless the solicitation is accompanied or preceded by a disclosure statement. The disclosure statement must contain adequate information which means information of a kind and in sufficient detail to enable a hypothetical reasonable investor typical of holders of claims, to make an informed judgement about the plan. Code Section 1125 (a) (1). The assignor-claimants have not been shown to have been given sufficient information by Phoenix Capital that they might make an informed judgement about the offer made to them. That much is required.

It seems clear that Judge Abram was concerned with the timing of the purchases in view of information uncovered by *The Wall Street Journal*. The Bankruptcy Code does not, however, protect ignorant trade claimants from not investigating the value of the claims they hold. We have not found another case, although there may be others, that disallowed a transfer on the grounds outlined in Judge Abram's holding.

Bankruptcy judges also have intervened when claims are purchased for the purpose of obtaining control of the debtor. In 1986 a company called EPA, Inc. mailed solicitations to all unsecured creditors of LTV Energy Products (a subsidiary of the LTV Corporation). They offered to purchase the claims for thirty-three cents on the dollar. Four hundred fifty such creditors agreed and Notices of Transfer were filed. At the same time, EPA and its parent company formulated a plan that would pay one-hundred cents on the dollar to unsecured creditors (including itself). Judge Lifland denied the transfer. It was done on the grounds that the transfers were part of a scheme. It could be viewed as a plan of reorganization to which EPA was soliciting consents prior to a disclosure statement. The few cases cited are not common. Absent these unusual motives, transfers are routinely granted.

Functions of the Private Debt Market

The most obvious benefit that post-petition investors bring to the bankruptcy process is liquidity. As pointed out, liquidity is a relative concept. The public market is always more liquid than the private claims market. This may be a significant deterrent for investors seeking to enter the private arena. Original claimants have different investment objectives and horizons than professional investors. Liquidity permits opportunities to exit their holdings. Without this, pre-petition investors, as well as trade claimants and banks, would be frozen in place. Financial markets for distressed securities would be severely undermined without the liquidity supplied by post-petition investors. This is particularly true in view of the sheer size and number of bankruptcy filings over the last couple of years, and the expected number of future filings.

In addition to the liquidity that post-petition investors generate in public securities' markets, they also create a market (albeit inefficient) in private claims. This is the area of trade claims, bank claims and private placements. These markets, to the extent they existed pre-petition (mainly bank debt and private placements), would almost certainly evaporate after the filing of a petition if it were not for the post-petition investor.

Benefits for the Seller

The most important benefit the seller of distressed claims receives is cash. The seller can trade its claim for cash, though at a discount. The alternative is to wait for an uncertain payment under an uncertain plan of reorganization (or liquidation) at an uncertain time in the future. For the trade creditor, this could be crucial, if not a matter of survival. Consider the small garment manufacturer or designer in the Federated case. A large bad debt left outstanding could be tantamount to driving the creditor out of business. Thus, the prospect of cash and risk-transfer are ordinarily sufficient motivation to encourage the original claimant (particularly trade) to sell. It is true, however, that most Chapter 11 bankruptcy debtors continue to pay their trade claimants in order to ensure continued access to goods.

The original claimant may also be motivated to sell because its accountant (in the case of banks or insurance companies, the regulators) has forced them to write the claims down to a value below what the claims are worth to the post-petition investor. This establishes potential tax loss values.

Conversely, there are negatives associated with selling a claim in a bankruptcy. As pointed out, the inefficiencies inherent in the market make pricing of the claim somewhat risky. This is particularly true for the non-professional investor or uninformed claim holder. In addition, the typical trade (and to some extent bank) claimant is not nearly as well equipped with resources and expertise in these matters as would be the bankruptcy investor. Apart from these limitations, the original claimant also faces uncertainty and delay with the court process. The claimant is usually unfamiliar with bankruptcy filings and procedures. Some claimants (banks particularly) will hire bankruptcy counsel to assist them. Most others (particularly all trade claimants) forego the additional decrease in value from incurring professional fees by permitting the buyer to prepare all documentation and court filings. Finally, Bankruptcy Court delays sometimes trigger "put" clauses in purchase contracts. The seller must repurchase the claim if the buyer so demands. In a bankruptcy where claim prices have been fluctuating, the delay effectively gives the buyer a free call on the claim.

Benefits for the Buyer

The post-petition investor is betting that a plan (or distribution) is confirmed before the carrying costs (time value of money) eliminate the spread. The spread is the difference between the distribution value and the price the investor was able to negotiate with the transferee. The discount associated with private debt is usually deeper than the discount of public debt to offset these uncertainties.

The investor must be cautious when investing in private debt. Inefficiencies in the market require the investor to make an extra effort. They must verify value, estimate reorganization time horizons and appraise potential off-sets and other demands the debtor or other creditors might assert against the claim. Additionally, private markets are not as fluid as their public market counterparts. This is especially true for "secondary private markets." They consist of purchases and sales by "non-original" claimants. Thus, the investor in private debt must be ready for the long haul that confirmation demands.

One must exercise diligence and thoroughness concerning the claim being purchased to avoid "merchandise defects." This is not burdensome with trade claims; however, with bank/LBO debt, the task is extremely important. The investor must guard against lender liability claims, fraudulent transfers, counterclaims, set-offs and tainted claims. Of course, the prudent investor will negotiate meaningful seller representations and warranties without relinquishing much of the discount.

6

The Performance of Distressed Securities

One reason for increased attention in distressed securities has been the perception that returns are very attractive. Hickman (1958) reported that the greater risk in lower grade debt was consistent with higher absolute returns. There is no shortage of anecdotes about fortunes made on bankrupt railroad securities, the REIT crisis, or specific situations such as Toys-R-Us. High returns earned by investors on more recent bankruptcies (Itel, Wickes, AM International and Storage Technology) added to the perception that this area was worth serious consideration. In addition, the increased supply of highly liquid, prominent company names to the bankruptcy ledger has given the field a sense of legitimacy.

What has been poorly understood are the exceptional skills required to be successful. The serious investor must have the necessary valuation skills and resources to analyze the credit risk, the likelihood of a successful reorganization and the legal complications of distressed exchanges. Also the Chapter 11 reorganization laws and precedents, contingency claims on assets, fraudulent conveyances of liability payments and the uncertainties of the reorganization-negotiation process must be understood. Concerning the latter, one cannot assume that the absolute priority doctrine, with respect to the hierarchy of claims and recoveries, will hold in the final settlement. See Eberhart, Moore and Roenfeldt

(1990) and Weiss (1990) for a discussion of deviations from the absolute priority doctrine. This "doctrine" or "rule" implies that a senior claim in a reorganization must be paid in full before a junior claimant receives anything. In fact, deviations from this rule are the norm rather than an exception.

The keys to success are the same skills common to any asset valuation process, plus some very specialized ones. They are as follows:

- knowledge of the fundamental earning power of the underlying assets of the distressed firm

- understanding the quality of management

- knowledge of the external environment

- a knowledge of debt priorities

The successful investor also must possess or have continual access to the following things:

- a number of specialized legal and economic resources

- patience to wait out the tedious reorganization process

The last attribute is important. The workout and reorganization process can take several years.

Our examination of published studies on distressed investing, and our own recent tests, confirm the potential for superior returns. They also show that all forms of investing and strategies will not produce acceptable returns. Usually, investing blindly in either the equities or debt of companies after the distressed condition becomes apparent will not work well. If the investor can eliminate a significant proportion of the firms that deteriorate further, then above average returns are likely. We find that investors have done very well over the period 1982–1989 and even over the past four years (1986–1989). They fared less well in the past two years (1989 and 1990).

Target and Minimum Rates of Return

Anyone who has analyzed the distressed security market must conclude that this is not a market for amateurs. In order to attract new investment dollars, it is necessary to earn extraordinary returns. The risky nature of the business, and the costly skills required, lead to high minimum required rates of return.

We queried our investor sample about their minimum and target rates of return. Results were as expected. The target rates of return were higher, on average, than the minimum. Some of the respondents gave identical answers to both questions. The most common response was a target return of 30 percent and a minimum return of 20–25 percent. About one-third of the respondents had a 30 percent target return. The other two-thirds split evenly below and above 30 percent (Exhibit 6.1). Two-thirds of the investors required a minimum rate of return of either 20 or 25 percent.

Historical Performance: Review of Literature

Equity Returns

A few studies have examined investment performance of distressed equity securities. Altman (1969) examined sixty-seven Chapter X and XI equity situations. If the equity holder retained some interest in the firm after reorganization, then the total return was higher than the average yield as measured by the S&P 500 Index. A small number (22 of 67) of equity holders survived as much as five years after the bankruptcy filing. Only 18 survived after 10 years. The average drop in price of bankrupt securities was 25 percent from the month-end before bankruptcy to the month-end after filing. Clark & Weinstein (1983) found an even greater drop in stock price for approximately the same time frame as well as significant price drops on the date of the bankruptcy filing.

Exhibit 6.1   Target and Minimum Rates of Return On Distressed Security Investing (based on 49 Respondents)

Target Rate of Return (%)	Respondents		Minimum Rate of Return (%)	Respondents	
	Number	Percentage		Number	Percentage
<20	0	0	<20	2	4
20	4	8	20	15	31
25	11	23	25	16	33
30	16	33	30	10	20
35	5	10	35	4	8
40	9	18	40	2	4
>40	4	8	>40	0	0
Total	49	100		49	100

Another performance study analyzed 50 firms over the period 1979–1983. This was first reported by Moeller (1986) and discussed in Ramaswami and Moeller (1990). Rates of return in the sample were compared with the performance of a leading mutual fund that invests in both traditional and bankrupt securities. A comparison was also made with the S&P 500 Index. Returns were measured from the first trading date following filing to the legal completion date of the bankruptcy process. Moeller found the average duration of the bankruptcy process was 21.5 months. The average annual return on the 50 stock sample was 28 percent. This compared to 8.5 percent for the mutual fund and 21.5 percent for the S&P 500. The variance of return, however, for the bankrupt equity sample was very large. Moeller did not test for significance. Thus, the mean return on the sample may not have been significantly different from the S&P Index or even from the benchmark mutual fund. Indeed, Moeller's results are consistent with the findings of Morse & Shaw (1988). The latter concluded that random equity investing did not produce abnormal returns.

Moeller and Ramaswami found, as did I (Altman, 1969), that the equity return of firms achieving a successful reorganization was exceptional (over 49 percent on an average annual basis). These authors proceeded to examine the factors that determined a successful reorganization, in order to build a predictive model. Drawing on the works of White (1983) and Casey, McGee and Stickney (1986), Ramaswami and Moeller set up a logistic classification model. This distinguishes between firms likely to reorganize successfully and those that will liquidate. Casey, et. al., found that a firm's proportion of net "free" assets (unsecured or unpledged) at bankruptcy filing and the change in profitability in the years preceding bankruptcy, were the most important determinants of reorganization success. This model's accuracy was only fair at 58.5 percent.

Ramaswami and Moeller used these two Casey, et. al., variables and added others. They measured assets (size) and growth. Reference is to the growth rate of the industry compared to the entire manufacturing sector, between the bankruptcy filing and reorganization (liquidation) date. They also measured the firm's age at filing (a proxy for managerial experience) and the monthly total return on their long-term corporate bonds. The latter variable measures the opportunity cost to creditors in permitting the firm to survive. The authors found that net "free" assets and the relative growth rate of the industry in the post-bankruptcy period were the only significant variables. Unfortunately, the predictability tests of their model were inconclusive. They analyzed a small sample of only eight bankrupt companies.

Morse and Shaw (1988) investigated 162 bankrupt equity situations between 1973 and 1982. Of their original sample, about 25 percent had been liquidated. Only one of the liquidated firms provided any returns to stockholders. From a sample of 56 firms, they concluded that no significant abnormal returns or losses were earned over a three-year period after bankruptcy. They found that the systematic (Beta) risk of the sample did increase after the filing of bankruptcy from 1.08 to 1.35. This was found *not* to be significant. There was, however, a dramatic increase in the total return variability. They also concluded that the new 1978 Bankruptcy Code had no significant impact concerning their samples' decisions or resolutions.

It should be pointed out that Morse & Shaw found some high positive three-year post-bankruptcy residual rates of return (up to 125 percent) for their pre-1978 sample. Due to the high inconsistency of returns, the average results were not significantly different from zero.

Debt Studies

Long & Hradsky (1989) examined the performance of defaulted issues from two years before to two years after default. Their sample included straight defaulted (non-convertible) debt and some distressed exchange issues over the period 1977–1987. They compared returns on their sample with the Blume-Keim (1987, 1989) index of lower grade bonds. Excess returns were calculated on a monthly basis by subtracting the Blume-Keim total return index from that of each security's total return. Weighted average cumulative absolute and abnormal returns were calculated. Abnormal returns are those in excess of the comparable period's return on a portfolio of junk bonds.

Their results show excess returns start to be negative eighteen months before default. They decline steeply five months before filing and bottom out about six months after. Curiously, they then rise for several months, falling again between months 10 and 16 and then continue upward to month 24. This trend is shown in Exhibit 6.2. A strategy of buying just after default results in a positive abnormal return of about 7.5 percent over the two-year post-default period. Returns for the first six months following default result in a *negative* abnormal return of nine percent. The abnormal gain from purchasing in month 6 and holding to

Exhibit 6.2 Cumulative Excess Returns on Defaults Only, 1977-1988

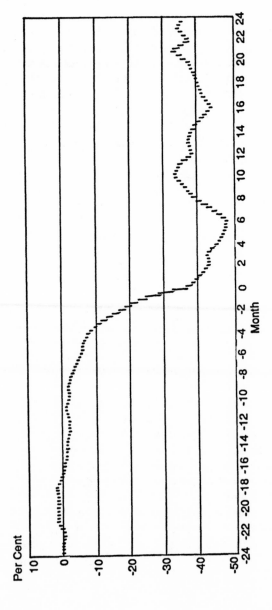

Source: Hradsky and Long (1989).

24 months is an impressive 16 percent. Distressed exchange issues also show a recovery after the exchange, but only after the 17th month.

In a preliminary study, we (Altman, 1989) found similar debt securities' results to that of Long & Hradsky. Our results on equities, however, were more promising than Morse & Shaw. The sample included only those companies that had both debt and equity outstanding at the time of default. It was restricted to a sample of 14 large companies. This study covered the period six months prior to two years after default. Both debt and equity absolute and residual returns were studied. All types of securities, including equity, senior and subordinated debt, showed positive excess residual returns for the two-year period after default. These ranged from 21.5 percent for equities, to 18 percent for senior debt and to 7 percent for junior debt (Exhibit 6.3). The benchmark portfolios were the Blume-Keim low grade debt index for bonds and the S&P 500 Index for equities. Similar to Long & Hradsky, we found the first six months after default resulted in negative residual returns. We observe again that the 18-month period (from month six to 24) saw exceptional performance. This is not surprising. There was a significant overlap of securities surveyed in the two debt studies (Long & Hradsky and Altman).

Of interest is the excellent equity returns indicated in Exhibit 6.3 as compared to my earlier (1969) study and the one by Morse & Shaw. Three items of caution should be noted. First, only large companies are analyzed where the likelihood of liquidation under Chapter 7 is small. The two other studies included a wider range of firm sizes. Second, no tests for significance were performed. The results might be insignificant, although positive. Third, the test period did not include 1989 and 1990, when prices of distressed securities were falling.

New Test of Distressed Debt Investment Strategies

These studies considered the formal bankruptcy or default date as the trigger for the investment. Our liberal definition of distressed debt securities (Chapter 1) involves those issues selling at a significant yield spread over U.S. Treasury bonds. Since a proportion of distressed securities eventually default, the usual yield-to-maturity criteria seems less relevant than the current yield. For our next test, we defined a distressed security as one that has a current yield of at least 10 percent above the intermediate term Treasury bond rate. For example, in June 1978 the T-Bond rate was 8.25 percent and our distressed criteria became 18.25

Exhibit 6.3

Cumulative Average Returns on Various Types of Bankrupt Securities (% Returns)

				Months			
Actual Returns	*No. of Issues*	*–6 to 0*	*–1 to 0*	*0 to 6*	*0 to 12*	*0 to 24*	*6 to 24*
All Equities	17	(68.09)	(31.25)	3.97	27.75	45.08	40.79
All Debt	20	(46.36)	(27.24)	(5.73)	21.89	40.52	46.27
Senior Debt	6	(27.18)	(23.38)	6.72	30.48	50.63	45.74
Junior Debt	14	(54.68)	(28.90)	(11.07)	18.72	36.40	46.72
*Residual Returns**							
All Equities	17	(70.89)	(37.24)	(3.51)	9.71	21.52	22.52
All Debt	20	(53.27)	(28.42)	(16.15)	3.34	9.91	23.89
Senior Debt	6	(30.43)	(24.99)	(5.47)	9.43	17.78	23.13
Junior Debt	14	(63.06)	(31.79)	(20.73)	1.37	6.86	24.55

*Note: residual return equals absolute performance less relevant opportunity cost, i.e., high yield index for debt and S&P 500 index for equity.

percent. We also categorized securities with a 20 percent or greater current yield as distressed. The proportion of these securities, however, was small. The lowest spread (6.3 percent) was in June 1982 when the T-Bond rate was 13.7 percent. Since October 1985, the intermediate-term T-Bond rate had been below 10 percent, thus fitting our parameters perfectly.

We included 310 issues in our distressed debt security analysis over the 11-year sample period (June 1978–June 1989). Once identified as a distressed security, we tracked the issue's total returns (interest plus price change) at six-month intervals for up to three years. Interest is not included if the issue defaults and is traded "flat." The results of our various investigations are contained in Exhibit 6.4. We list the absolute return at the various time intervals. We also cataloged the residual return, adjusted by the benchmark portfolio of low-grade bonds. For this standard, we used the Blume-Keim Index, which was available from 1978–1988. We used the average of the Merrill Lynch and Salomon Brothers high-yield indices for 1989.

Naive investment strategy results (selecting all debt securities when they first became distressed) are shown in panel A of Exhibit 6.4 and in Exhibit 6.5. As expected, the returns are poor for all time intervals up to 36 months. Absolute returns were negative for the first six-month interval. They increased to a respectable average return of about 12 percent per year for both the two- and three-year time intervals. The residual returns are significantly negative for all intervals (at the .05 level—95 percent confidence). These results are not surprising since 57.4 percent (178 of 310 issues) defaulted after the initial distress indication. The average time to failure was a little over six months; hence, the negative average return for the first six-month period.

In Panel B of Exhibit 6.4, we remove defaults from the computation and the returns become vastly improved (Exhibit 6.6). The returns were 29.7 percent, 67.6 percent and 90.3 percent for the one-, two- and three-year period intervals. This equals an approximate compound return of 30 percent per year over two years and 25 percent per year over three years. The residual returns were also positive and significantly different from zero for all intervals, except the first six-month period. If we could choose distressed securities that do not default, the target return rate of 25–30 percent per year would be achieved.

The observed performance was quite poor during the initial six-month period. Thus, we examined the performance starting from six months after distress and proceeding until 36 months after (a two-and-

Exhibit 6.4 Performance Results for Various Strategies of Investing in Distressed Debt Securities (1978-1989)

A. Invest in All High Yield Spread Issues

	Gross Return (%)/Months After Distress						Residual Return (%)/Months After Distress					
	6	12	18	24	30	36	6	12	18	24	30	36
Return	(7.2)	2.0	9.2	22.7	29.6	35.2	(14.1)	(15.2)	(16.4)	(9.7)	(12.5)	(18.1)
Standard Deviation	42%	54%	63%	71%	70%	74%	41%	52%	61%	69%	66%	67%
No. of Issues	310	251	199	160	114	83	310	251	199	160	114	83
Significant (.05)							Yes	Yes	Yes	No	Yes	Yes

B. Invest in All Non-Defaulting High Yield Spread Issues

	Gross Return (%)/Months After Distress						Residual Return (%)/Months After Distress					
	6	12	18	24	30	36	6	12	18	24	30	36
Return	7.1	29.7	45.4	67.6	80.2	90.3	0.4	10.5	14.8	30.1	28.6	26.8
Standard Deviation	34%	45%	48%	45%	46%	47%	32%	43%	48%	47%	49%	50%
No. of Issues	132	93	76	67	49	39	132	93	76	67	49	39
Significant (0.5)							No	Yes	Yes	Yes	Yes	Yes

C. Invest in All High Yield Spread Issues After Six Months

	Gross Return (%)/Months After Distress					Residual Return (%)/Months After Distress				
	6	12	18	24	30	6	12	18	24	30
Return	6.0	13.3	23.7	36.0	35.4	(1.9)	(2.0)	2.3	5.5	(4.3)
Standard Deviation	46%	64%	64%	70%	73%	46%	62%	61%	67%	66%
No. of Issues	251	198	159	113	82	251	198	159	113	82
Significant (.05)						No	No	No	No	No

* See legend on page 66.

Exhibit 6.4 (continued)

D. Invest in All Distressed High Yield Issues with Positive 6 Months Price Change

	Gross Return (%)/Months After Distress						Residual Return (%)/Months After Distress				
	6	12	18	24	30		6	12	18	24	30
Return	5.5	8.9	18.2	30.2	33.9		(2.8)	(6.6)	(2.8)	(3.2)	(3.0)
Standard Deviation	30%	41%	49%	56%	57%		29%	38%	44%	50%	50%
No. of Issues	96	80	69	47	40		96	80	69	47	40
Significant (.05)							No	No	No	No	No

E. Invest in Positive Zeta Distressed High Yield Issues

	Gross Return (%)/Months After Distress						Residual Return (%)/Months After Distress					
	6	12	18	24	30	36	6	12	18	24	30	36
Return	15.4	23.6	45.7	43.2	68.1	79.1	3.1	1.1	15.1	8.2	22.1	22.7
Standard Deviation	52%	65%	54%	42%	55%	57%	50%	62%	51%	39%	49%	51%
No. of Issues	10	9	9	9	8	8	10	9	9	9	8	8
Significant (.05)							No	No	No	No	No	No

F. Invest in Zeta > -1 Distressed High Yield Issues

	Gross Return (%)/Months After Distress						Residual Return (%)/Months After Distress					
	6	12	18	24	30	36	6	12	18	24	30	36
Return	17.6	24.2	37.3	44.9	68.4	72.9	5.4	1.0	7.9	9.8	20.7	23.8
Standard Deviation	43%	51%	57%	54%	55%	60%	42%	50%	56%	48%	49%	57%
No. of Issues	31	29	26	24	17	16	31	29	26	24	17	16
Significant (.05)							No	No	No	No	Yes	No

*See legend on page 66.

Exhibit 6.4   (continued)

G. Invest in Zeta > -2 Distressed High Yield Issues

| | Gross Return (%)/Months After Distress | | | | | | Residual Return (%)/Months After Distress | | | | | |
	6	12	18	24	30	36	6	12	18	24	30	36
Return	2.0	11.9	21.2	28.3	42.5	52.2	(8.3)	(11.3)	(7.8)	(6.0)	(3.1)	(5.7)
Standard Deviation	47%	54%	60%	58%	69%	75%	44%	52%	58%	53%	61%	68%
No. of Issues	46	38	35	32	23	20	46	38	35	32	23	20
Significant (.05)							No	No	No	No	No	No

$$*t = \frac{\bar{X}}{6/\sqrt{N}}, \text{ at .05 level. approximately 2.}$$

Exhibit 6.5 Investment in All High Yield Spread Issues (1978-1989)

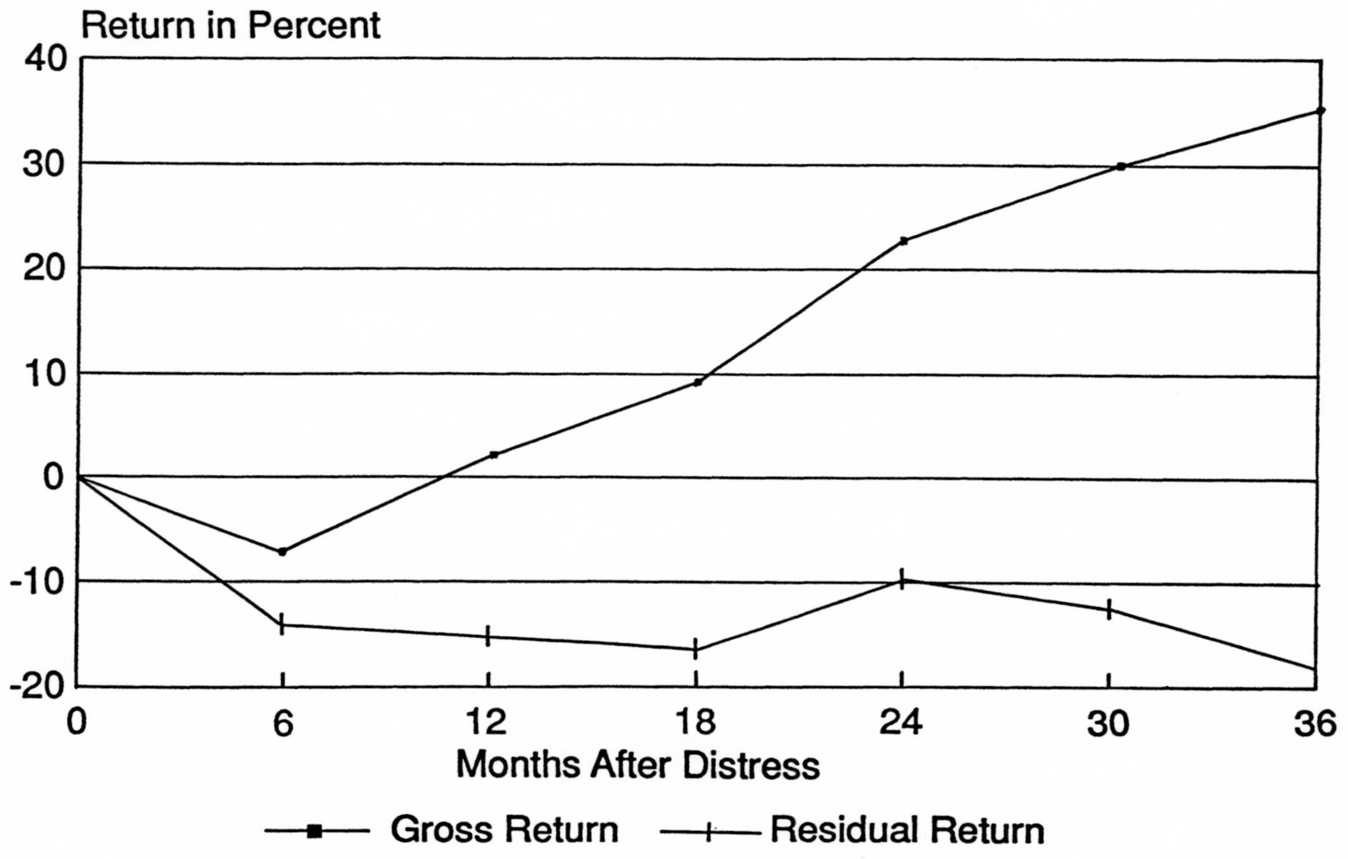
Return in Percent
40
30
20
10
0
-10
-20
0
6
12
18
24
30
36
Months After Distress
Gross Return
Residual Return

Exhibit 6.6   Investment in All Non-Defaulting Distressed Issues (1978-1989)

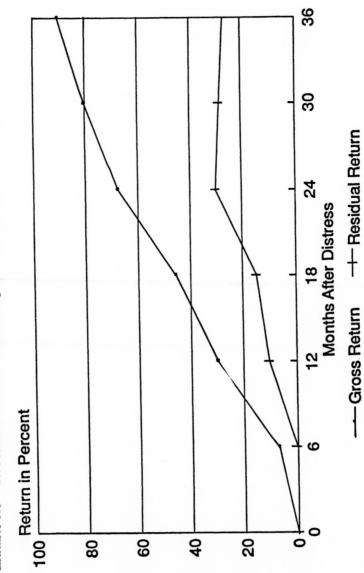

one-half-year period). The results are listed in Panel C of Exhibit 6.4. The absolute returns were good, resulting in 35.5 percent over two years (a 16 percent compound annual return). The residual returns varied from positive (at 18 and 24 months), to negative (at 6, 12 and 30 months). None of these residual results were significantly different from zero due to the high variability of return rates. The first six-month period often has problematic results, especially if the firm deteriorates further toward demise. Recall that over half of our sample failed. That average period to default was six months after the first yield-spread sign of distress.

In Panel D (Exhibit 6.4), we simulate an investment strategy. This selects only those securities that increased in price over the first six-month period after the distressed classification. This included 31 percent (96 of 310) of the issues. We measured the performance from six months after filing. Absolute returns are good. All residual returns were negative, although low and not significantly different from zero. This appears consistent with returns from our typical junk bond portfolio over the same period. It should be noted that returns on our benchmark junk bond portfolio were good for all but the 1989 period.

The Zeta® Credit Evaluation Tool

It is certainly unlikely that investors can always avoid defaults when investing in distressed securities. And we cannot perform traditional credit analysis in our statistical testing of the entire 310 firm sample. We can, however, apply a calculated credit scoring model to our sample on a consistent and objective basis. We chose the ZETA® credit scoring method to do this. The ZETA® credit scoring system was derived by Altman, Haldeman and Narayanan (1977). It is an established tool utilized by an increasing number of financial and industrial organizations (available from ZETA Services, Hoboken, N.J.).

ZETA® builds on earlier bankruptcy classification works (i.e., Altman, 1968, 1983). It combines traditional financial measures with a multivariate technique known as discriminant analysis. This leads to an overall "credit score" for each of the firms being examined. This model form is as follows:

$$ZETA = a_o + a_1 X_1 + a_2 X_2 + a_3 X_3 \ldots a_n X_n$$

where Zeta = overall credit score

$X_1 \ldots X_n$ = Explanatory variables [ratios and market measures]

$a_o \ldots a_n$ = Weightings or coefficients

It was derived from a comparison of over 100 industrial firms. Of those firms approximately half filed for bankruptcy reorganization. The other half represented a healthy, control group of firms. The final ZETA® model included seven financial measures.

ZETA® Score Variables

X_1 = Profitability—earnings before interest and taxes (EBIT)/total assets

X_2 = Stability of earnings measure—standard error of estimate of EBIT/TA (normalized) for 10 years.

X_3 = Debt service capabilities—EBIT/interest charges

X_4 = Cumulative profitability—retained earnings/total assets.

X_5 = Liquidity measure—current assets/current liabilities

X_6 = Capitalization levels over time—five-year average market value of equity/total capitalization.

X_7 = Size—total tangible assets, normalized

The model was very accurate in assigning firms from the original sample of bankrupt and non-bankrupt companies. Accuracy for the bankrupt group was 96 percent for one annual statement before bankruptcy. It was 70 percent for five annual statements before bankruptcy. More importantly, the model has proven to be very accurate in later tests.

The lower the firm's ZETA® score, the more the model indicates that it is "in distress." Negative ZETA®s do not indicate certain default or bankruptcy. The lower the score, however, the greater the similarity between that particular firm and those that have gone bankrupt in the past. The average ZETA® score for past bankrupt firms in 1984–1988 was -3.63 one year prior to bankruptcy. It was -6.44 at the time of filing (see Exhibits 6.7 and 6.8).

The average ZETA® score of bonds rated by Moody's and S&P during 1980–1989 is given in Exhibits 6.9 and 6.9a. Note that the average ZETA® score decreases in a consistent manner as the bond rating decreases. The average B rating is equivalent to a ZETA® score of about -2.0. Note the trend in the average ZETA® score for five years before bankruptcy (Exhibit 6.10) and their relationship to the ZETA® equivalent to Moody's bond ratings.

Investing In Distressed Debt Using ZETA® Scores

We used ZETA® cut-off scores ranging from zero (0), to -1, and -2 for selecting a group of companies. The rate of return achieved on this portfolio is shown in Panels E–G of Exhibit 6.4. We were able to derive ZETA® scores for only 134 of the 310 issues. Those 134 issues were scrutinized for various hurdle rates for investment selection. ZETA® scores varied from 1.63 to -11.64. The low ZETA® score range attests to our selection of these companies' securities as distressed.

There were only 10 issues with positive ZETA® scores. The results of these selections are given in Panel E and Exhibit 6.11. Returns are generally excellent with positive residuals for all the time intervals after distress was first detected. But the number of observations is too small to make any practical, definitive statements. The 30- and 36-month residuals are significant at the .25 level but not significant at the .05 level (due to sample size and variability).

The results are also quite positive with a ZETA® cut-off score of -1. The number of observations increases to 31 (Panel F). Note the significant positive residual returns for the 30- and 36-month intervals at the .05 and .10 levels, respectively. The results are impressive, perhaps more so than those for a positive ZETA® score cut-off.

In Panel G of Exhibit 6.4, the ZETA® cut-off strategy of -2 is used. While the absolute returns are good, note that the residual returns deteriorate as the cut-off score lowers. They are negative, although not significant, over the entire interval range.

The purpose of these exercises was to show how a prudent, disciplined, analytical approach can be successfully used in the distressed security arena. A technique such as ZETA® could be combined with other types of analysis to increase the number of the relevant securities eligible for investment. This is appropriate since ZETA® scores are unavailable for over half of the issuing companies.

Junk Bond Portfolio Selections

ZETA® scores also can be used as a risk-reducing strategy for junk bonds. The performance of junk bonds since June 1989 has been the subject of much concern. Commentators have characterized the market as "in disarray," "traumatic," "illiquid" and a poorly performing asset class. In 1989, junk bond performance was far below other fixed income and equity indices. The actual absolute total return for 1989, however,

Exhibit 6.7 Average ZETA® Credit Scores At Date of Bankruptcy (1984-1988)

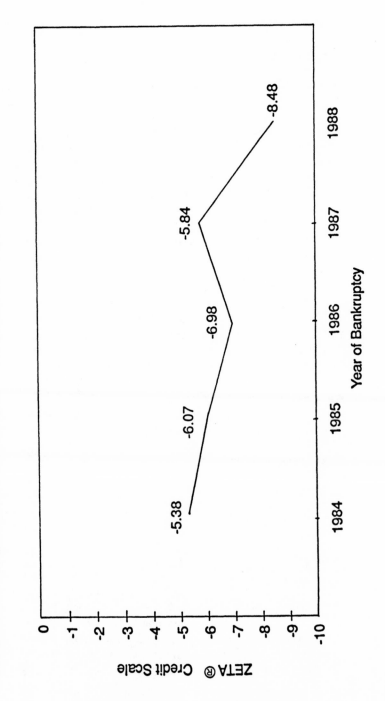

Exhibit 6.8 Trend in ZETA® Credit Scores Bankruptcies Between 1984–1988

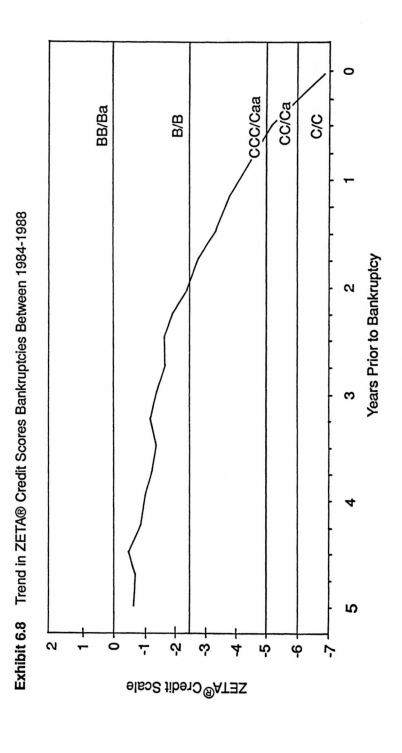

Exhibit 6.9

Average Zeta Scores by Rating Agency and by Rating Category

Senior Debt Bond Rating

	1990	1989	1988	1987	1986	1985	1984	1983	1982	1981
Moody's										
Aaa	8.10	8.09	9. 08	9.34	9.54	10.75	11.55	10.90	10.54	9.87
Aa	7.25	7.30	7.68	7.36	7.36	8.03	7.77	7.74	7.57	7.61
A	5.58	5.61	5.88	5.33	5.05	5.32	5.48	5.35	5.42	5.60
Baa	2.95	2.87	3.34	2.77	2.97	3.30	3.42	2.96	2.88	3.43
Ba	-0.42	-0.35	0.81	0.90	1.47	0.66	0.75	0.81	1.29	1.00
B	-2.30	-2.16	-1.88	-2.01	-1.25	-1.50	-1.62	-2.18	-1.62	-0.69
Caa	-1.71	-3.35	-3.97	-4.62	-6.32	-7.63	-6.95	-4.50	-4.97	-3.69
NR	0.75	0.79	-0.05	-0.52	-0.22	0.35	1.33	1.09	1.36	—
S & P										
AAA	7.85	7.81	8.76	8.95	8.78	9.95	11.01	10.80	10.34	10.03
AA	7.14	7.08	7.25	7.02	6.82	7.55	7.48	7.58	7.29	7.58
A	5.48	5.48	5.87	5.29	5.19	5.34	5.47	5.20	5.39	5.65
BBB	2.80	2.80	3.25	2.94	2.87	3.26	3.51	2.83	2.71	3.61
BB	-0.29	0.03	0.85	9.59	1.47	1.08	0.86	0.78	1.09	1.38
B	-1.89	-2.02	-1.53	-1.70	-0.59	-1.88	-2.08	-1.56	-1.43	-0.79
CCC	-5.82	-5.74	- 8.19	-6.27	-8.36	-5.24	-4.35	-4.23	-4.23	-2.59
NR	1.66	2.15	3.30	2.40	2.83	4.20	4.52	0.82	0.64	—

Source: Zeta Services Inc., Bond Rating Analysis Book, Spring 1990.

Exhibit 6.9a

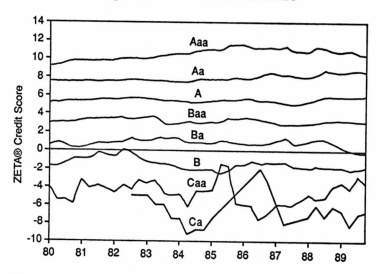

ZETA® Equivalents of Moody's Rating
Average Scores for the Last Ten Years

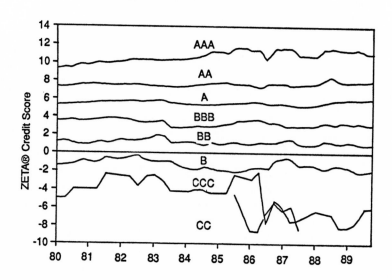

ZETA® Equivalents of S&P's Rating
Average Scores for the Last Ten Years

Exhibit 6.10 Average Zeta® Credit Scores for Bankrupt Companies (1984-1988)

Years Prior to Bankruptcy	All Bankruptcies All Yrs.	All Yrs.	Non-Fraud, Non-Legal Bankruptcies					
			1988	1987	1986	1985	1984
0	−6.44	−6. 90	−8.48	−5.84	−6.98	−6.07	−5.38
1	−3.63	−4.11	−5.60	−3.81	−2.97	−3.61	−3.72
2	−2.15	−2.50	−3.56	−2.23	−1.86	−2.20	−2.10
3	−0.96	−1.38	−2.46	−1.51	−1.10	−0.52	−0.81
4	−0.62	−1.03	−1.85	−0.58	−0.82	−0.67	−0.65
5	−0.24	−0.71	−1.00	1.06	−0.76	−1.75	−0.24

Exhibit 6.11 Investment in Positive ZETA Distressed Issues (1978-1989)

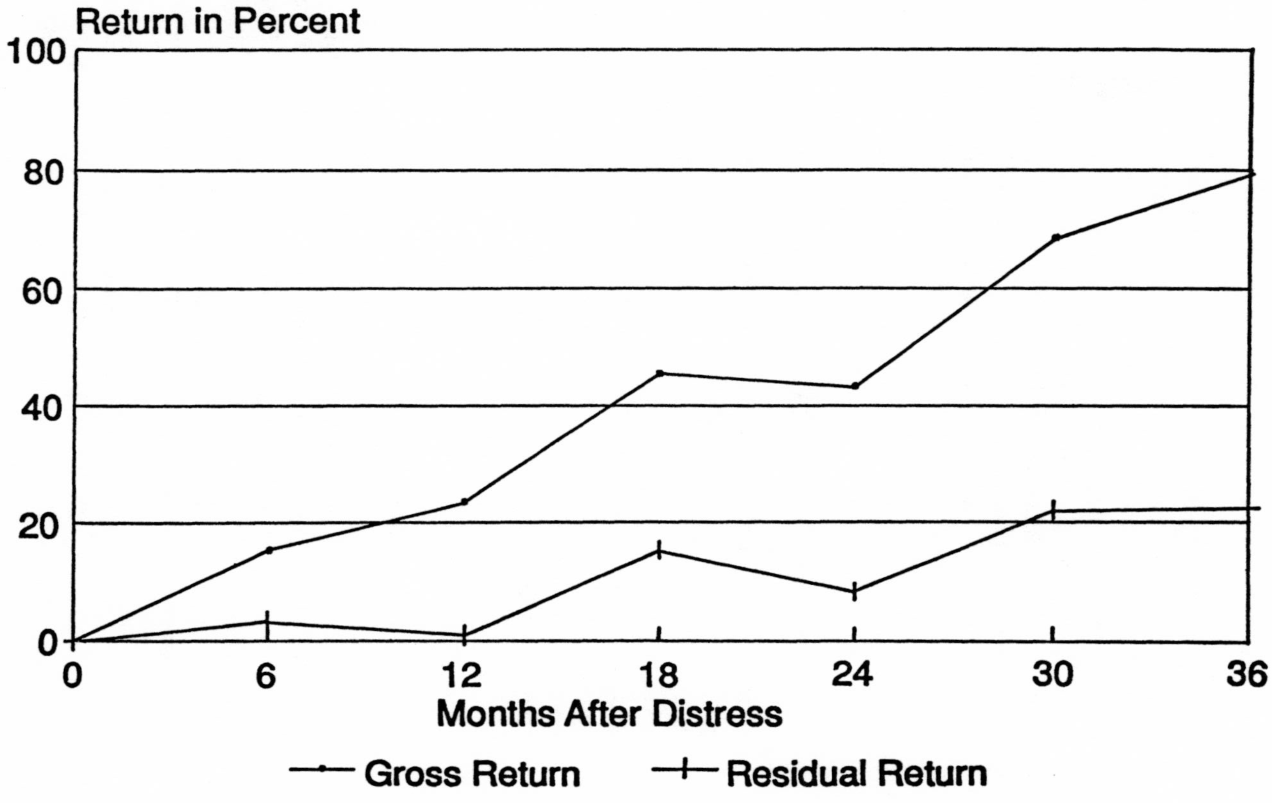

was just slightly negative with the average mutual fund recording a return of -.089 percent. Other junk bond indices compiled by securities firms were also slightly negative for the year. According to Lipper Analytical Service, the average Fund lost -6.60 percent over the one-year period April 1, 1989–March 31, 1990.

An increasing default rate and a distinct lack of liquidity have been the primary reasons for this market's poor performance. Highly visible defaults, such as Allied and Federated Stores, Integrated Resources and Hillsborough Holdings occurred. Others such as Southland, Western Union and Interco were selling at distressed prices. While the truly distressed companies' securities suffered most, all junk bonds were, to some extent, tarred with the same brush. As expected, default rates increased and the liquidity premium required by investors soared.

Can Rigorous Credit Analysis Help?

Would a special effort to reduce the investor risk amongst a diversified junk bond portfolio have helped to improve overall returns during this market decline? We seek to answer this question by assessing bond performance selected by the ZETA® credit scoring approach. ZETA®, as described earlier, is a multivariate approach. It uses a set of seven financial indicators. Each one is weighted by a statistical technique developed specifically to assess the credit risk and distress potential of U.S. industrial companies.

The ZETA® Test

Exhibits 6.9 and 6.9a showed the average ZETA® score for each of the published S&P and Moody's bond rating groupings over the last 10 years. The ZETA® equivalent scores for the various bond ratings have been quite consistent over this period. Note that a score of zero is roughly coincident with a bond rating of BB. A score of -1.0 is somewhere between BB (Ba) and B. In our 1977 tests, we found that a score of zero maximized the accuracy of bankruptcy classification up to five years before the actual filing. Later tests substantiated those initial results.

Our next test involved the selection of junk bond issues with ZETA® scores of -1.0, -0.5 or 0.0 as of year-end 1988. We assessed total performance over the 12-month period, calculating ZETA® scores. We assessed the scores for year-end 1988 based on data available March 31, 1989. The simulation began on that date. We selected cut-off scores between 0.0 to -1.0. These serve the dual purpose of selecting credit worthy companies and providing a sufficient number of issues.

The one-year total return performance of our ZETA® selected portfolio was then compared with various other asset classes. Included were two widely cited junk bond indices, the 10-year U.S. Treasury Index and the S&P 500 Stock Index. The most relevant comparison is with the junk bond indices. The purpose of the test is to assess whether a credit quality approach to portfolio selection can enhance returns in a falling junk bond market. We also compared the ZETA® portfolios with the average junk bond mutual funds' performance. It should be noted, however, that mutual funds normally have lower average returns than securities' indices due to management and transaction costs.

Exhibit 6.12 lists the one-year (April 1, 1989-March 31, 1990) performance of various indices vs. the ZETA®-selected portfolios. The ZETA® portfolio performance was vastly superior to both the Merrill Lynch 175 Index and the First Boston High Yield Index. For ZETA®'s greater than 0.0, the total return was 11.23 percent with complete data available on 114 issues. If our criterion was lowered to ZETA®'s -0.50, raising relevant issues to 129, the return is similar at 11.30 percent. Finally, if the criterion was changed to ZETA® greater than -1.0, there were 168 observations with returns of 9.65 percent. The comparable junk bond indices' total return were -0.02 percent (Merrill Lynch), -3.88 percent (First Boston) and -6.60 percent for the average of 85 funds followed by Lipper Analytical Services.

The ZETA® portfolio (0.0 and -0.5) outperformed all 85 of the high current yield mutual funds followed by Lipper during this period. Only one fund with a return of 9.62 percent was even close to ZETA®'s 9.65 percent performance (-1.0). Keep in mind that the ZETA® portfolio returns are not impacted by management or transaction costs. Still, ZETA® outperformed the high-yield funds and indices.

The standard deviations of the ZETA® portfolios are slightly less than those of the other junk bond indices and considerably less than Treasury bonds and S&P 500 indices. These are based on the variance of quarterly returns for that one-year period. The average return results of ZETA® vs. the junk bond indices are significantly different, although we do not have the standard deviations from within the other indices. The ZETA® portfolios' performance were slightly lower than the U.S.

Exhibit 6.12 Total Return Performance For A Portfolio of Bonds Selected By the Zeta® Approach Compared to Various Portfolio Index Returns (for the period April 1, 1989–March 31, 1990)

Portfolio	Number of Issues or Funds	One-Year Total Returns (%)
Zeta ≥ -0.0	114	11.23
Zeta ≥ -0.5	129	11.30
Zeta ≥ -1.0	168	9.65
Merrill Lynch 175 Index of High Yield Bonds	175	-0.02
First Boston High Yield Index	349	-3.88
U.S. Treasury (10-year)	—	12.06
S&P 500 Stock Index	500	19.28
High Current Yield Mutual Funds	85	-6.60

Sources: Zeta Services, Merrill Lynch, First Boston, Standard & Poor's and Lipper Analytical Services.

Exhibit 6.13 Distribution of Ratings for the Issues with a ZETA ≥ -1

	Observations	
Rating	Number	Percentage (%)
BB+	21	12.50
BB	38	22.62
BB-	14	8.33
B+	20	11.90
B	22	13.10
B-	27	16.07
CCC+	5	2.98
CCC	1	0.60
CCC-	3	1.79
CC	0	0.00
C	0	0.00
NR	17	10.12
	168	100.00

Treasury 10-year Bond Index (12.06 percent). The leading index over this one-year period was the S&P 500 Index (19.28 percent).

It could be argued that the selected ZETA® portfolios merely matched the best performing junk bond sector (i.e., BB-rated bonds). The latter returned 9.31 percent for the one-year sample period. As Exhibit 6.13 shows, the ratings of our ZETA® -1.0 portfolio comprised about 43 percent BBs with 57 percent either lower rated or non-rated. Therefore, the ZETA® portfolio was more diversified and wider based than the junk bond portfolio.

The results indicate that a disciplined credit evaluation technique can lead to significantly higher portfolio returns. This is especially true in the difficult market conditions of high-risk debt securities. One should not condemn the entire junk bond market when the return is poor and below historical averages. The key to high-yield, high-risk corporate bond market performance is paying attention to fundamental risk characteristics and using established tools of analysis.

## 7

An Index of Defaulted
Straight Debt Securities[*]

A formal return index spanning time is another standard of performance in distressed securities. Indices exist for all major asset classes. These include equities, investment and low-grade corporate bonds, convertible bonds, municipal securities and government securities. For the equities market, many indices of different sizes exist. The Dow-Jones Industrial Index covers very few securities. The NYSE Index contains the entire New York Stock Exchange. Value Line and the Wilshire 5000 Index are larger still. One, the Quintero Index (R.R. Quintero & Co.), follows bankrupt stocks only. There are also many bond indices. Most put either investment-grade or low-grade securities into a single basket. Some securities firms, such as Merrill Lynch and Co. and Salomon Brothers, Inc., break down the return measures by individual bond rating catego-

---

[*]   Eric Katzman and Thierry Genoyer of NYU, Stern School of Business, contributed a great deal to the construction and calculation of this index. The index is now published and maintained as the Altman-Merrill Lynch Index of Defaulted Debt Securities.

ries, and First Boston's high-yield index includes a small number of defaulted bonds.

A Defaulted Straight Corporate Debt Index

In order to assess how defaulted debt securities have performed in recent years, we constructed a total return index on these straight (non-convertible) corporate issues. It was comprised of companies that either have filed for reorganization or have defaulted on the interest due. We originally constructed a monthly index over the four-year period 1986!1989 (inclusive)* and have since extended the index through July 1990. The number of securities that comprised our index ranged from 23 in January 1986 to 116 as of September 1989 and was 128 in June 1990. Because the number of securities was so so small in 1986, we have eliminated the index performance results for that year in this study. Our sample period is therefore January 1987 to July 1990 (about 3.5 years). The first observation of any issue was either January 1987 (if the default came prior to that date) or the first month after the default (if it came after the start of the sample period). After a firm emerges from Chapter 11 or its securities are exchanged for others or cash, the original bond is no longer tracked by our index.

The prices used in our index compilation are from the Standard & Poor's monthly *Bond Guides*. these prices are supplied to S&P by Interactive Data Corporation on issues traded on the NYSE and ASE, using actual trades recorded. In addition, the S&P staff consults traders in these securities from the various brokerage houses. For O-T-C issues, prices are usually bids with matrix pricing utilized for nontraded issues. There is reason to believe that some S&P prices respond slowly to significant firm unique events such as the announcement of a corporate restructuring, the filing of a bankruptcy petition, or the filing of a plan or reorganization. And there may even be differences between the bid prices used and trader-quotes. Because we need a consistent, historical

---

*   This four-year sample period was discussed briefly in the Altman/Foothill Report on Investing in Distressed Securities, April 1990, Los Angeles, CA. Copies of this report are available from the author or the Foothill Group in Los Angeles.

database, despite these discrepancies, we choose to utilize the S&P data for our index calculations.

We constructed three versions of our index. The first was a market value weighted average index. The second was a market value weighted index without two very large bankruptcies, Texaco and Public Service of New Hampshire (PSNH). The third was an arithmetic (equally weighted) average. Texaco was eliminated in the second index because of its huge size and the special nature of its bankruptcy. PSNH was also isolated to assess its impact on 1989 returns.

Our indices are essentially wealth measures, since they assume that the index was bought at the start of each month and sold as of the end of the month. The monthly returns are cumulated to arrive at the end of sample period index level. Because there are no interest payments over the relevant holding periods, we need make no assumptions about reinvested cash flows. The index is therefore directly comparable to other total return indexes measured over the exact same horizons. On the other hand, it is not comparable to some average returns such as mutual fund net asset value changes.

Each index commences with the level at December 1986 equalling 100. The arithmetic index rose from 100 at the start to 149.7 as of July 1990. The two market weighted indices performed considerably better in the first two years but fell off in 1989 and 1990, ending at a somewhat lower level of 132.5 in July 1990. The market weighted index (DDW) and the arithmetic index (DDU) defaulted debt indexes as well as indexes for high yield "junk" bonds and the S&P 500 stock index is shown in exhibits 7.1 and 7.2. We utilized the Merrill Lynch high yield debt Master Index as the comparable bond index. Note the far superior results of the defaulted debt indexes compared to both the S&P and Merrill Lynch indexes in 1987 and 1988 and the inferior performance in 1989 and 1990. The arithmetic defaulted debt index has done fairly well in the first seven months of 1990, rising 19 percent, while the market-weighted index fell by 1.3 percent.* The entire three-and-a-half-year period rate of return as well as the individual years are listed in Exhibit 7.3. Returns between July and October, however, fall rather severely and

---

* The large increase in the arithmetic index in 1990 was caused by several very small bond issues rising significantly in March.

Exhibit 7.1

Defaulted Debt Indexes*

Month	Market Weighted	Percent Change	Arithmetic Average	Percent Change
Dec-86	100.000		100.000	
Jan-87	109.802	9.802%	113.544	13.544%
Feb-87	121.367	10.533%	122.234	7.653%
Mar-87	125.946	3.773%	126.045	3.11%
Apr-87	127.523	1.252%	122.360	−2.924%
May-87	128.086	0.442%	129.039	5.458%
Jun-87	131.797	2.897%	133.553	3.498%
Jul-87	139.051	5.503%	143.226	7.243%
Aug-87	139.775	0.521%	146.344	2.177%
Sep-87	136.351	−2.450%	149.204	1.954%
Oct-87	124.194	−8.916%	122.905	−17.626%
Nov-87	128.188	3.216%	123.160	0.208%
Dec-87	137.846	7.534%	124.886	1.401%
Jan-88	139.836	1.443%	131.366	5.188%
Feb-88	147.445	5.442%	138.957	5.779%
Mar-88	152.013	3.098%	142.765	2.741%
Apr-88	156.846	3.180%	147.853	3.564%
May-88	155.424	−0.907%	144.793	−2.070%
Jun-88	166.943	7.411%	157.026	8.449%
Jul-88	165.047	−1.136%	152.978	−2.578%
Aug-88	160.398	−2.81%	151.209	−1.156%
Sep-88	160.280	−0.073%	149.079	−1.409%
Oct-88	157.692	−1.615%	145.222	−2.587%
Nov-88	166.885	5.830%	147.399	1.499%
Dec-88	174.358	4.478%	150.683	2.228%
Jan-89	166.568	−4.468%	149.661	−0.678%
Feb-89	159.928	−3.986%	144.407	−3.511%
Mar-89	159.596	−0.207%	143.709	−0.484%
Apr-89	162.866	2.049%	146.711	2.089%
May-89	164.491	0.998%	146.332	−0.258%
Jun-89	164.302	−0.115%	146.306	−0.018%
Jul-89	168.344	2.460%	148.266	1.340%
Aug-89	164.816	−2.096%	146.331	−1.305%
Sep-89	151.727	−7.942%	135.778	−7.212%
Oct-89	138.841	−8.493%	123.392	−9.122%
Nov-89	135.098	−2.696%	123.756	0.295%
Dec-89	134.223	−0.648%	125.236	1.195%

*Original compilation by Eric Katzman (NYU); modified by E. Altman and theirry Genoyer.

Exhibit 7.1   (continued)

Defaulted Debt Indexes*

Month	Market Weighted	Percent Change	Arithmetic Average	Percent Change
Jan-90	130.312	−2.914%	126.353	0.892%
Feb-90	126.558	−2.881%	125.528	−0.653%
Mar-90	131.608	3.990%	142.616	13.613%
Apr-90	133.524	1.456%	146.031	2.395%
May-90	131.842	−1.259%	143.899	−1.460%
Jun-90	129.541	−1.745%	144.906	0.700%
Jul-90	132.452	2.247%	149.109	2.901%

*Original compilation by Eric Katzman (NYU); modified by E. Altman and theirry Genoyer.

Exhibit 7.2 Defaulted Debt* (DD) Performance vs. High Yield** and S&P Stock Indexes (1986-1989)***

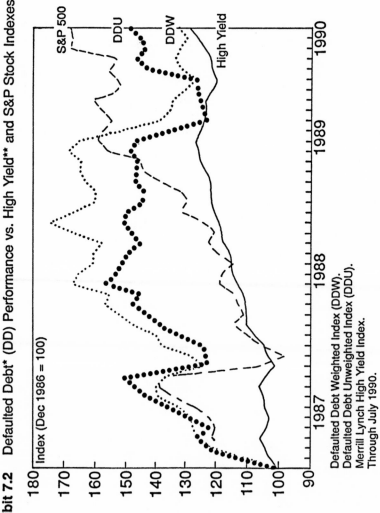

Defaulted Debt Weighted Index (DDW).
Defaulted Debt Unweighted Index (DDU).
Merrill Lynch High Yield Index.
Through July 1990.

Exhibit 7.3   Return on Defaulted Debt Securities Indices
(1987–1990)

Period	Average Number of Securities	Annual Return (Market Weighted Average)	Annual Return (Arithmetic Unweighted Average)	S&P 500 Stock Index	Merrill Lynch High Yield Index
1987	61	37.9%	24.0%	5.3%	4.7%
1988	89	26.5	20.7	16.6	13.5
1989	106	-23.0	-16.9	31.7	4.2
1990	126	-17.1	-2.9	-3.1	-4.4

1987–1990 Average (Annual)

Arithmetic	96	2.8%	5.1%	11.9%	4.3%

Source: Original compilation, E. Katzman, modified by E. Altman and T. Genoyer. Updated monthly results published in "This Week in High Yield," Merrill Lynch & Co., M. Fridson, Editor.

the arithmetic index was 127.4 and the weighted index was 119.9 as of the end of October 1990.

The individual year returns show two exceptional years (1987 and 1988) and one relatively poor year of performance (1989). Indeed, the annual rate of return on the market-weighted index was as high as 37.9 percent in 1987 and 26.5 percent in 1988 or as low as -23.0 percent in 1989. The unweighted index returns were between 24.9 percent and -16.9 percent. the average annual return over the four-year period was 10.0 percent (weighted) and 12 percent (unweighted)"assuming 1990 returns so far are for the entire year. The defaulted debt indexes perform in a similar manner to the S&P 500 Index, with the latter recording a slightly higher average annual return of 14.2 percent for the four-year period. The high yield index had the lowest total return with an average annual return of 6.7 percent (Exhibit 7.4).

As of November 1990, we began to publish and maintain the Altman/Merrill Lynch Defaulted Debt Index (see Altman and Fridson, 1990). This index is our DDW version and comprised about 130 issues from 50 companies. It is updated on a monthly basis and published in Merrill Lynch's "This Week in High Yield."

Market Value Weighting and Return Bias

The market value indexes are based on the amount outstanding for each issue multiplied by its price at the start of each month. The index in my earlier report was calculated on weights based on prices at the end of the month. We have determined that end-of-month weightings inflate the returns in each month. It is interesting how the statistical design of an index can have such a profound effect. For example, the previously reported annual rates of return for 1987–1989 were 53.0 percent, 44.5 percent, and 2.4 percent, respectively, vs. those listed in Exhibit 7.3. In every year, the earlier reported returns are substantially higher. The start-of-month weighting is the conventional methodology.

Size and Returns

Observing the returns, it appears that the large market capitalization issues performed better over the first two years of the sample period than did the smaller capitalization issues. In the past year and a half, however, the market-weighted average index underperformed the arithmetic average index. The market-weighted index reflects that available supply of investments. Because most stock and bond market indexes are market weighted, we refer to that index primarily as our benchmark for defaulted debt securities. The arithmetic index implied an equal amount of invested dollars in each issue at the beginning of each month. As expected, the market-weighted index without Texaco and PSNH did substantially worse than when those securities were included. This was most notably true in 1989.

Diversification Benefits: Correlation with Other Strategies

Including distressed firm debt securities in a larger portfolio has potential for adding a positive return asset class which have low correlations with other assets in the portfolio. Investors can diversify across asset classes to reduce total return variability.

An ignored aspect of distressed security investing is the relationship that these securities have within a larger portfolio of different asset classes. The firm-unique risk of these securities is important in explaining their movement over time. Uncorrelated with other assets, these investments may afford attractive diversification accruing benefits to the manager investing in similar asset classes, such as equities and high-yield bonds. Our test results support this concept.

Based on total returns, the distressed security weighted average index displayed relatively low correlations with the S&P 500 equity index (0.50) over the period 1987–1990. It was somewhat higher with the Value Line equity index (0.59) that includes smaller stocks. The distressed security weighted average index also displayed surprisingly low correlations with the Merrill Lynch high-yield debt index. The correlations are listed in Exhibit 7.4.

One example of how these benefits might work is for a pension fund portfolio manager to invest assets with different managers specializing in relatively safe investments like government bonds, as well as with more risky asset classes like equities, junk bonds and defaulted debt. While not a natural hedge, distressed securities do appear to have the potential to add a positive element to the overall risk/return tradeoff of a portfolio diversified across asset classes.

Exhibit 7.4   Correlation Matrix Between Defaulted Debt
Security Returns and Various Equity and High
Yield Bond Returns

(Monthly Return Observations, 1987-1990)*

	Defaulted Debt	S&P 500 Equity	Value Line Equity	Merrill Lynch High Yield
Defaulted Debt	1.00	0.50	0.59	0.56
S&P 500 Equity	0.50	1.00	0.87	0.56
Value Line Equity	0.59	0.87	1.00	0.69
Merrill Lynch (HY)	0.56	0.56	0.69	1.00

*Original compilation by E. Katzman (NYU) and modified by E. Altman and T. Genoyer (NYU).

## 8

Fallen Angels: Are They All Created Equal?

Previously, we have discussed and analyzed defaulted (no-yield) and distressed high-yield bonds. Downrating of bonds from the so-called investment-grade bond rating to the non-investment-grade or "junk" bond classes is a type of distress. It is caused by the deterioration of the company's credit quality. We now investigate the anatomy and performance of downgraded bonds, sometimes referred to as the fallen angel market.

For 80 years, the corporate debt market has been categorized according to the credit worthiness of the issuer and the individual issue characteristics. Independent agencies assign individual bond evaluations. The three earliest rating agencies were formed in 1909 (Moody's), 1922 (Standard & Poor's) and 1923 (Fitch). For a detailed discussion of these agencies and the rating process, see Ederington and Yawitz (1987). Ratings are also applied to insurance company debt holdings by the National Association of Insurance Commissioners. Those ratings on both public and private issues were modified in 1980 from four to six categories. The ZETA® system discussed in Chapter 6, has been adapted to assist in this process.

The bond rating classification was expanded to investment-grade vs. non-investment-grade designations. The euphemism "junk bonds" was added in the mid-1970s to designate the latter's higher risk, lower rated status. It should be noted that low-rated bonds have existed ever since ratings were first introduced. The top four categories (AAA/Aaa, AA/Aa, A/A and BBB/Baa for S&P and Moody's respectively) had been thought of as investment-grade bonds, seemingly the more desired type of security. Early studies show lower grade bonds produce significantly higher returns (e.g., Hickman, 1958). Many financial institutions are prohibited from investing in the non-investment-grade categories (BB/Ba, B/B and CCC/Caa). Life insurance companies are required to set aside higher bond loss reserves for the lower grade securities.

There are three main types of issues within the non-investment-grade or "junk bond" population. In total, these amount to over 1500 issues and about $200 billion outstanding. First are smaller, unseasoned issues that flourished in the early and mid-1980s and now equal about 20–25 percent of the high-yield junk bond market. The second is the most important and controversial segment of the junk bond market. These are newly issued bonds created from large, corporate restructurings such as LBO's and leveraged recapitalizations. These account for over 65 percent of the new issues since 1985. These proportions of the total outstanding market continue to be valid in 1990.

The third segment comprises bonds originally issued as investment-grade securities. Due to issuer deterioration there is a downrating from investment to non-investment-grade. Known as "fallen angels," they were considered "angelic" at birth but have fallen from the graces of the credit community to junk status. While fallen angels are part of the junk bond market, certain securities firms refuse to include this segment in their "junk" calculations. They claim that if they were not original issue junk, they should not be analyzed with the rest of the high-yield bonds. I do not agree with this separation. In the mid-1970s, virtually all the junk bond market was comprised of these fallen angels, hence the name "junk" became popular. The fallen angel segment grew with the total size of the junk bond market. It reached a peak of $39 billion in June 1987. In the last four years, the junk bond proportion of fallen angels has shrunk from 31 percent in 1985, to 28 percent in 1987 and about 20 percent as of June 30, 1989 (Exhibit 8.1). There are two reasons for the recent reduction in size of the fallen angel segment. One is the significant electric public utility upgrades in June 1989 ($2.4 billion). The other is the upgrades of Texaco's large outstanding debt in April 1988.

We estimated the amount of the fallen angels based on data from Merrill Lynch's Master High Yield Debt List and from discussions with various practitioners. As of June 30, 1989, there was approximately $151 billion par value of outstanding publicly traded, straight high-yield debt. There was another $50 billion of private debt with registration rights. This brought the total to $201 billion. From the Standard & Poor's *Bond Guides*, we found only $117.2 billion of the $151 billion rated public debt. Further analysis showed that of the $117.2 billion, $23.0 billion (19.6 percent) were fallen angels. Extrapolating the $23 billion to a proportion of the $151 billion total public debt, we estimated that the fallen angel population could be as much as $29.7 billion. The likelihood is that the majority of private high-yield debt ($50 billion) was recently issued, not fallen angels.

Therefore, fallen angels comprised about 14.7 percent of the 200 billion dollar straight high-yield debt market as of June, 1989. Public utilities were only 10 percent of the fallen angel total dollars outstanding, down from 15 percent two years earlier.

In terms of the issue number, we estimate that fallen angels comprised 30 percent of the 1404 public issues. The proportion of fallen angel issuers was 15 percent of the high-yield market in 1989, compared to about 10 percent in 1987. The average size of fallen angel issues in 1989 was lower than the average for the entire market. This is the reverse of just two years earlier.

Purpose of the Research

This chapter's objective is to analyze the pre- and post-downrating performance of those bonds which become fallen angels. We are concerned with the junk bond segment of the markets performance, both in absolute and relative terms. The time criteria is from just before the downrating to two years after. Are these bonds different from the junk bond market as a whole? Does a security that becomes a junk bond perform as any other non-investment-grade security? Within this category, are the differences in performance dependent upon the reason the bonds were downrated? Does this depend on whether the bond is from an industrial company or a public utility? Where does the bond "land" when it falls amongst other junk bonds? In addition, the study will consider the wealth loss suffered by bondholders when firms have been involved in high leveraged restructurings that resulted in significant downratings.

Exhibit 8.1 Fallen Angel (FA) Proportion of the High Yield Debt (HYD) Market

Fallen Angel Totals		*December* 1985	*June* 1987	*June* 1989
Rated Issues	$ Amount in MM	$23,165	$38,783	$29,688
	Number of Issues	350	380	413
	Number of Issuers	72	90	116
Utilities	$ Amount in MM	$8,758	$5,783	$2,841
	Number of Issues	196	143	87
	Number of Issuers	13	10	8
Total FA Dollars		$23,165 = 31.1%	$38,783 = 28.3%	$29,688 = 19.6%
Total HYD Outstanding		$74,514	$136,952	$151,580
Total FA Issues		350 = 29.9%	380 = 24.3%	413 = 29.4%
Total HYD Issues Outstanding		1,170	1,567	1,404
Total FA Issuers		72 = 14.8%	90 = 10.2%	116 = 15.3%
Total HYD Issues Outstanding		488	883	757

Evolutionary vs. Revolutionary Downratings

Fallen angel debt's basic distinction is the reduction to non-investment-grade status. Before 1984, downratings were almost exclusively due to earnings quality deterioration and to a lesser ability to service corporate debt. Usually, this was caused from within the firm. In some cases, it was from an external shock that precipitated concerns about an entire industry. Examples are the oil crisis, serious agricultural problems, or nuclear power plant problems for public utilities. We refer to these downratings as evolutionary credit deteriorations (CD) as contrasted from the more dramatic revolutionary change due to a single event.

The single event, or revolutionary change, is a more recent development. This can lead to a massive downrating in the outstanding indebtedness of the firm. The risk that this will or has already taken place is called "event-risk" (ER). It is usually associated with a large financial restructuring of the firm with debt/equity ratios increasing from normal levels to as much as 10:1. The average in 1980-1986 was 6:1 for restructurings, especially in LBO's (see Jensen, Kaplan and Stiglin, 1989). Event-risk occasions include leveraged buyouts, leveraged recapitalizations and other defenses against hostile takeover attempts that result in massive new debt issues. In most cases, the basic earning capacity of the firm's assets is unchanged or slightly increased.

Event-risk became an important issue in the late 1980s. Standard & Poor's began to evaluate individual companies and issues on the risk that an event will alter its bond rating. They now publish a rating from one to five as to event-risk.

Downrating is related to the event-risk type of fallen angel. Evolutionary downratings are usually of a one or two tick type, (e.g., BBB- to BB+ - one tick or BBB to BB+ - two ticks). Revolutionary fallen angels may see their bonds fall eight or more ticks (e.g., A+ to B is a 10-tick drop). Standard & Poor's first refined their ratings to include pluses and minuses in 1974. Our sample will consist of about 10 percent of these issues receiving a drop of 8 or more ticks.

Another fallen angel distinction is whether it is a public utility. Public utilities are thought to have little default risk. Exceptions were the Washington Power Authority's (WPSS) default and Public Service of New Hampshire's Chapter 11 filing in 1987. No other major public utility has defaulted on its debt obligations since the depression. A downrating to non-investment-grade status might not be construed in the same manner as a non-utility bond. Hence, its pre- and post-market behavior may be different. A final means of stratifying the fallen angel population is the specific bond downrating result (i.e., to BB vs. B or CCC).

Some Basic Questions for Investors About Fallen Angels

Investors in fixed income, investment-grade corporate bonds are always concerned with downratings. These events translate into capital depreciation. Until recently, investors relied upon traditional credit evaluation techniques to anticipate such changes. Their success in selling before the price drop is questionable and inconsistent. With the emergence of the sudden, event-risk decline, forecasting rating decreases has become more difficult and, sometimes, more devastating. During the period 1985-1988, it was reported that over $32 billion of investment-grade debt had been downgraded to junk bond status. This resulted in losses exceeding $5 billion (Forsyth, 1988). Before bonds are formally downgraded, the news of a possible major restructuring (using debt financing) will cause prices to fall dramatically. In October of 1988, RJR Nabisco's management announced its intention to take the firm private through an LBO. RJR's $5.4 billion of A-rated paper was placed on S&P's *Credit Watch List* and Moody's indicated it was reviewing its A1 rating. Spreads jumped roughly 200 basis points on some outstanding issues and prices fell almost 20 percent. The actual rating change did not occur until March 1989.

Beside the investor disappointment in experiencing a downrating, how should the old bondholder or prospective new investor view the outlook of fallen angels? Do these bonds do better, worse, or about the same as other corporate bonds, particularly other junk bonds? Does it make a difference if the cause for the downrating was an event type, revolutionary change or a more fundamental debt service coverage deterioration? Is a new fallen angel public utility likely to perform differently than either existing junk bonds or those that are non-utility downgrades? We will examine the evidence to resolve these concerns.

One supposes an event-risk fallen angel is a better investment than one that fell due to evolutionary changes. The earning power is still intact. The gradually deteriorating firm could move further toward default. If LBO's and other highly leveraged restructurings can add tax benefit value and operating efficiency, then upgrades are more likely than in the non-event-risk case. Conversely, if one believes the market will discount the bad information (deteriorating earnings or vastly increased leverage burdens) and events and changes that occur at random are unforeseeable, then one fallen angel won't perform differently from others nor distinctively from other comparable investments.

Prior Studies on Fallen Angels

While fallen angels have been around for a long time, little empirical attention has been given to this segment of the corporate bond market. Absolutely nothing has been published about investment performance coinciding with the time of downrating or periods after that date. The few studies that highlighted fallen-angel debt focused on their default rate statistics.

For example, Fridson and Wahl (1986) analyzed the default rate of fallen angels vs. original issue high-yield bonds for the period 1978–1985. Their calculations showed that fallen angels had a higher average annual default rate (2.66 percent vs. 1.18 percent) when measured by averaging the annual default rates. The difference narrowed considerably (2.02 percent vs. 1.51 percent) when the default rate was measured by dividing the average annual volume by a weighted average of outstanding yearly amounts. When calculated in this manner, the original issue high-yield sector had the higher default rate. It was 1.60 percent per year vs. 0.89 percent for fallen angels (1.73 percent vs. 0.66 percent by the weighted average method). This showed the average issue size of fallen angels was greater than the average size of original issue debt. This is no longer the case.

Exhibit 8.2 comprises defaults from 1970 through 1988 by original bond rating. In addition, the bond rating status is observed as of one year before and six months before filing. This table is listed by number of issues and shows about one-third of defaults were originally issued as investment-grade. All but one (Johns Manville), became fallen angels before default. In dollar amounts, just over 50 percent are original issue investment-grade debt.

Long and Hradsky (1989) examined a sample of defaulting issues over the period 1977–1988. They calculated that annual default *loss* to investors, on a market weighted average basis, was 1.63 percent per year for all issues. It dropped to 1.15 percent per year when fallen angels were eliminated. Apparently fallen angels contributed 48 basis points per year to default losses, or 29 percent of the total. Their data included distressed exchange issues.

Exhibit 8.2

Rating Distribution of Defaulting Issues at Various Points Prior to Default
(Through June 1990)

Including Texaco's Default

Original Rating	AAA	AA	A	BBB	BB	B	CCC	CC	Total
Number	5	19	32	41	45	140	64	4	350
Percentage	1.43%	5.43%	9.14%	11.71%	12.86%	40.00%	18.29%	1.14%	100%

Rating One Year Prior	AAA	AA	A	BBB	BB	B	CCC	CC	Total
Number	0	0	2	25	35	178	100	9	349
Percentage	0.00%	0.00%	0.57%	7.16%	10.03%	51.00%	28.65%	2.58%	100%

Rating 6 Months Prior	AAA	AA	A	BBB	BB	B	CCC	CC	Total
Number	0	0	2	16	18	154	149	20	359
Percentage	0.00%	0.00%	0.56%	4.46%	5.01%	42.90%	41.50%	5.57%	100%

Excluding Texaco's Default

Original Rating	AAA	AA	A	BBB	BB	B	CCC	CC	Total
Number	0	9	28	41	45	138	64	4	329
Percentage	0.00%	2.74%	8.51%	12.46%	13.68%	41.95%	19.45%	1.22%	100%

Rating One Year Prior	AAA	AA	A	BBB	BB	B	CCC	CC	Total
Number	0	0	2	25	35	157	101	9	329
Percentage	0.00%	0.00%	0.61%	7.60%	10.64%	47.72%	30.70%	2.74%	100%

Rating 6 Months Prior	AAA	AA	A	BBB	BB	B	CCC	CC	Total
Number	0	0	2	16	18	133	149	20	333
Percentage	0.00%	0.00%	0.59%	4.73%	5.33%	39.35%	44.08%	5.92%	100%

Fridson (1989) analyzed the expected rating upgrade experience of original issue high-yield debt vs. fallen angels. Original issuers of the junk bonds unjustifiably expected to improve their financial and operating profiles for later upgrades. On average only 1.8 percent per year were upgraded over the period 1976–1986. Paradoxically, 5.2 percent per year of the fallen angels were returned to investment-grade (i.e., were rebounding angels). The gain from original issue low-grade debt that achieved upgrade was equal to an average of 50 basis points per year. By inference, the increase was almost 150 basis points per year for the rebounding angels. Neither calculation includes the downgrading or defaulting loss to investors on original issue junk bonds or fallen angels. As we (Altman, 1989) and others have shown, investors lost 120–140 basis points per year from defaults. This is also discussed in Chapter 2. No one has forecasted the gain or loss per year from rating changes across the entire spectrum. This is the subject of a new research project currently being investigated.

Fridson (1989) presents part of the reason so-called "rising stars" of the junk bond market do not achieve upgrades. The entrepreneurs who run these firms have no interest in obtaining investment-grade status. Often, when the firm is approaching upgrade, it will re-lever or de-equify, using creditor funds, to achieve growth and equity return objectives.

Empirical Results

We examine fallen angels' return behavior for the six months before, and up to 24 months after, the downrating month. The 24-month post-downrating period is arbitrary. Anything beyond that interval would severely limit the number of observations. Downrating constitutes the month Standard & Poor's lowered the classification to BB+ or below from BBB− or above. Data was compiled on 414 fallen angel issues over the period 1984–1988. The sample comprised 108 different issuers including 51 event-risk companies and 13 public utilities. A list is given in Exhibit 8.3. Note that some fallen angels are not listed due to lack of market price data after the rate change (e.g., Beatrice, Holiday Inns). The downrated amounts, in terms of tick numbers, is given in Exhibit 8.4 as is the rating change frequency distribution.

Exhibit 8.3   Fallen Angel Companies, 1984–1988

Fallen Angel Companies
1984-1988

Company	Downrating Date
1984	
American Sugar	2/84
Storage Technology	2/84
Ticor	2/84
Vought Corp.	5/84
Central Maine Power	6/84
Continental Illinois	6/84
Crane Company	7/84
Montana Power	8/84
Valero Energy	8/84
Valero Natural Gas	8/84
AMEX, Inc.	10/84
Bethlehem Steel	10/84
Continental Group	11/84
ARA Services	12/84
Western Union Telegraph	12/84
1985	
Warner Communications	1/85
American Smelting & Refinery	3/85
Federal Paper Board	3/85
Guardian Industries	3/85
Home Group	3/85
Arkansas Power & Light	4/85
Control Data	4/85
Louisiana Power & Light	4/85
Mississippi Power & Light	4/85
New Orleans Public Service	4/85
UniDynamics	4/85
ANR Pipeline	5/85
Armco Inc.	5/85
Colorado Interstate Gas	5/85
Commercial Credit	6/85
DCS Capital Corp.	12/85
Pembroke Capital Co.	12/85
Texaco Capital	12/85
Texaco Inc.	12/85
Tidewater Oil Co.	12/85
Union Carbide	12/85

Exhibit 8.3 continued

1986

Inland Steel	1/86
National Steel Corp.	1/86
Moran Energy	3/86
Norton Simon, Inc.	3/86
ACF Industries	4/86
Phillips Petroleum	4/86
Gulf State Utilities	5/86
Amerada Hess	7/86
ASARCO	7/86
Hanna Mining	8/86
NL Industries	8/86
Colt Industries	9/86
Armstrong Rubber	10/86
Colorado National Bancshares	10/86
Copperweld	10/86
Midland-Ross Corp.	10/86
Owens-Corning Fiberglass	10/86
Entex	11/86
Fruehauf Corp.	12/86
Revco	12/86

1987

Greyhound Leasing & Financial	1/87
Allied Stores	2/87
Marthon Oil	2/87
Texas Oil & Gas	2/87
USX Corp.	2/87
Southdown Inc.	3/87
Texas American Bancshares	3/87
Owens-Illinois	4/87
Zenith Electronics	4/87
Arkansas Power & Light	5/87
Borg-Warner Corp.	5/87
Louisiana Power & Light	5/87
Mississippi Power & Light	5/87
New Orleans Public Service	5/87
Orient Express Hotels	5/87
Clark Equipment	6/87
Leaseway Transportation	6/87
MCorp.	7/87
Burlington Industry	9/87
Rio Grande Ind.	9/87
First Republic Bank	10/87
IFRB Corp.	10/87
Jim Walter	10/87
McDermott Inc.	11/87
Southland Corp.	11/87

Exhibit 8.3   continued

1988

Bucyrus-Erie	1/88
American Medical Int'l	2/88
International Technology	2/88
ONEOK	3/88
Pulte Home Corp.	3/88
Pulte Home Credit	3/88
Singer Co.	3/88
Bell & Howell Group	4/88
Santa Fe Natural Resources	4/88
Federated Department Stores	5/88
Flexi-Van Leasing	5/88
Victoria Bancshares	5/88
American Standard	6/88
US Gypsum	6/88
USG Corp.	6/88
Stevens (JP) & Co.	7/88
Stop & Shop Cos.	7/88
Pneomo Corp.	8/88
Fort Howard Corp.	9/88
Cenvill Investors	10/88
Southern Pacific Railroad	10/88
Southern Pacific Transportation	10/88
St. Louis Southwestern Railroad	10/88
Texaco & New Orleans RR	10/88
Eagle Picher Industries	11/88
Kroger Co.	11/88
Maxus Energy Corp.	11/88
Southern Pacific Corp.	11/88
Insilco Corp.	12/88
Interco	12/88
National Distillers & Chemical	12/88
Quantum Chemical	12/88

Source: Standard & Poor's *Bond Guides*, 1984-1988.

Exhibit 8.4   Distribution of Downratings, 1984–1988

Ticks	Number of Issues	Downgrade	Number of Issues
1	113	AAA to BB-	1
2	126	AA- to B	7
3	29	A+ to BB	11
4	17	A+ to B+	2
5	35	A+ to B	12
6	24	A to BB+	1
7	29	A to BB	2
8	8	A to BB-	10
9	10	A to B+	5
10	15	A to B	4
11	7	A- to BB+	1
12	-	A- to BB	5
13	1	A- to B+	4
		A- to B	2
Total	414	A- to B-	1
		BBB+ to BB+	4
		BBB+ to BB-	3
		BBB+ to B+	4
		BBB+ to B	3
		BBB+ to CCC+	4
		BBB+ to CCC	1
		BBB to BB+	52
		BBB to BB	7
		BBB to BB-	6
		BBB to B+	10
		BBB to B	18
		BBB to CCC+	1
		BBB- to BB+	113
		BBB- to BB	71
		BBB- to BB-	18
		BBB- to B+	10
		BBB- to B	19
		BBB- to B-	1
		BBB- to CCC+	1
		Total	414

Exhibit 8.5   Total Return Performance: Fallen Angels 1984-1988

Average Arithmetic Returns

Months Relative to Downrating Date

	-6 to 0	-2 to 0	-1 to 0	0 to 1	1 to 6	6 to 12	12 to 24	0 to 6	0 to 12	0 to 24
1984	2.54%	-2.19%	0.25%	1.86%	10.62%	9.18%	14.07%	12.58%	22.31%	36.62%
1985	6.45	2.10	0.69	4.05	5.69	18.97	9.15	9.86	29.89	43.52
1986	8.98	2.11	0.47	0.96	4.22	3.40	10.02	5.17	8.51	18.22
1987	-2.30	-5.78	-4.39	0.49	-4.47	4.17	–	-0.04	-0.48	–
1988	2.24	0.50	-0.34	-0.45	2.55	–	–	0.01	–	–
Total	3.56%	-0.77%	-0.96%	-0.45%	2.68%	9.72%	10.41%	4.44%	14.86%	33.77%
Standard Deviation	7.88	6.67	5.26	4.72	10.23	13.08	9.72	11.41	19.56	8.53
# Issues	401	414	414	414	389	341	204	385	341	214

Average Weighted Returns

Months Relative to Downrating Date

	-6 to 0	-2 to 0	-1 to 0	0 to 1	1 to 6	6 to 12	12 to 24	0 to 6	0 to 12	0 to 24
1984	2.03%	-1.63%	0.76%	2.24%	10.29%	7.81%	12.76%	12.69%	21.14%	34.38%
1985	4.87	0.28	-0.58	1.95	9.06	12.84	9.06	10.93	25.08	36.75
1986	3.25	1.03	0.62	2.21	6.04	5.94	11.91	8.36	14.55	26.94
1987	-0.7	-3.6	-3.1	0.08	-5.24	3.8	–	-5.06	-1.06	–
1988	0.88	-1.04	-1.55	-0.85	2.43	–	–	-0.09	–	–
Total	2.52%	-0.44%	-0.73%	1.26%	4.73 %	7.87%	10.99%	6.08%	17.46%	31.64%
# Issues	401	414	414	414	389	341	204	385	341	214

Exhibit 8.6   Event-Risk vs. Credit Deterioration Fallen Angels: Total Return Performance 1984-1988

Event Risk

	Months Relative to Downrating Date									
	-6 to 0	*-2 to 0*	*-1 to 0*	*0 to 1*	*1 to 6*	*6 to 12*	*12 to 24*	*0 to 6*	*0 to 12*	*0 to 24*
Arithmetic	3.75%	1.41%	-0.02%	0.02%	6.37%	6.68%	9.97%	6.15%	13.69%	25.68%
Weighted	1.19	-0.004	-0.49	0.49	7.96	6.6	11.41	6.57	14.61	27.67
Standard Deviation	7.67	5.32	6.26	4.22	8.13	8.78	8.45	8.69	13.22	13.31
# Issues	124	126	126	126	108	80	61	108	80	61

Credit Deterioration

	Months Relative to Downrating Date									
	-6 to 0	*-2 to 0*	*-1 to 0*	*0 to 1*	*1 to 6*	*6 to 12*	*12 to 24*	*0 to 6*	*0 to 12*	*0 to 24*
Arithmetic	3.22%	-1.72%	-1.37%	2.39%	1.25%	10.62%	10.58%	3.79%	15.18%	37.00%
Weighted	3.71	-0.95	-1.02	2.14	1.15	9.06	10.31	2.92	13.16	33.43
Standard Deviation	7.94	6.97	4.7	4.76	10.59	14.02	10.15	12.22	21.07	19.31
# Issues	277	289	289	289	277	262	153	277	263	153

Exhibit 8.7   Utility vs. Non-Utility Fallen Angels: Total Return Performance 1984-1988

Utilities

	Months Relative to Downrating Date									
	-6 to 0	*-2 to 0*	*-1 to 0*	*0 to 1*	*1 to 6*	*6 to 12*	*12 to 24*	*0 to 6*	*0 to 12*	*0 to 24*
Arithmetic	2.23%	-3.07%	-2.40%	3.48%	0.85%	14.18%	10.16%	4.43%	18.73%	41.21%
Weighted	2.82	-2.72	-2.29	3.12	0.73	13.48	10.22	3.92	17.3563	37.63
Standard Deviation	8.24	7.22	5.18	3.02	5.45	11.19	5.31	7.24	16.79	19.01
# Issues	172	177	177	177	181	114	86	176	173	96

Non-Utilities

	Months Relative to Downrating Date									
	-6 to 0	*-2 to 0*	*-1 to 0*	*0 to 1*	*1 to 6*	*6 to 12*	*12 to 24*	*0 to 6*	*0 to 12*	*0 to 24*
Arithmetic	4.55%	0.94%	0.10%	0.33%	4.2 2%	5.17%	10.62%	4.47%	10.89%	27.72%
Weighted	2.43	0.21	-0.29	0.72	6.02	5.79	11.29	6.79	14.44	30.17
Standard Deviation	7.45	5.65	5.06	5.28	12.77	13.31	12.2	13.93	21.32	15.71
# Issues	229	238	237	237	208	167	118	210	169	118

Total Return Performance

Fallen angels returns for intervals six months before the downrating, up to 24 months after, are given in Exhibit 8.5. The data is presented in arithmetic averages, assuming an equal amount is invested in each issue (top panel). Averages based on market weights are also given in the bottom panel. Exhibit 8.6 examines behavior by event-risk vs. non-event-risk categories. Exhibit 8.7 gives results by utilities vs. non-utilities. Exhibit 8.8 notes the effects of results by BB vs. B-rated fallen angels.

See Exhibit 8.5 for the entire sample. Fallen angels gained 3.56 percent (interest + price change) on an average arithmetic basis for the six months before the downrating. They lost -0.77 percent and -0.96 percent for the two-month and one-month periods respectively before the event. The gains were less positive and the losses were less negative when based on the weighted average calculations.

The fallen angel totals recovered slightly in the one-month period after downrating. Absolute returns of 14.86 percent (arithmetic) and 17.46 percent (weighted) for one year after downrating were posted. The two-year percentages were 33.77 percent (arithmetic) and 31.64 percent (weighted).

Credit Deterioration vs. Event-Risk

The sample's credit deterioration (CD) arithmetic return increased 3.22 percent for the six-month period prior to the downrating. The event-risk (ER) category increased by 3.75 percent (Exhibit 8.6). The CD group fell more than the event-risk issues for the two- and one-month periods prior. This was not unexpected. Credit deterioration is a gradual phenomenon, observable by the market, causing continuous price declines. Event-risk is not easily prophesied, despite S&P's efforts to quantify it. The credit deterioration issues are likely to appear on the Standard & Poor's *Credit Watch List* several months before the actual downrating. This is also true for many event-risk issues. Most of the average decline had taken place during the two months prior to the downrating. It was surprising that the event-risk issues' total return did not show a larger price drop in the months before the downrating. Apparently the interest returns offset price declines two months before the downrating. It approximated the price decline of the downrating month.

Event-risk (ER) companies recover more than the CD firms during the first six months after the downrating. Exhibit 8.6 shows a first six-month return of 6.15 percent (ER) vs. 3.79 percent (CD). For the 12- and 24-month periods, the situation was reversed. CDs outpaced their event-risk counterparts by 15.18 percent vs. 13.69 percent (one-year) and 37.00 percent vs. 25.68 percent (two-years). The one-year divergence (1.49) is minor. The market value weighted averages have a slight superiority for the event-risk class. Neither the arithmetic or market weighted results are significantly different for one-year after downrating. The two-year post-differential greatly favors the credit deterioration sample.

Pre-Downrating Loss in Wealth

Upon examining the pre-downrating price and return behavior of the event-risk fallen angels, an interesting facet emerges. A smouldering controversy surrounds the wealth transfer between the equity holders and the existing bondholders. The equity holders benefit from the buyout firm's offered premium. The existing bondholders suffer from the restructured entities increased leverage. RJR Nabisco bondholders have sued the buyout firm and the old management responsible for their sizeable losses. How pervasive are those losses and what are the magnitudes involved?

Evidence on bondholders losses, due to takeovers and high leveraged restructurings, is unclear. There are many stories told of horrific losses (e.g., Forsythe, 1988). Takeover critics argue that large premiums received by the target firm's shareholders merely represent a redistribution of wealth from existing bondholders. As reported by Jarrell, Brickley and Netter (1988) and Amihud (1989), however, the evidence does not support this wealth transfer hypothesis. Denis and McConnell (1986) found no bondholder losses, of either the acquiring or the target firms. Their conclusions were based on a sample of 132 mergers in the period 1962–1980. Lehn and Poulsen (1987) found evidence for the redistribution theory based on a study of 108 leveraged buyouts (only nine of which had bonds outstanding) from 1980 to 1984. They noted a negative return (-1.16 percent) for the period from 10 days prior to 10 days after the buyout. While these are significant results, they are not dramatically negative and the sample size is very small. Warga and Welch (1990) investigated LBO effects on bondholders and stockholders for a sample of 43 bonds issued by 16 companies in the 1985–1988 period. The find

Exhibit 8.8 Price Changes in the Pre-Downrating Period: Event-Risk Sample

Period	Average Price Change	Standard Deviation	N	Distribution	
				<-5%	>+5%
-6 to 0	-0.884%	7.460	124	32	25
-2 to 0	-0.329%	5.295	124	21	20
-1 to 0	-0.887%	6.234	126	16	7

that while the old bondholders experience significantly negative residual returns after the LBO offer announcement, these losses are considerably less than equity holder gains.

Marais, Schipper and Smith (1987) found that the announcement of going private had a small negative effect on bond prices. Their larger sample involved 26 non-convertible bonds. While we do not look at LBO's per se, our event-risk downrating sample is considerably greater with 124 observations.

We observed the price behavior of our event-risk sample for the six-month period before the downrating. Average price changes (not returns) listed in Exhibit 8.8 were actually quite modest. They were: -6 months to 0, -2 months to 0, and -1 month to 0 (i.e., -0.88 percent, -0.33 percent and -0.88 percent, respectively). In Exhibit 8.6, the gross return was positive for the six-month prior period. The accrued coupon payment, based on an average annual coupon yield of 9.50 percent, more than offset the small price decreases. Once again, there is no significant evidence of the postulated redistribution effect in terms of absolute returns. But, if we had adjusted the absolute return for what could have been earned on similar risk investments, the residual return would no doubt have been significantly negative.

A small average negative price change (under -1.0 percent) for the six-month prior period is little solace to the bondholders suffering a loss of over 10 percent. Fifteen of the 124 issues fell by over 10 percent. Another 17 fell between 5 and 10 percent. Approximately one-quarter of the issues had a minimum five percent price loss. On the other hand, 25 issues enjoyed a price increase of at least five percent. It was startling that almost half the issues increased in price. Sometimes, the rise resulted from expectations (the issue being called) or from an actual tender offer coinciding with the restructuring. Indenture changes in the bonds could benefit the bondholder despite the increase in overall leverage. Finally, the restructuring might have been announced before the six-month period prior to the downrating. The primary drop in price also could occur more than six months prior, therefore outside our measurements. Warga and Welch (1990) estimate that the LBO takes place an average of five months after the announcement of the takeover.

Utilities vs. Non-Utilities

For the six-month period prior, utilities performed worse than non-utilities, gaining only 2.23 percent vs. 4.55 percent (Exhibit 8.7). For the two- and one-month prior periods, the utilities loss was -3.07 percent and -2.40 percent. Non-utilities gained 0.94 percent and 0.10 percent, respectively. The market seemed to anticipate the utility rating change earlier than it did for the non-utilities. This is understandable. Utilities are not susceptible to takeover event-risk as was common for non-utilities.

The utilities recovery was better than the non-utilities for both the 12- and 24-month periods (18.73 percent vs. 10.89 percent and 41.21 percent vs. 27.72 percent). The mean test difference (comparing utilities and non-utilities) for 12-months was 3.77 and for 24-months was 5.77. Both are significant at the .05 level. This implies that fallen angels could be considered an asset class after the downrating, and utilities are the preferred segment over non-utilities. We will examine the *relative* performance of all our various fallen angels. This will shed more light on their attractiveness as investments.

BB vs. B-Rated Downgrades

We will now look at our sample of fallen angels from another viewpoint. Observe the performance of bonds falling to the highest level of junk bonds (BB) vs. those falling to the lower level (single-B). CCC-rated bonds were so few in number (7) that we will not pursue that category. BB-rated bonds are still considered credit worthy. This is the reason for our separation. In many periods, original issue BB-rated bonds performed the best of any rating class (Altman, 1989). BB fallen angels in the post-downrating period could be the same case. It's likely that the amount of the downrating (i.e., the number of downticks) is lower for BBs than for single-Bs. Hence, the trauma of the drop is also less. However, if the market has completely digested the information of the downrating, any future movements will be random.

The total return results of our analysis is given in Exhibit 8.9. (Exhibit 8.13 will show the analysis for residual returns.) We observe that the return decline in the pre-downrating period is significantly lower than for single-B bonds. For example, in the two months before the downrating, BBs fell by just -0.58 percent vs. -2.66 percent for single-Bs. The immediate one-month post downrating performance is also superior for BBs (+2.27 percent vs. -0.08 percent). Over the first six months after the downrating, there is virtually no difference in performance. Thereafter, BBs again perform better. For one year the BB's 16.54 percent return is significantly better than the B's 9.50 percent.

Exhibit 8.9 BB-Rated vs. B-Rated Fallen Angels: Total Return Performance 1984-1988

BB-Rated

	Months Relative to Downrating Date									
	-6 to 0	*-2 to 0*	*-1 to 0*	*0 to 1*	*1 to 6*	*6 to 12*	*12 to 24*	*0 to 6*	*0 to 12*	*0 to 24*
Arithmetic	4.35%	-0.20%	-0.59%	2.27%	2.16%	10.96%	11.23%	4.68%	16.54%	36.68%
Weighted	2.56	-0.13	-0.50	1.83	3.81	9.00	11.20	5.93	16.15	34.24
Standard Deviation	7.82	6.31	4.36	4.00	9.96	13.83	9.12	11.16	20.09	17.77
# Issues	295	308	308	308	287	266	174	287	267	174

B-Rated

	Months Relative to Downrating Date									
	-6 to 0	*-2 to 0*	*-1 to 0*	*0 to 1*	*1 to 6*	*6 to 12*	*12 to 24*	*0 to 6*	*0 to 12*	*0 to 24*
Arithmetic	1.30%	-2.66%	-2.25%	-0.08%	4.40%	5.67%	6.79%	4.14%	9.50%	21.13%
Weighted	2.38	-1.24	-1.38	-0.01	7.13	5.34	10.25	7.01	13.30	25.75
Standard Deviation	7.80	7.42	7.33	5.72	9.90	8.74	11.22	11.35	16.36	16.32
# Issues	99	99	99	99	91	71	40	91	71	40

Exhibit 8.10 Average Residual Performance for Fallen Angels (1984-1988)

Months Relative to Downrating Date	Performance[1] Residual (%)	Standard Deviation	No. of Issues	Difference from Zero Test
-6 to 0	-4.37	7.21	401	-12.1*
-2 to 0	-2.53	5.45	414	-9.4*
-1 to 0	-1.89	5.04	414	-7.6*
0 to 1	-0.34	4.39	414	-1.5
0 to 6	-1.84	11.44	385	-3.2*
1 to 6	-1.28	10.29	389	-2.5*
6 to 12	-1.17	11.95	341	-1.8
0 to 12	-2.79	18.14	341	-2.8*
0 to 24	0.38	16.15	214	0.3

[1]Relative to the Blume-Keim high yield index.
* Significant at .05 level.

This continues for the two-year post period with BB's recording an exceptional 36.68 percent average performance. This is 15.5 percent better than the 21.1 percent B returns. Therefore, for almost every measurement interval, BB fallen angels outperform Bs.

The superior BB performance might be caused by the importance of public utility bonds represented in the BB category. There is likely to be a smaller proportion of public utilities in the B-rated class. We find that 155 of the 309 (50.2 percent) issues that dropped to BB were public utilities compared to 22 of the 99 (22.2 percent) issues that dropped to B.

Because public utility downgrades outperformed non-public utilities, we conducted tests on our BB vs. B downgrades without any public utilities. The results show that BBs still outperform Bs, but the margin is somewhat lower. For example, for the 24-month period after the downrating, BBs realized a 31.1 percent positive return. This compared to 21.1 percent for Bs (a 10 percent differential). Both were for non-utility firms only. Recall that the BB vs. B differential for all issues was about 15 percent. Thus BBs tend to outperform lower rated fallen angels across the board for all industries.

Findings consistent with the new bond rating class (BB vs. B) are found also when analyzing the number of downticks. The performance by those issues with the smallest downticks (i.e., 1–3) was -0.71 percent in the two months prior vs. -3.14 percent for 4–6 downticks. A surprisingly positive 1.59 percent was found for issues with greater than six downticks. It appears that the largest downticks represent the smallest pre-downrating loss to investors. They also represent the largest residual losses in the post-downrating period.

Relative Performance: Excess Return Analysis

In Exhibit 8.10 we compare the return performance of our fallen angel total population with the Blume-Keim high-yield index. This allows us to calculate excess or residual returns (losses) for various period intervals. Residual returns are negative for most intervals, except for a slightly positive 0.38 percent over the entire 24-month period after the downrating. The significant pre-downrating negative performance is to be expected. The small post-downrating negative residuals are generally significantly different from zero. This is true except for the first month and months six to 12. It indicates that fallen angels seem to perform about the same when compared to high-yield bonds. Investors shun

Exhibit 8.11

Average Residual Results for Event-Risk (ER)
Fallen Angels vs. Credit Deterioration (CD) Issues
(1984-1988)

Period Relative to Downrating	Sample	Performance[1] Residual (%)	Standard Deviation	No. of Issues	Difference[2] in Means Test
–6 to 0	ER	–5.18	8.33	124	–1.08
	CD	–4.26	6.65	277	
–2 to 0	ER	–1.66	5.09	126	2.24*
	CD	–2.91	5.55	289	
–1 to 0	ER	–1.69	6.31	126	0.47
	CD	–1.98	4.38	289	
0 to 1	ER	–0.79	4.40	126	–1.34
	CD	–0.16	4.39	289	
0 to 6	ER	–1.42	8.12	108	0.53
	CD	–1.99	12.49	277	
1 to 6	ER	–0.21	7.33	108	1.51
	CD	–1.68	11.21	277	
6 to 12	ER	–0.16	7.98	80	1.19
	CD	–1.59	12.91	262	
0 to 12	ER	–1.03	12.63	80	1.25
	CD	–3.35	19.45	262	
0 to 24	ER	–3.13	12.30	61	–2.33*
	CD	1.78	17.25	153	

[1] Sample total return minus Blume-Keim high yield index.

$$^2\ Z = \frac{X_{ER} - X_{CD}}{(S_{ER}^2/N_{ER} + S_{CD}^2/N_{ER})^{1/2}}$$

*Significant at .05 level.

fallen angels for the first year after the downrating. There is little difference between fallen angels and high-yield bonds for the longer two-year post-downrating period.

The pre-downrating relative performance is decidedly negative, -4.37 percent, for the six months prior and -2.53 percent for the two months prior. This indicates market recognition prior to the downrating date.

Event-Risk vs. Credit Deterioration

Exhibit 8.11 lists the residual results by event-risk vs. non-event-risk causes. The event-risk issues perform poorer for the six-month period prior to the downrating. The difference is -5.18 percent vs. -4.26 percent. Both the event-risk and credit deterioration issue results indicate statistically significant negative performance for this six-month period. One month after the downrating, the event-risk issues reverse their comparative return performance and outperform the non-event-risk issues (-1.03 percent vs. -3.35 percent for 12-months after). Both do worse than junk bonds generally over the one-year post-downrating. This "superior" event-risk performance, however, does not persist and after 24-months the event-risk issues do considerably worse than junk bonds (-3.13 percent) and certainly worse than non-event-risk issues. The latter posted a slight increase of 1.78 percent, vis-a-vis junk bonds, not significantly different from zero.

Utilities vs. Non-Utilities

The reason for the non-event-risk superior two-year post-downrating performance is probably due to the impressive public utility residual results of +6.5 percent (Exhibit 8.12). Most of the non-utilities' poor performance is in the first 12 months while the utilities perform very well in the second year. Both utilities and non-utilities do relatively poorly in the six months prior to the downrating.

BB vs. B

As we saw with the absolute returns analysis, BBs also outperform single-Bs in terms of residual performance. For example, Exhibit 8.13 shows that the negative performance of BBs in the two months before

Exhibit 8.12 Average Residual Results for Utility (U) vs. Non-Utility (NU) Fallen Angels (1984-1988)

Period Relative to Downrating	Sample	Performance[1] Residual (%)	Standard Deviation	No. of Issues	Difference[2] in Means Test
–6 to 0	U	–4.80	6.50	172	–0.99
	NU	–4.10	7.70	229	
–2 to 0	U	–3.20	5.70	177	–2.02*
	NU	–2.10	5.20	238	
–1 to 0	U	–2.70	4.80	177	–2.86*
	NU	–1.30	5.10	237	
0 to 1	U	0.04	2.30	177	2.40*
	NU	–0.90	5.40	237	
0 to 6	U	–0.20	4.50	176	2.79*
	NU	–3.20	14.80	210	
1 to 6	U	–0.69	4.10	181	1.33
	NU	–1.90	13.40	208	
6 to 12	U	0.20	10.40	174	2.25*
	NU	–2.70	13.20	167	
0 to 12	U	–0.50	13.20	173	2.35*
	NU	–5.10	21.80	169	
0 to 24	U	6.50	15.80	96	5.27*
	NU	–4.60	14.70	118	

[1] Relative to Blume-Keim high yield index.

$$^2 Z = \frac{X_U - X_{NU}}{(S_U^2/N_U + S_{NU}^2/N_{NU})^{1/2}}$$

*Significant at .05 level.

Exhibit 8.13 Returns on Fallen Angels by Amount of the
Downrating (Absolute Arithmetic Returns)

| Period | *Number of Downrate Ticks** | | |
	1-3 (N)	*4-6 (N)*	*>7 (N)*
−6 to 0	3.87 (256)	2.64 (76)	3.39 (69)
−2 to 0	−0.71 (269)	−3.14 (76)	1.59 (70)
−1 to 0	−0.87 (269)	−2.40 (76)	0.22 (70)
0 to 1	2.59 (269)	0.68 (76)	−0.78 (70)
0 to 6	4.18 (248)	5.86 (73)	3.85 (63)
0 to 12	16.27 (237)	12.49 (61)	10.55 (44)
0 to 24	38.01 (146)	26.92 (35)	22.29 (33)
	Residual Returns		
−6 to 0	−3.51	−6.01	−5.73
−2 to 0	−2.26	−4.32	−1.64
−1 to 0	−1.63	−3.27	−1.42
0 to 1	0.27	−0.83	−2.13
0 to 6	−1.76	−0.89	−3.21
0 to 12	−2.08	−4.37	−4.39
0 to 24	3.24	−6.08	−5.45

(N) Number of observations
*One tick represents the smallest possible S&P change, e.g., BBB− to BB+, 4 ticks, e.g.,
BBB to BB−, etc.

the downgrade (-2.12 percent) is significantly "less than" Bs (-4.08 percent). Without utilities, it was -1.59 percent for BBs vs. -3.30 percent for Bs.

The dramatic difference is that BBs outperform all junk bonds by 2.64 percent for the two years after the downgrade. This compares with the negative -9.45 percent for single-Bs, resulting in a return difference that is significant at the .01 level. Finally, it should be noted that the positive residual performance of BBs, although impressive (+2.64 percent) is not significantly different from junk bonds.

Downtick Performance

Our final test of downrating performance examines the relationship between performance and the amount of the downrating. We classified the degree of downrating by number of ticks (i.e., 1-3, 4-6, greater than 7). The results are listed in Exhibit 8.13. For the post-downrating period, the performance is inversely related with the amount of the downrating. Fallen angels with just 1–3 downticks outperform junk bonds by 3.24 percent for the 24-month period with a very respectable 38.01 percent absolute return. The residual performance is below junk bonds generally for the four to six and greater than seven downtick observations (-6.08 percent and -5.45 percent, respectively). There doesn't seem to be much performance difference between fallen angels of four or more downticks and junk bonds.

Major corporate restructurings and event-risk type of downratings are consistent with large downtick amounts. It is not surprising that these results are consistent with prior analysis of event-risk situations (Exhibit 8.6).

Concluding Remarks

Fallen angels make up a significant, although diminishing, segment of the high-yield debt population, recently about 20 percent. Since the event date of the downrating is clearly evident, investors and analysts can focus on the performance before and after the downrating. Our investigations indicate that for long periods after the downrating, fallen angels perform in a similar manner to the overall high-yield debt population. For shorter periods, of up to one year after the downrating, there appears to be significant negative performance of fallen angels. The data indicates that the reason for the downrating, event vs. non-event-risk causes, does impact the relative returns with a slight long-term preference for non-event-risk downratings. This was probably due to the performance of public utility downrated issues. They did quite well over the two-year period after the downrating. We also find that bonds falling to BB significantly outperform those falling to B. The amount of the downrating is inversely related with post-downrating returns.

Fallen angel debt issues are an important segment of the corporate debt market. They may increase in their proportion of the high-yield sector if the economy goes into a serious recession. Once the downrating takes place, the issues become increasingly relevant for investors who specialize in junk bonds and, as such, deserve continued attention

## 9

Default Rates and Fixed Income Performance

We referred earlier to junk bond defaults and their contribution to the distressed securities market. We now investigate this fascinating area from a fixed income performance context. A discussion of the level and significance of junk bond default rates will attempt to set the record straight in this continuing debate.

The assessment of three primary risk characteristics determine the required yields on various types of fixed income securities. They are as follows:

- sensitivity of prices to interest rate changes,

- perceived differences in the liquidity of the issues, and

- their inherent default risk.

The hierarchy of returns on debt securities should reflect the typical risk vs. return tradeoff. Higher returns are required for the riskier classes. The riskiest debt securities, in liquidity and default risk terms, are the lower rated corporate bonds. Until recently, high-yield junk bonds had the highest paybacks to investors, whether measured by portfolio indices or fixed income mutual fund performance averages. This historical hierarchy was upset in 1989. BBB (Baa) investment-grade bonds did best over the past ten years (1980–1989). For this complete discussion, see Altman, 1990a.

Junk bonds are made up of three types of issues. About 20–25 percent of the market is of original issue investment-grade securities. Their credit profile has deteriorated and their bond ratings drop to the low-rated categories. We discussed these "fallen angels" in Chapter 8. Another 25 percent comes from original low-grade issues that use the proceeds for growth and investment purposes. The balance is comprised of bonds issued for large corporate restructurings, particularly in the period 1986–1989. This B-rated category is the dominant and most controversial junk bond today. Also, with the recent slump in the junk bond market, the amount of new public issuance in 1990 has dropped to a trickle (under $500 million). Highly leveraged, publicly financed corporate restructurings have all but stopped.

The problems of many junk bond issues resulted in record yield spreads over Treasuries in 1990, as high as 8–10 percent. These spreads reflect increased concerns about both liquidity and default prospects of a large number of issues.

Here, we concentrate on the following:

- recent attention in the measurement of principal and interest of corporate issuers

- the history and forecast of defaults and the ramifications for investor returns.

Since virtually all defaulted bonds are rated non-investment or "junk" grade just before their distress date, we will highlight the junk bond statistics and controversy.

The significance of defaults, particularly amongst the high-risk high-yield junk bond market has never been more important. There is widespread concern about the future viability of this $200 billion market. In 1989, $8.1 billion of corporate debt defaulted or was exchanged for lower yielding and lower priority securities (involving 37 companies and 80 issues) and the number and amounts are much higher in 1990. Measured the traditional way, this amounts to a default rate of about 4 percent in 1989 and over 8 percent in 1990. Several billion dollars of additional securities are severely distressed. Financial institutions, including commercial banks, are creating junk bond underwriting and trading departments in increasing numbers. This provides a full complement of advisory and corporate financing services to clients and attractive underwriting fees can also be earned (averaging three percent on low-rated issues). Even though the public has redeemed many of the open-end, high current yield, junk bonds, the number of these mutual funds is still large (approximately 85 as of September 1990). Net asset values of these public mutual funds were $21.3 billion, down from a high of $35 billion in June 1989.

A large number of studies have chronicled the default incidence of bonds. The controversy over appropriate measurement of defaults and their implications has never been greater. Wall Street researchers, and an increasing number of academics, display heightened interest in this market. Why should there be such a controversy over the default phenomenon? This has been discussed in depth ever since the classic work by Hickman (1958). The reasons are simple. Emotion breeds and the media thrives on controversy. Sadly, in their quest to stir up newsworthy events, some journalists create confusion.

Junk bonds, more than other corporate financing mechanisms, have conjured up passionate supporters and intense persistent detractors. This is because they were used in the highly leveraged corporate restructurings and hostile takeover movement of the 1980s. The default risk to investors is foremost in the debate. How risky have these instruments been? Has the market changed enough to make past measurements less important? The clash between traditional measurement methods and the more recent mortality/aging concepts have sparked academic and media controversies, creating several new works and formal commentaries.

First, discussion of the traditional method for measuring defaults of junk bond portfolios is in order. Then we will compare the recent default innovations results and return measurement procedures. These new studies are consistent in their findings. Interpretations by various practitioners and the press are prone to differences. We discuss attempts to estimate future defaults and their impact on investor returns. Finally, we assess the implications of the record yield spreads required by investors as of mid-1990.

Traditional Measures of Default Rates and Losses

Central to our discussion is the accurate measurement of default risk tradeoffs between the required risk premiums and returns. The market has accepted the distinctions between investment-grade and non-investment-grade categories. Bonds receive precise ratings within four classes of investment-grade debt and three classes of lower-quality junk bonds. Despite the finer distinctions, all published analysis before 1988 concentrated on either the entire corporate bond or the high-yield, non-investment-grade sector. Traditional measurement of default rates is calculated on an average annual basis. Individual rates for each year are combined with rates for other years to form the estimate. The rate for each year is based on the dollar amount of defaulting issues in that year. It is divided by the total population outstanding as of some point during that year. Each year is usually given equal weight in calculating the average, although the yearly default rate is market weighted.

Default Rates

Exhibit 9.1 lists the average annual default rate compilation on low-rated debt for the period 1970–1989. Shorter intervals within the entire 20-year period are also shown. The average for the period 1970–1989 was 2.5 percent while the 1978–1989 average rate was 2.1 percent. The rate increased to 3.4 percent for the past five years (1985–1989). Exhibit 9.2 lists the average annual default rate on *all* corporate straight debt for selected periods from 1900 through 1989. Note, these estimates are not strictly comparable because various researchers use different criteria for measuring default rates. Nevertheless, the data is instructive and permits the reader to observe trends over a long period. As Vanderhoof et. al., (1989) points out, the average differences from 1900 through 1944 vs. 1945 to the present are great and easily statistically significant. The bond markets are, in many ways, not the same. Yet, in terms of recoveries from default, the results over the two large sample periods are very similar.

Default Losses

The more relevant default statistic for most investors is not the rate of default but the amounts lost from defaults. Altman and Nammacher (1987) measured the amount lost from defaults. This assumed the investor had purchased the issue at par value, sold the issue just after default, and lost one coupon payment.

The average annual default loss over the sample period 1978–1989 has been approximately 1.5 percent per year. It was 1.26 percent for 1974–1989, with a higher rate at 2.77 percent for the most recent five

Exhibit 9.1

Historical Default Rate–Low Rated, Straight Debt Only 1978-1990 ($ Millions)

Year	Par Value Outstanding	Par Value Default	Default Rate
1990	$210,000	$18,354.00	8.740%
1989	201,000	8,110.30 (1)	4.035%
1988	159,223	3,944.20	2.477%
1987	136,952	7,485.50 (1)	5.466% (1)
1986	92,985	3,155.76	3.394%
1985	59,078	992.10	1.679%
1984	41,700	344.16	0.825%
1983	28,233	301.08	1.066%
1982	18,536	577.34	3.115%
1981	17,362	27.00	0.156%
1980	15,126	224.11	1.482%
1979	10,675	20.00	0.187%
1978	9,401	118.90	1.265%
Total	$790,271	$25,300.45	

Arithmetic Average Default Rate 1970 to 1989 2.485%
Arithmetic Average Default Rate 1978 to 1989 2.096%
Arithmetic Average Default Rate 1983 to 1989 2.706%

Weighted Average Default Rate 1970 to 1989 3.179%
Weighted Average Default Rate 1978 to 1989 3.201%
Weighted Average Default Rate 1983 to 1989 3.383%

(1) $1.841.7 million without Texaco, Inc., Texaco Capital, and Texaco

---

Exhibit 9.2   Total Corporate Debt Default Rates, 1900–1989

Period	Total Corporate Debt Default Rate (%)
1900–1909	0.90
1910–1919	2.00
1920–1929	1.00
1930–1939	3.20
1940–1949	0.40
1950–1959	0.04
1960–1967	0.03
1968–1977	0.16
1978–1989	0.34
Averages (Unweighted)	
1900–1944	1.65
1945–1989	0.14
Averages (Weighted)	
1900–1944	1.82
1945–1989	0.26

Sources: Hickman (1958), Atkinson (1967), Fitzpatrick and Severiens (1978), Hill and Post (1978), and Altman (1987). The latter is updated for 1988 and 1989. For tables listing the default rate in each year 1900–1987 and the averages for bonds 1900–1944 vs. 1945–1987, see Vanderhoof, Albert, Tenenbein and Verni (1989).

---

years (Exhibit 9.3). In 1990, the loss rate was about 7.26 percent. Compared to defaults, the loss is a lower percentage. Defaulting debt, on average, sells for less than 40 percent of par at the end of the defaulting month. The recovery rate in 1988 was 43.6 percent and in 1989 was 38.3 percent (Exhibit 9.4). The recovery rate on certain lower priority debt fell dramatically in 1989 (Exhibit 9.5) and also again in 1990.

The 40 percent average recovery rate is similar to the Hickman (1958) findings for 1900–1943 defaults. Recovery rates in 1989, however, have declined. An additional important item is the amount lost from other crisis situations, such as distressed exchange issues. Fridson, Wahl and Jones (1988) did look at the loss on distress exchange issues and losses from defaults. They found that the average annual loss for the

Exhibit 9.3

Default Rates and Losses High Yield Debt Market 1985-1990

Year	Par Amount of Default ($MM)	Default Rate (%)	Weighted Price After Default	Weighted Coupon (%)	Weighted Default Loss (%)
1990	18354.0	8.74	23.4	12.94	7.26
1989	8110.3	4.03	38.3	13.40	2.76
1988	3944.2	2.48	43.6	11.91	1.54
1987	7485.7	5.47*	75.9	12.07	1.65*
1986	3115.8	3.39	34.5	10.61	2.40
1985	992.1	1.68	45.9	13.69	1.02
Average	7,000.4	4.30*	43.6	12.44	2.77*

* Including Texaco. Without Texaco, default rate and default loss for 1987 would have been 1.34% and 0.89% respectively.

Exhibit 9.4

Default Loss to Investors (Based on 69 Defaulting Issues in 1989)

Background Data		Arithmetic Calculation	Weighted Calculation
Average Default Rate 1989	=	4.03%	4.03%
Average End of Month Price After Default	=	35.97	38.31
Average Loss of Principal	=	64.03%	61.69%
Average Coupon Payment	=	12.93%	13.40%

Default Loss Computation	Arithmetic Calculation	Weighted Calculation
Default Rate	4.030%	4.030%
X Loss of Principal	0.640	0.617
Loss from Principal	2.580%	2.486%
+ Coupon X Def. Rate	0.261%	0.270%
Default Loss 1989	2.841%	2.756%

1974-1989 Statistics	Loss	No. of Years	Wgt.
Default Loss 1974-1988	1.162%	15	0.938
Default Loss December 1989	2.756%	1	0.063
Average Default Loss 1974-1989 (Equal Weight)	1.262%	16	1.000

Exhibit 9.5

Recovery Rates* on Defaulted Debt by Seniority (1985-1989)

Year	Secured	Senior	Senior Subordinated	Subordinated
1989	$82.69 (9)	$53.70 (16)	$21.53 (18)	$24.56 (29)
1988	67.96 (13)	41.59 (20)	29.23 (11)	36.42 (18)
1987	12.00 (1)	70.52**(29)	51.22 (9)	40.54 (7)
1986	48.32 (7)	40.84 (7)	31.53 (8)	30.95 (33)
1985	74.25 (2)	34.81 (2)	36.18 (7)	41.45 (13)
Arith. Avg.	66.451 (32)	55.292**(74)	31.614 (53)	32.118 (100)
Std. Dev.	18.722	26.457	19.87	15.423

( ) Number of issues in parentheses.
*Price per $100 of par value at end of default month.
**Without Texaco, 1987 Recovery = $29.77.
  Arithmetic Average Senior Recovery = $43.11.
  Standard Deviation of Senior Recovery = 20.781.
  Compilation by E. Altman & D. Chin, New York University.

period 1978–1987 was 1.88 percent. Their specific base and reference population was original issue high-yield debt. Long and Hradsky's (1989) default loss calculation, including distressed exchange issues, averaged 1.6 percent per year for the period 1977-1988. Vanderhoof et. al., point out that during 1900–1943, 105 of 549 "defaults" (19 percent) never experienced a legal default. This was because the contracts were modified before failure took place. Two-thirds of these modifications were accomplished when the bond was about to mature.

Questions Related to the Traditional Method

The traditional method for assessing default rates and losses has considerable relevance for fixed income securities performance. However, it does present some controversial questions and potential biases. The more recent history of defaults is useful for assessing subsequent year loss rates and setting aside adequate reserves for these losses. It becomes problematic for longer term assessment, especially if the inputs are possibly biased.

It could be argued that both the numerator (calendar-year defaults) and denominator (amount of bonds outstanding) are subject to change in the future. For example, if the amount of outstanding bonds, particularly those comprising the high-yield "junk" bond sector, fall or do not grow, then the default rate would increase. This is especially true during a recessionary period. This is occurring in 1990 as firms repurchased over $5 billion of their own bonds and new issues have been less than $500 million. The market has shrunk a bit. We maintain that investors can estimate market size and loss reserves from traditional default rate calculations for the next year or so. Longer term estimates may require a different perspective.

Total high-yield bonds outstanding will continue to shrink as long as the combination of calls, exchanges, upgrades and collateralized bond obligations (CBOs)exceeds new issues and downgrades. Refinancing with private debt or equity on non-exchanged defaults continues the process. A convincing argument, during the years when the market was growing rapidly, was that the default rate tended to be understated.

One could say the opposite trend will take place in the early 1990s and beyond. This would occur as the market's new issues decrease and past defaults are purged from the market. Therefore, we could observe an overestimate of the average default rate in 1992 and beyond.

There is another problem with the traditional method. It is the aggregation of bonds across all ratings that is used to calculate the total corporate default rate. Non-investment-grade, low-rated categories must also be calculated to determine high-yield bond default rates and losses. It seems more appropriate to analyze bond performance in a less aggregated way (i.e., across individual credit quality classes such as bond ratings, AAA, AA, A, etc). The mortality rate technique (Altman, 1988 and 1989) is constructed to use this simpler structure, assessing longer term performance.

Another major criticism of the traditional method is its lack of consideration of time dependency (aging effect). The average annual method considers all issued and outstanding junk bonds the same. The age of a bond will have some bearing on its future default probability. Investors should be concerned with the cumulative possibility of default over time as well as next year's expected default rate and loss.

Finally, all historic examinations suffer from the criticism that current market conditions are quite different from the past. Simply to extrapolate past results for use in the future without reference to present conditions is unwise.

Mortality/Aging Approaches

To answer many of the queries about the traditional default rate method, two recent studies have given both answers and confusion. Altman's (1988, 1989) mortality technique and Asquith, Mullins and Wolff's (1988, 1989) aging approach have shed new light on default rates. They also have caused an enormous amount of controversy from various interpretations by interested parties. We will first summarize these two studies and then comment on their methods and findings. A later work by Douglass & Lucas (Moody's, 1989) adds to our information about the mortality of bonds and defaults. In reviewing these studies, we will examine their results.

Our initial mortality work (Altman, 1988) assessed the cumulative rates and losses for all corporate bonds issued between 1971–1986. It was later updated through 1989 (Altman, 1990b). Defaulted bonds were separated into individual rating groups. This assessment included investment-grade as well as non-investment-grade issues. Market weighted results assessed the mortality of bonds where the original population changed over time due to calls, sinking funds and defaults. The mortality result, updated to 1989, is a table (Exhibit 9.6) that shows the cumulative rates over a ten-year investment horizon. The junk bond market is relatively young, starting in 1977. Thus, results for long horizons (e.g., 7–10 years) would be based on just a few years of original issuance data. For example, 10-year rates could only be calculated for bonds issued in 1977 and 1978, nine-year results for bonds issued in 1977–1979, etc.

Asquith et. al., argued that the traditional technique had many potential pitfalls. It was better to measure defaults, including distressed exchange issues, by tracking specific year rating groups. They concentrated only on all junk bonds lumped together, although there is some data presented by individual ratings. They also used a market value approach. In addition, they calculated the proportion of each cohort year's issuance that was eventually exchanged or called. A representative table of their primary results is shown in Exhibit 9.7.

To complete the picture, Douglass and Lucas (Moody's, 1989) did a type of mortality analysis. Their study analyzed the default rate of *issuers*, not issues or their dollar amounts. The study's motivation was to determine bond ratings for structured securities such as collateralized obligations. This relies on the market value of a corporate bond pool. A variation on using marked values as collateral is to use the cash flow from the collateral pool. This is the usual method in CBO evaluation. The payment likelihood of a structured portfolio derives directly from the cash flow generated by corporate bonds or bank loans.

Moody's mortality approach differs from Altman's in that they assess default frequency based on the bond rating at the start of some period and not at birth. For example, the one-year Moody's rate for Ba-rated bonds is based on the number of issuers defaulted that were rated Ba as of January 1 of the default year.

Comparison of Results

Compare the results from Exhibit 9.6 (Altman's mortality rates) and Exhibit 9.7 (Asquith's aged defaults). One can see that the cumulative mortality rate for B-rated debt (the dominant junk bond category) in the 10th year is 32.9 percent. The aged approach shows about 32.4 percent in the 11th–12th year. If we assess the 10th year aged results, the default percent is 29.3 percent (see Exhibit 9.8). The latter number is derived by taking the 1977, 1978 and 1979 cohort groups and tracking them for 10 years, then comparing the weighted average of the combined three-year (1977–1979) cohort groups. If we equate the 10-year single-B rated debt

Exhibit 9.6   Cumulative Mortality Rates by Original S&P Bond Rating Covering Defaults and Issues from 1971-1989

Years After Issuance

Original Rating	1	2	3	4	5	6	7	8	9	10
AAA	0.00%	0.00%	0.00%	0.00%	0.00%	0.15%	0.20%	0.20%	0.20%	0.20%
AA	0.00	0.00	1.21	1.46	1.63	1.63	1.86	1.86	1.96	2.07
A	0.00	0.34	0.62	0.68	0.68	0.78	0.93	1.00	1.12	1.12
BBB	0.03	0.63	0.97	1.57	1.87	2.22	3.22	3.22	3.40	4.10
BB	0.00	1.08	1.54	4.80	5.23	6.92	12.09	12.09	12.09	15.04
B	1.08	2.58	5.58	8.84	11.56	15.69	20.97	23.76	30.92	32.94
CCC	1.39	3.21	7.63	22.37	24.55	N/A	N/A	N/A	N/A	N/A

Exhibit 9.7 Aged Defaults for High Yield Bonds Grouped by Year of Issue

Panel A: % of Par Amount Defaulted in nth Year After Issue

Issue Year	1st	2nd	3rd	4th	5th	6th	7th	8th	9th	10th	11th	12th	Total
1987	0.00	0.00	0.00	0.00	0.00	0.00	0.00	7.71	3.63	19.27	3.30	0.00[1]	33.92
1978	0.00	8.32	0.00	1.39	0.00	7.91	4.85	3.12	5.55	1.39	1.73[1]	–	34.26
1979	0.00	0.00	5.54	1.11	2.38	6.73	1.98	0.00	5.78	1.19[1]	–	–	24.70
1980	0.00	0.57	2.45	0.00	0.00	13.90	6.30	1.88	2.45[1]	–	–	–	27.56
1981	0.00	6.05	0.00	8.06	6.85	0.00	0.00	0.00[1]	–	–	–	–	20.97
1982	1.00	2.41	1.61	11.49	0.00	9.44	0.00[1]	–	–	–	–	–	25.94
1983	0.00	0.00	6.08	7.83	4.80	0.50[1]	–	–	–	–	–	–	19.21
1984	2.20	1.99	2.03	3.06	0.00[1]	–	–	–	–	–	–	–	9.38
1985	0.00	0.80	2.28	0.45[1]	–	–	–	–	–	–	–	–	3.53
1986	2.73	3.84	1.57[1]	–	–	–	–	–	–	–	–	–	8.14

May be incomplete, i.e., entire sample may not have been outstanding for x years.
Source: P. Asquith, D. Mullins and E. Wolff, "Original Issue High Yield Bonds: Aging Analysis of Defaults, Exchanges and Bonds," *Journal of Finance*, September 1989.

as comparable to the entire junk bond market, the mortality rates are slightly above the aged results. Since the number of actual issues is so tiny compared with the amount issued in more recent years, it is not terribly conclusive. We also compared mortality and aged results for a five-year horizon. We found that the mortality single-B results show a cumulative rate of 11.5 percent vs. 12.2 percent for the aged technique (Exhibit 9.8). Hence, the results again are quite similar.

One could argue that single-B issues are representative of the junk bond market since they dominate the double-B and triple-C ratings in terms of the number of issues. This was not always the case. Exhibit 9.8 also shows the weighted average mortality rate results. The 10-year results are less meaningful (triple-Cs have not been in existence for this long). For the five-year period, the weighted average mortality rate for all junk bonds is 9.1 percent. This is due to the low double-B rates and the small market values of CCC bonds.

Asquith et. al., do list some results by individual bond ratings. They show, for example, that B-rated debt had a cumulative default rate of 55.7 percent (1977 cohort), 34.15 percent (1978) and 21.4 percent (1979). Since these rates are only through 1988, it is difficult to calculate what would be the 10-year results for each rating group. Still, a weighted average of the 1977–1979 results would be similar to the results reported earlier. Exhibit 9.8 also shows that Moody's issuer aging results are similar to the other studies. Their 10th year single-B's were about equal to that of the mortality rates (market value average) and equal to the aging's overall results. Moody's does find high five-year cumulative results for single and double-Bs. If the aging approach implies increased marginal rates with the passage of time, Moody's 5- vs. 10-year results seem to question this.

Cheung and Bencivenga (1989) use the mortality approach and concentrate on original issue high-yield bonds over the period 1977–1988. Bonds were grouped by year of issue, by security priority, by original S&P rating and by bonds pursuant to a LBO, acquisition or recapitalization. In addition to mortality rates, they also calculated actual returns that were compared with five-year Treasuries. Their results were based on dollar amounts, rather than par amounts. When an issue defaulted, they conservatively treated the loss based on the entire dollar amount at issuance, rather than the outstanding amount at default. They include distressed exchange issues in their default statistics.

**Exhibit 9.8   Comparative Junk Bond Mortality/Aged Default
Statistics: Four Recent Studies**

Rating	Mortality (Altman) 1971–1989 (%)	Aging (Asquith) 1977–1988 (%)	Original Issuers (Moody's) 1970–1988 (%)	(Cheung) 1977–1988 (%)
5-Year Cumulative Default Rate				
Ba/BB	5.2	NA	8.3	2.5
B/B	11.5	NA	22.3	11.0
Caa/CCC	24.6	NA	47.3	22.4
Total (Wgt. Avg.)	9.1	12.2[1]	11.8	8.0
10-Year Cumulative Default Rate				
Ba/BB	15.0	NA	14.2	10.4
B/B	32.9	NA	29.3	35.5
Caa/CCC	NA	NA	51.3	NA
Total (Wgt. Avg.)	NA	29.3[2]	17.4	NA

[1] Based on Combined 1977–1984 Issuance.

[2] Based on Combined 1977–1979 Issuance.

We conclude, based on the above comparisons, that the mortality/aging results are similar. There are certainly some differences in methodology and sample periods.

Aging and Defaults

Claims by Asquith et. al., are that the effect of bond age on default rates is "clearly evident" and that default rates "rise over time." Since the timing of defaults has been coincident with the larger total market size, they argue that the traditional method is biased. We do not dispute that a growing market size will distort the formerly accepted rates. The amount is unclear and its implications not easily adjusted for. For example, the average annual default rate for the last five years has been about 3.4 percent per year (Exhibit 9.3). It has been about 2.1 percent for the last dozen years. With 10-year cumulative mortality rates of about 33 percent, the recent 2.5 percent to 3.5 percent annual rates are "on target."

The aging process intuition on corporate bond default rates is clear. As bonds age, the probability of firms exercising their call option on outstanding bonds increase. If we assume that there is a greater likelihood of more credit-worthy companies calling than less credit-worthy firms, then the remaining population of cohort bonds will have a greater probability of future default than did the original population. This has not yet been empirically measured or tested.

Rating agencies, like Moody's and S&P, would argue that age makes no difference as long as the bond's current rating is the same as its initial rating. For example, a Ba bond at birth has the same default probability as a five-year old Ba bond. If all new Ba bonds have a higher probability of slipping to a lower rating (i.e., after five years) than they do of rising to a higher rating, then the expected default rate will rise over time. This bond rating "drift" propensity has not yet been demonstrated or tested. Douglass and Lucas (1989) found the opposite. The default rate on issues of a given rating decreases over time. I hope to analyze this "drift" effect in a subsequent study.

To closely analyze the aging process, we observe the pattern of defaults for each year's rating group. In Exhibit 9.7, we see Asquith et. al.'s yearly results. It is difficult to find much of an aging pattern. For example, the first seven years of the 1977 cohort all had zero percent default rates. The second year rate in 1978 was 8.32 percent which was higher than any later year. The third year rate was high, about equal to its sixth and ninth years. By observing each individual cohort, a consistent aging pattern does not emerge. It is true that the Asquith et. al., results show that when you average all the first years, all the second years, etc., you find a clearer aging pattern. Even here, the results are not that evident, with the average second and third year default rates about equal to the fifth, seventh and eighth (Asquith, et. al, 1989).

Blume and Keim (1989) argue that the aged default rates do not account for their "critical" dependence on prevailing economic conditions. They suggest that analysts should adjust or control for this systematic variation in default rates. They find that there is no aging effect if one adjusts for overall economic conditions.

If we observe the mortality results in Exhibit 9.6, the aging phenomenon is even less evident. For single-B issue mortalities, the yearly (marginal) rates are relatively constant. They are about two to three percent from the third to the tenth year after issuance. There are higher rates in the seventh and ninth years. BB rates are fairly constant for the second through fifth years. Then they increase for the sixth and seventh years but fall back thereafter and rise again in the tenth year. These results, however, are sensitive to individual issue defaults, especially if they are very large ones. There appears to be even less of an aging effect for investment-grade defaults in the long term. While there does appear to be some aging effect, it is not very consistent across or within rating classes. Another conclusion is that there is some bias inherent in the traditional approach to default measurement, but not enough to make short-term forecasting invalid.

As you increase the horizon on any investment in risky bonds, the cumulative default rate will rise. That is not the same thing as saying that a bond of a certain age and rating (e.g., six-years old with a BB rating) has a higher probability of default in the next four years than a younger bond in the same risk category.

Returns

Up to now, we have only discussed the risk dimension of investing in corporate bonds. In order to provide a complete analysis of comparable investment attributes, it is essential to observe total returns of assets in different risk classes. By adjusting returns for risk, net return analysis is possible. Of the published studies on default risk, attempts have been made to assess returns using traditional methods and using the mortality approach. Recent papers by Goodman (1989) and Blume and Keim (1989) assess returns using the aging approach. Asquith et. al., (1989) does not attempt to measure returns themselves, citing data problems.

All the above studies conclude that after adjusting for default risk, all corporate bonds, especially junk bonds, return positive spreads vs. long-term Treasury bonds. This is consistent with the earlier works of Hickman and Atkinson.

The traditional average annual approach shows that the compound average return spread during 1978–1989 favors junk bonds by about 1.0 percent (down from 2.4 percent through 1988). This compares to an expected yield spread of 4.16 percent over the same period (Exhibit 9.9). These are total return numbers of portfolios with different durations measured for finite time periods. The results are impacted by changes in interest rates, market credibility changes, calls and liquidity issues. Losses from defaults averaged between 1.2 and 2.8 percent for the sample period. The difference between the average yield spread and the average return spread (3.17 percent per year) is reasonable given other risk factors.

Exhibit 9.9

Annual Returns, Yields and Spreads on Long-Term (LT) Government
and High Yield (HY) Bonds

Year	HY	Return (%) LT Govt	Spread	HY	Promised Yield (%) LT Govt	Spread
1989	1.62	15.99	(14.37)	15.41	7.93	7.48
1988	13.47	9.20	4.27	13.95	9.00	4.95
1987	4.67	(2.67)	7.34	12.66	8.75	3.91
1986	16.09	24.08	(7.99)	14.45	9.55	4.90
1985	22.51	31.54	(9.03)	15.40	11.65	3.75
1984	8.50	14.82	(6.32)	14.97	11.87	3.10
1983	21.80	2.23	19.57	15.74	10.70	5.04
1982	32.45	42.08	(9.63)	17.84	13.86	3.98
1981	7.56	0.48	7.08	15.97	12.08	3.89
1980	(1.00)	(2.96)	1.96	13.46	10.23	3.23
1979	3.69	(0.86)	4.55	12.07	9.13	2.94
1978	7.57	(1.11)	8.68	10.92	8.11	2.81

Arithmetic Average:

| 1978-1989 | 11.58 | 11.07 | 0.51 | 14.40 | 10.24 | 4.16 |

Compound Average:

| 1978-1989 | 11.19 | 10.20 | 0.99 | | | |

The above approach could be critiqued as being too aggregative and not evident for individual year yield and return spreads. Still, in assessing expected returns and losses from defaults over the near-term horizon, average annual rates provide measurable estimates.

The mortality rate idea is conducive to return estimation. It assumes a buy-and-hold strategy over some time horizon (e.g., 10 years). The assumption of reinvesting all cash flows from coupons, calls, maturities and default recoveries in the same asset risk class is made. Exhibits 9.10 and 9.11 show the results of return spreads assuming initial coupons on T-bonds of 8.75 percent. They show the actual spreads of each bond rating class over the sample period. Actual opportunity costs, call and recoveries are factored into the table's results. Note that all rating classes show positive return spreads with B and CCC-rated bonds doing best for short horizons up to three to five years. The power of compound interest more than offsets even the high B-rated mortality rates. These results do not include distressed exchange issues. Since a large percentage of distress exchange eventually default, not including exchanges in our mortality returns does not affect our results materially (see comments by Asquith, et al.).

Goodman (1989) simulates Altman's and Asquith, et al.'s cohort groups by assuming various call rates, interest rate spreads and recovery rates on defaults. She concludes that the mortality/aging studies are similar in terms of simulated returns and that the return spreads of junk bonds are uniformly positive.

Blume and Keim Study

All of the studies use simulated results in order to estimate the actual results. Asquith and others criticize simulations as not always realistic. In order to answer that critique, Blume and Keim (1989) take the Asquith 1977 and 1978 cohort groups and calculate actual returns. Results show that investors in all newly issued high-yield "junk" bonds (in 1977–1978) still outperformed intermediate-term Treasuries by almost one percent per year. The 8.51 percent actual yield earned by the 1977–1978 cohorts was about 2.6 percent less than the promised yield. The comparable yield on intermediate-term Treasury bonds averaged 7.60 percent over the 1977–1988 period. Intermediate-term T-bonds are used since the duration of these government bonds is comparable to high-yield junk bonds.

Exhibit 9.10

Expected Return Spread on Net Investment in Corporate Bonds over Risk Free Government
Bonds for Years Ended 1989
(In Dollars)

Bond Rating at Issuance

Years After Issuance	AAA	AA	A	BBB	BB	B	CCC
1	$0.46	$0.77	$1.07	$1.70	$3.14	$3.94	$7.04
2	1.01	1.70	2.28	3.33	6.36	8.07	16.06
3	1.67	2.59	3.76	5.60	10.64	11.47	27.27
4	2.49	3.83	5.67	8. 67	12.19	15.15	29.65
5	3.46	5.41	7.95	11.94	17.71	20.09	46.98
6	4.51	7.37	10.62	15.72	22.68	24.00	N/A
7	5.82	9.40	13.80	19.84	20.75	26.45	N/A
8	7.51	12.28	17.80	26.09	30.19	33.09	N/A
9	9.56	15.63	22.66	33.43	39.90	27.49	N/A
10	12.00	18.51	28.51	41.39	37.80	37.03	N/A

Exhibit 9.11 · Realized Return Spread on Net Investment in Corp. Bonds Over Risk-Free Governments

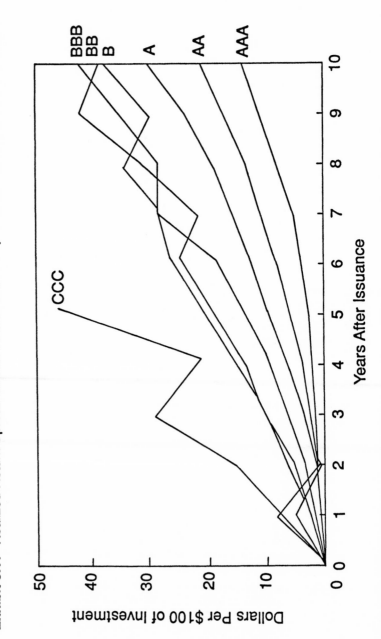

Assuming cash flows of the 1977–1978 high-yield bonds were re-invested in their own junk bond index, Blume and Keim calculated a total return of 10.37 percent. It was almost the same if reinvested in either high-grade corporates or long-term Treasury bonds. This information shows positive return spreads for junk bonds. The Blume-Keim results answer the critique of the (Asquith, Mullins and Wolff) study's failure to measure returns on the 1977–1978 newly issued junk bonds. Their results are adjusted for calls and distressed exchange issues. Asquith, et. al., estimate one-third of the 1977–1978 cohorts had defaulted or exchanged and another one-third had been called.

Cheung and Bencivenga Study

Cheung and Bencivenga (1989) calculate actual returns on their sample of original issue high-yield bonds. They conclude that each class of bonds outperformed comparable five-year Treasury bonds. For most of the years in their analysis, the promised yield spread exceeded the actual return spread. The forecasted yield spread reflects the incremental default loss and uncertainty about the amount of the loss. This confirms that the actual spreads reflect only the latter uncertainty-risk premia. They do not mention liquidity risk in their analysis. They do note that promised spreads have risen dramatically in the most recent years, 1987 and 1988.

Concerning the priority of claims, Cheung and Bencivenga find that seniority within the capital structure has no bearing on the absolute levels of promised yields vs. actual returns.

Positive Spreads

Most analysis reports positive junk bond return spreads over long periods of time, even after adjusting for default risk. Items such as liquidity and duration differences, default recovery and call uncertainties explain net-of-default-loss return differences. Many of these differences, between risk free Treasuries and corporate debt, are difficult to precisely measure. Observation of individual year return vs. yield spreads (Exhibit 9.9) shows that in five of the last 12 years, returns on Treasuries were greater than on high-yield bonds. The compound return spread over the period 1982–1988 favors Treasuries.

High yield debt has many equity features, including a call option on the firm's assets should the bonds default. Recent correlations between returns on junk bonds and equities have been higher than in the early 1980s, and it is becoming increasingly useful and important to analyze high yield debt as a separate asset class.

The above descriptions have generated a great deal of interest from both practitioners and the press. Two thoughtful commentaries by Kao (1989) and Marmer (1989) add to our understanding of the similarities and differences of the aging and mortality results.

And Now for the Future

Historical data is the basis of all these studies and are not necessarily accurate guides for future default rates. In some aspects, the corporate debt market, particularly junk bonds, is very different today than it was a decade ago. We could face a serious recession yet. We should not turn our backs on the past, however, especially if there are lessons and methodologies, not to mention results, useful for projections.

There has been one study that attempted to project future default rates and losses on junk bonds. It estimated rates of return on nine different asset classes. Wyss, Probyn and de Angelis (1989), in their study for DRI/McGraw-Hill, assessed the default frequency on 573 high-yield bond issuers that had debt outstanding at the end of 1988. Balance sheet and income statement data was available from the *Compustat* database. Their study projected these firms' balance sheets and cash flows under four different economic scenarios for the five-year period 1989-1993. The economic simulations were based on various degrees of economic downturns. These included the following:

1. a soft-landing downturn with no recession but a moderate increase in prices
2. a mild recession of two quarters in late 1989
3. a big recession in 1990 with a peak to trough decline in real GNP of 3 percent but declining interest rates
4. an inflationary recession similar to the 1981–1982 severe downturn

Using forecasts of individual industry performance, projections were derived for their default risk measure (i.e., current assets less changes in cash-flow over each quarterly period). They called this an "available-liquidity" measure. When this measure is negative for four consecutive quarters, the company is pushed into "default." The DRI group calculated an expected default rate. They did this by (1) summing the default issuer's debt and dividing by the amount of debt outstanding for the entire 573 firm sample and (2) at the start of the calendar year dividing the number of defaults by the total number of companies.

Returns on junk bond portfolios were measured by assuming that junk bonds yield a constant 350 basis point spread over 10-year U.S. Treasury bonds. It was also assumed that defaulted bonds were sold at 40 cents on the dollar in the same quarter as the default. The total return was the sum of the coupon payments, plus any price change in that period, minus net losses associated with defaults. Any increase (decrease) in the value of the portfolio was reinvested (disinvested) in the same portfolio. They assumed no redemptions on the debt outstanding at the start of their five-year horizon, nor did they differentiate between senior or subordinated debt holders.

Default rates for the first three economic scenarios were remarkably similar to the cumulative five-year rate from our earlier mortality rate results. In terms of dollars, it equalled about 13 percent in all cases. In terms of number of defaults, they were 67, 69 and 69 of the 573 firms for scenarios 1, 2 and 3 respectively. This finding is similar to previous historical studies. The worst case inflationary-recession scenarios show a five-year cumulative default rate of about 19 percent. This is about four percent per year in dollar terms. Eighty-one companies (14 percent) defaulted.

In terms of total returns, high-yield "junk" bonds outperformed all other asset classes. This included long and short-term government bonds, high-grade corporate bonds, mortgages, domestic CDs and domestic equities. The time frame was the five-year horizon under the first three scenarios. Only under the fourth, severe economic condition scenario did junk bonds do worse than some other asset classes. Then, it was only the short-term money market assets that outperformed junk bonds. The DRI study's conclusion was that risks associated with high-yield bonds remain similar to historical experience. A diversified portfolio of such bonds is an attractive investment compared with other asset classes, even in a recessionary environment.

It is not the purpose of this chapter to report in detail about every investigation. The DRI report is the only one attempting a forecast; therefore, it is important to emphasize its questionable methods and its relevant findings. On the plus side, the study deals with actual issuers and a large representative sample of junk bond issuing industrial firms. It is based on asset and liability structures and does not include assumptions about assets sales or debt repayments. As such, it is a liquidity-cash flow oriented fundamental analysis. It also includes short-term capital gains based on interest rate movements. It does not, however, impute any contagion effects that a series of events (e.g., defaults) might have on the rest of the market.

The DRI study runs into questionable "realities" in its dependence on industry driven forecasts. It does not impute any firm specific attributes. All firms in a given industry are assumed to perform the same. Such things as a particular firm's competitive position vis-a-vis its industry's counterparts is ignored. This could be important if a highly leveraged firm finds itself at a disadvantage regarding price cuts by less leveraged industry competitors.

The definition of default, when current assets are negative for four consecutive quarters, is arbitrary. It says nothing about a firm's ability to raise new capital or to sell assets to meet commitments. It assumes that the credit community's reaction to specific problems is irrelevant. It suggests that bankers and other creditors depend upon a firm's liquidity in determining credit standards. Since this author is particularly skeptical about liquidity measures as predictors of default, this assumption is troublesome. The DRI study authors point out they were not building a model to assess a firm's probability of default.

A Different Kind of Simulation

Simulations (the DRI study) attempt to plan the future based on a given state or condition and various total performance estimates. Others estimate the future based on a qualitative feel for the marketplace after observation of past default rates. Examples of the latter are (1) the recent S&P publication (1989) that assumes a possible default rate of 10-15 percent in a given recession year (Hessol, 1989, p.11) and (2) Baldwin (1989) of Moody's similar remarks. These estimates, even if accurate in some specific future year, do not tell the entire story since yield spread analysis and the impact on returns is left out.

A different approach simulates the theoretical break-even default rate. This results in a default risk adjusted return on junk bonds equal to an investment in risk-free government bonds. For example, a portfolio of 12 percent coupon junk bonds, which incurs a default rate of 6.0 percent in a 12-month period and has a consequent loss rate of 3.96 percent, will break-even when the promised yield spread is 4.2 percent between junk bonds and T-Bonds. The investor earns the 4.2 percent spread on the 94 percent of the portfolio that does not default which offsets the 3.96 percent default loss. Exhibit 9.12 shows various required yield spreads that result in break-even rates for a number of different default rate and recovery rate scenarios. Even if the default rate exceeds the break-even yield spread amount, causing returns to be below risk-free opportunities, the absolute return to junk bond holders will usually be positive. For example, a 10-percent default rate could translate into $20 billion of par value defaults. For those who believe a 10-percent default rate is possible, a 5-percent promised yield spread will result in a return spread of -1.60 percent but still a positive return of 5.40 percent in that year.

These results are based on one-year returns without influence of other factors (e.g., interest rate changes, market contagion effects, liquidity problems, etc). For instance, in 1988 the yield spread was 4.95 percent at the beginning of the year and the default rates and losses were 2.48 percent and 1.65 percent, respectively. The return spread was not, however, 3.30 percent (4.95 percent minus 1.65 percent) but 4.3 percent (Exhibit 9.9). In 1986, despite a promised yield spread of 4.90 percent and a 2.4 percent default loss rate, the return spread favored governments by a whopping 7.99 percent as interest rates fell dramatically. Long-term governments reacted more positively than junk bonds. In 1989, one of the causes of the poor junk bond performance was market liquidity problems. Another was the large amount of defaults, and near defaults, which had a negative impact on other junk bond prices. This trend was further exacerbated by the dramatic flight to quality coincident with the stock market decline of October 13, 1989.

Some market observers, including this author, expect that historical recovery rates will decrease in the future as the market evolves and default rates increase. Exhibit 9.12 also indicates break-even conditions with recovery rates varying between 20 and 50 percent.

As of May 1990, the yield spread between junk bonds, and T-Bonds was in the 7.0–7.5 percent range. Many analysts feel that the junk bond market today consists of two or three different groupings of issuers. They are the better quality issues (with lower yield spreads), the so-called average junk bond and high-risk issues selling at 1000 or more basis points above T-bonds. At the end of 1990, however, the average junk bond had spreads of over 1000 basis points.

Examining Exhibit 9.12, if one assumes a 30 percent recovery after default, a default rate of about 9.0 percent is implied. If an investor does not believe that such high defaults (over $18 billion) are likely, there

Exhibit 9.12

Breakeven Conditions for Total Returns on Junk Bonds vs. U.S. Treasuries

Default	*Default Loss*			*Required Yield Spreads %*		
	Recovery Rates			*Recovery Rates*		
Rate (%)	*20%*	*30%*	*40%*	*20%*	*30%*	*40%*
2.0	1.72	1.52	1.32	1.8	1.6	1.4
3.0	2.58	2.28	1.98	2.7	2.4	2.0
4.0	3.44	3.04	2.64	3.6	3.2	2.8
5.0	4.30	3.80	3.30	4.5	4.0	3.5
6.0	5.16	4.56	3.96	5.5	4.9	4.2
7.0	6.02	5.32	4.62	6.5	5.7	5.0
8.0	6.88	6.08	5.28	7.5	6.6	5.7
9.0	7.74	6.84	5.94	8.5	7.5	6.5
10.0	8.60	7.60	6.60	9.6	8.4	7.3
15.0	12.90	11.40	9.90	15.2	13.4	11.6

(Assuming a 12% Junk Bond Coupon and Various Default Recovery Rates)

appears to be attractive investment opportunities. If an additional risk premium of one to two percent is required by investors, due to the liquidity risk factor, then a seven to eight percent default rate expectation was implied by the May 1990 yield spreads. The junk bond market's vulnerability in a recessionary period is also of concern for many investors. To them, the current yield spread may seem reasonable. Finally, the historic 40 percent recovery rate may not be achievable in the future. Senior debt holders, primarily commercial banks, will become proficient in retaining priority status of bankruptcy or out-of-court settlement cases. The presence of lower priority-subordinated securities may also dilute the historic recovery rates.

The recovery rate on defaulted debt has declined in recent years. This is based on the price just after defaults. Exhibit 9.13 lists the recovery rate by seniority of the debt issue for the period 1985–1989. Note that the secured debt holder received, on average, 66 percent of par value after default. The senior debt holder received 55 percent and both the senior subordinated and the subordinated debt averaged just 32 percent of par. These are total, weighted averages with most defaults only involving one or two layers of debt. For those companies with a complex layered capital structure, the expected higher recovery rate for the more senior issues are manifest. The low recoveries in 1989 reflect higher debt levels relative to asset values of recent defaults. The capital structures of these firms are more complex. Hence, we assumed a 30-percent recovery rate in our current assessment of the market.

In 1990, recovery rates continued to fall with subordinated cash-pay bondholders recovering under 20 percent of par value. Non-cash pay bonds also recovered about 20 percent of their accrued values at the time of default.

Concluding Remarks

This chapter summarizes and integrates the findings of several studies. These included the measurement and implications of junk bond default rates, default losses and returns to investors. The results of these studies are enormously important. They influence investors, underwriters and firms who contemplate using this form of financing to grow or restructure their operations. The actual and anticipated default experience of corporate bonds will impact the cost of debt capital of new borrowers. It will also effect their ability to take on marginal investment projects. Not only will financing rates be affected by changes in risk perceptions, but

Exhibit 9.13 Recovery Prices* on Defaulted Debt by Seniority (1985-1990)

Year	Secured		Senior		Senior Subordinated		Subordinated			
							Cash Pay		Non-Cash Pay	
1990	$35.04	(7)	$32.02	(27)	$24.04	(28)	$17.93	(17)	18.99	(12)
1989	82.69	(9)	53.70	(16)	19.60	(21)	23.95	(30)	—	
1988	67.96	(13)	41.99	(19)	30.70	(10)	35.27	(20)	—	
1987	12.00	(1)	70.52**	(29)	53.50	(10)	40.54	(7)	—	
1986	48.32	(7)	37.09	(8)	37.74	(10)	31.58	(34)	—	
1985	74.25	(2)	34.81	(3)	36.18	(7)	41.45	(15)	—	
Average Total:	$53.38	(39)	$45.02	(102)	$33.63	(86)	$31.79	(123)	$18.99	(12)
Simple Average:	$35.16									

( ) Number of issues
* Price at end of default month
** Without Texaco,
   1987 recovery rate = $29.77;
   Average senior recovery = $38.23

the number of leveraged restructurings will be strongly impacted. In the final analysis, expected default rates and the yields required by investors appear to be the key to this market's future.

On the other hand, defaults and loss rates present continuous opportunities for the distressed debt investor. What for old bondholders is a regrettable occurance, is for others the food of existence. The so-called "vulture" investor is not, however, interested in seeing the distressed firm continue to deteriorate. On the contrary, the goal is to seek those firms and issues which will recover (i.e., rise like the "Phoenix" from the ashes). Those ideas have been explored in earlier chapters.

## 10

Outlook and Conclusion

Increasing supply and demand pressures of the distressed securities market appears promising for investors, especially in the medium to long-term. Near-term performance may be hampered by the continued increase of bankruptcies. Investors are likely to be cautious, with the lackluster performance of 1989 clear in their memories. We felt that prices could go lower in the short-term as the junk bond market faces a continued bumpy road. And, this was a correct forecast or prices on both junk bond and default issues continued to fall in 1990. But, good values in distressed issues appear to be already in evidence. The outlook should be brighter with important new demand forces participating in the market along with traditional investors. Superior returns earned on securities that have already been heavily discounted could result. Sound fundamental valuation analysis and the technical and psychological skills necessary to analyze complex issues will be more evidently important.

Supply Forces

Analysts are predicting corporate debt default rates will continue to accelerate in 1990 and into the next year. The restructuring excesses of the late 1980s in junk bond financing will take more time before the shake-out is completed. Some observers, such as Moody's and Standard & Poor's, have estimated that the default rate could reach 10 percent or

more in the coming years. This translates to a \$20 billion a year esti-
mate. We believe these forecasts are probably a bit high, but not incon-
ceivable. Indeed, the 1990 total as of December 1990 was approaching 9
percent! Recall the amount of distressed debt approximated \$50 billion
at the end of 1989. In reality, these securities are already "available" to
bottom-fishers. While further deterioration in prices for those issues that
default will no doubt occur, the fall presumably will not be to the same
extent as in the past.

Our comparison of current junk bond yield spreads over Treasuries
concludes the "market" is anticipating a near-term default rate in the 7-
to 9-percent range (see discussion in Chapter 9 and Altman, 1990b).
This depends on the risk premium investors demand for the liquidity
problem of these issues. If these premiums and estimates are above what
actually materializes, junk bond prices and selected distressed issues
prices will become firmer. Current legislative restrictions against certain
institutions holding junk bonds continues short run pressure on their
prices. These outside forces should not affect the basic earning power
and credit worthiness of individual company issues. It will, however,
make refinancing more difficult for all debtors. These short-term inefficiencies create even more opportunities for the patient, value-oriented
investor.

The increase in near-term defaults will swell the par value of this
sector. The market value will not conceivably increase as much since
recovery rates seem to be dropping. For those issues whose prices have
suffered along with the general deterioration in the market, large gains
appear possible if the firm doesn't default. There are many "no-prob-
lem" companies having "problem" yield spreads on their securities. This
is a major opportunity for the astute investor.

Estimating Supply from the Z-Score Bankruptcy Indicator

The Z-Score model is the predecessor of the ZETA® approach, men-
tioned earlier. It is specifically applicable to publicly held manufacturing
firms. This study was based on an analytical model still valid today,
built over 20 years ago (Altman, 1968). It shows as much as 10 percent
of the S&P 400 firms currently are at risk or showing signs of distress.
This is pictured Exhibit 10.1. The data shows the proportion of those
large corporations that have distressed financial profiles (i.e., a Z-Score

below 1.8). The aggregate results for the S&P 400 are indicative of trends, not precise estimates. Z-Score is comprised of five (5) components and has the following format and variable descriptions:

$$Z = 1.2X_2 + 1.4X_2 + 3.3X_3 + 0.6X_4 + 1.0X_5;$$

Z = overall index of corporate health;

X_1 = working capital divided by total assets;

X_2 = retained earnings divided by total assets;

X_3 = earnings before interest and taxes divided by total assets;

X_4 = market value of equity divided by book value of total liabilities; and

X_5 = sales divided by total assets.

Z-Score Model Description

$$\frac{\text{Variable}}{X_1} = \frac{\text{Working Capital}}{\text{Total Assets}}$$

Frequently found in studies of corporate problems, this is a measure of the net liquid assets of the firm relative to the total capitalization. Working capital is defined as the difference between current assets and current liabilities. Liquidity and size characteristics are explicitly considered. Ordinarily, a firm experiencing consistent operating losses will have shrinking current assets in relation to total assets.

$$X_2 = \frac{\text{Retained Earnings}}{\text{Total Assets}}$$

This is a measure of cumulative profitability over time, and the balance sheet figure is used. The age of a firm is implicitly considered in this ratio. For example, a relatively young firm will probably show a low RE/TA ratio because it has not had time to build up its cumulative profits. Therefore, it may be argued that the young firm is somewhat discriminated against in this analysis, and its chance of being classified as bankrupt is relatively higher than another, older firm. But this is precisely the situation in the real world. The incidence of failure is much higher in a firm's earlier years; over 50 percent of firms that fail do so in the first five years of existence. It should be noted that the retained-earnings account is subject to manipulation via corporate quasi-reorgani-

Exhibit 10.1 Chance of Bankruptcy Within S&P Industrials

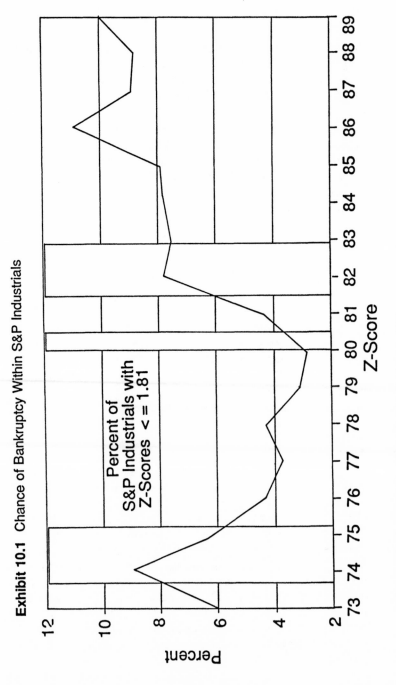

Percent of S&P Industrials with Z-Scores <= 1.81

Source: Quantitative Viewpoint, Merrill Lynch & Co., R. Bernstein, 1990.

zations and stock dividend declarations. It is conceivable that a bias would be created by a substantial reorganization or stock dividend.

$$X_3 = \frac{\text{Earnings Before Interest \& Taxes}}{\text{Total Assets}}$$

This ratio is calculated by dividing the total assets of a firm into its earnings before interest and tax reductions. In essence, it is a measure of the true productivity of the firm's assets, abstracting from any tax or leverage factors. Since a firm's ultimate existence is based on the earning power of its assets, this ratio appears to be particularly appropriate for studies dealing with corporate failure. Furthermore, insolvency in a bankruptcy sense occurs when the total liabilities exceed a fair valuation of the firm's assets with value determined by the earning power of the assets.

$$X_4 = \frac{\text{Market Value of Equity}}{\text{Book Value of Total Liabilities}}$$

Equity is measured by the combined market value of all shares of stock, preferred and common, while liabilities include both current and long-term. Book values of preferred and common stockholders equity may be substituted for market values when the latter is not available (Altman, 1983). The substitution of book values, especially for the common stock component, should be recognized as a proxy without statistical verification, since the model was built using market values (price X shares outstanding). The measure shows how much the firm's assets can decline in value (measured by market value of equity plus debt) before the liabilities exceed the assets and the firm becomes insolvent. For example, a company with a market value of its equity of $1,000 and debt of $500 could experience a two-thirds drop in asset value before insolvency. However, the same firm with $250 in equity will be insolvent if its drop is only one-third in value.

$$X_5 = \frac{\text{Sales}}{\text{Total Assets}}$$

The capital-turnover ratio is a standard financial ratio illustrating the sales generating ability of the firm's assets. It is one measure of management's capability in dealing with competitive conditions.

It should be noted that variables X_1, X_2, X_3, and X_4 should be inserted into the model as decimal fractions. For example, a working capital/total assets of 20 percent should be written as 0.20. The variable X_5, however, is denominated in number of times. For example, where sales are twice as large as assets, the ratio is written as 2.0.

Note also that the weights of each of the five ratios are not identical to those found in my original article (Altman, 1968). The denomination of the ratios in the original were different. The reader is referred to the original article for an in-depth description of the model.

A Z-score greater than 3.0 indicates a non-distressed firm profile while scores below 1.8 indicates distress. Scores between 1.8 and 3.0 are in the grey zone. The lower the score the more vulnerable the firm appears to be. Exhibit 10.2 shows the distribution of S&P 400 scores as of March, 1989. Note that the predominant score range is between three and five with a sizeable group below 1.8 (distress).

From Exhibit 10.1, we observe that in the last decade the proportion of distressed firms has increased from three percent to 10 percent. The signs of increased pressures are clear and many large companies are in a deeply distressed situation. Firms such as Western Union, Interco, Southland and others have seen their bond values fall precipitously. An actual default will not greatly impact their market price if the default is generally anticipated. The relative increase in distressed debt exchange issues has had a mitigating effect. Only a very small proportion of the bigger distressed companies will go bankrupt. Chapter 11 statistics will be lower, or at least deferred. This was not typical in the past.

Demand Forces

Although the poor performance of 1989 serves as a sobering force, the demand for distressed paper appears to be actively gaining strength. New buyers are selectively entering the junk bond and distressed debt markets. Existing institutions are expanding their efforts to raise capital. New sources of capital will search out established investors with a proven track record in this realm. Institutions such as pension funds, insurance companies, and equity mutual funds, will presumably expand their interest in junk bonds and distressed paper as good values materialize. Traditional equity investors are also looking carefully at the distressed segment as a type of "equity-play," with higher upside potential than low-rated bonds typically afford.

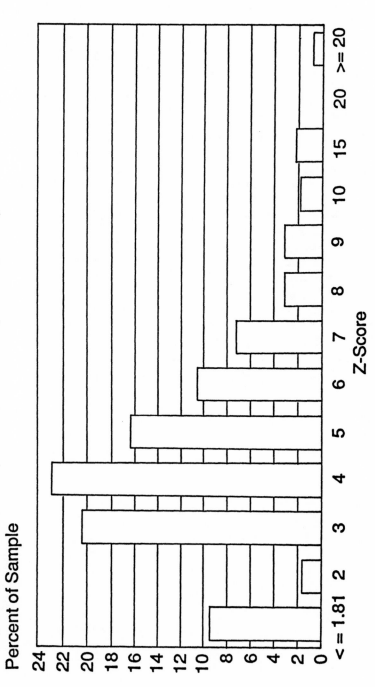

Exhibit 10.2 Distribution of S&P Industrials Z-Scores (As of March 1989)

Percent of Sample

Source: Quantiative Viewpoint, Merrill Lynch & Co., 1990 Compustat.

On a negative note, legislative and regulatory constraints on certain types of investors, such as insurance companies, could arbitrarily cause a reduction in demand for low-rated debt. This would drive prices even lower in the short run. Investors who are not effected by such restrictions may see prices on their portfolios fall temporarily. The upside opportunities will be greater in the mid- and long-term.

Questionnaire Response on the Outlook

We solicited our distressed investors for comment on the outlook for the "industry." We specifically asked: "With the increase in demand for distressed securities, are you optimistic/pessimistic or neutral about the future probability of earning excess returns?" We did not pursue the question in terms of their forecast duration. Twenty-six (26) of the 56 respondents were *optimistic*, while 11 were pessimistic and 19 neutral. This reflects an investor's natural tendency to be optimistic about their specialty. Because more than half of the respondents were pessimistic or neutral, the near-term outlook is most likely uncertain. Returns were good in the first six months after the surveys were filled out (in the first half of 1990), but very poor in the second.

Indeed, a number of the respondents wrote they were pessimistic or neutral about the short-term. However, they were very optimistic about the longer term prospects. This writer agrees with that forecast. The reasons are discussed throughout this book. The long-term outlook is bright with good values doubtlessly materializing.

Glossary of Terms

Business Failure Rate: The number of business failures in the economy per 10,000 firms listed by Dun & Bradstreet, New York City.

Chapter 11: The part of the Bankruptcy Code which specifies conditions and procedures for the reorganization of bankrupt companies.

Defaulted Securities: Those securities of firms which have not met the prescribed interest/principal payments to debtholders. Includes all firms operating under Chapter 11 as well as others in default but not in bankruptcy.

Distressed Securities: Those debt securities whose bonds are selling at a significant yield premium over risk-free securities, e.g., ten percentage points above the government bond rate.

Defaults: Rates and Losses: The rate or proportion of debt that has defaulted. Losses consider the default rate adjusted for recoveries (see below) and a non-paid debt coupon payment.

HLT Debt: High leveraged transaction debt that was issued, primarily by commercial banks, in order to finance corporate restructurings, such as LBOs. Trading of this debt in secondary markets has emerged in 1990 as an important source of liquidity for bonds and investors.

Prepackaged Chapter 11: Where most debt and equity claimants agree to a bankruptcy reorganization plan prior to the actual bankruptcy filing.

Private Bank Debt: The debt of distressed and defaulted companies owed to commercial banks and other financial institutions.

Private Trade Claims: Other private debt primarily owed to suppliers of the distressed or defaulted company.

Recovery Rates: The market value of defaulted debt just after default adjusted for the fact that a coupon payment is also lost; i.e., the amount that would be received if the bonds were sold at the end of

163

the default month minus one-half of the annual coupon amount, all divided by the par value of the bonds.

Reorganization: The process by which a firm attempts to restructure its assets, liabilities and equity capital in order to emerge from Chapter 11 as a going concern.

ZETA® Scores: Credit evaluation scores derived from a statistical model developed and distributed by Zeta Services, Inc. (Hoboken, N.J.)

References

Altman, Edward I., "Financial Ratios, Discriminant Analysis and the Prediction of Corporate Bankruptcy." *Journal of Finance*, Vol. 23, September 1968, 589–609.

Altman, Edward I., "Bankrupt Firms' Equity Securities as an Investment Alternative." *Financial Analysts Journal*, Vol. 25, July-August 1969, 129–133.

Altman, Edward I., *Corporate Bankruptcy in America*, Lexington, Mass.: Heath Lexington Books, 1971.

Altman, E.I., R. Haldeman and P. Narayanan, "Zeta Analysis, A New Model to Identify Bankruptcy Risk of Corporations." *Journal of Banking and Finance*, June 1977, 29–54.

Altman, Edward I., *Corporate Financial Distress: A Complete Guide to Predicting, Avoiding and Dealing with Bankruptcy*. New York: John Wiley, 1983.

Altman, E.I. and S.A. Nammacher, "The Default Rate Experience on High Yield Corporate Debt." *Financial Analysts Journal*, July–August 1985, 25–41.

Altman, Edward I. and Scott Nammacher, *Investing in Junk Bonds: Inside the High Yield Debt Market*, New York: John Wiley & Sons, 1987.

Altman, Edward I., *Default Risk, Mortality Rates and the Performance of Corporate Bonds*, Charlottesville, Va.: Research Foundation of the Institute of Chartered Financial Analysts, 1989.

Altman, Edward I., "Investment Performance of Bankrupt Debt and Equity Securities: Preliminary Results," presented at *Max L. Heine Symposium on Investing in Bankrupt Securities*, NYU Stern School of Business (April 1989).

Altman, Edward I., "Measuring Corporate Bond Mortality and Performance," NYU Salomon Center Brother Working Paper #477, June, and *Journal of Finance*, September 1989, 909–922.

Altman (1990a), "How 1989 Changed the Hierarchy of Fixed Income Security Performance." *Financial Analysts Journal*, May–June 1990, 9–20.

Altman, "Setting the Record Straight About Junk Bond Default Rates," *Journal of Applied Corporate Finance*, Summer 1990.

Altman, Edward I. and Martin S. Fridson, "An Introduction to the Altman-Merrill Index of Defaulted Securities," EXTRA CREDIT, Merrill Lynch and Co., November 1990, 10–16.

Amihud, Yakov, "Leveraged Management Buyout and Shareholders' Wealth" in Y. Amihud ed., *Leveraged Management Buyouts; Causes and Consequences*. Homewood, Illinois: Dow-Jones Irwin, 1989.

Atkinson, T.R., *Trends in Corporate Bond Quality*, New York: National Bureau of Economic Research, 1967.

Asquith, Paul, David Mullins and Eric Wolff, "Original Issue High Yield Bonds: Aging Analysis of Defaults, Exchanges and Calls," Vol. 44, No. 4, *Journal of Finance*, September 1989, 923–953.

Baldwin, Christopher, Conference on Investing in Turnarounds, *Corporate Finance Institute*, December 4–5, 1989, New York.

Blume, Marshall E., and Donald B. Keim, "Risk and Return Characteristics of Lower Grade Bonds," *Financial Analysts Journal*, (July–August 1987), 26–33.

Blume, M. and D. Keim, "Risk and Return Characteristics of Low Grade Bonds," 1977–1987, *Financial Analysts Journal*, July–August 1987 and updates, R. White Center Working Paper, 1989.

Blume M. and D. Keim, "Realized Returns and Defaults on Lower Grade Bonds: The Cohort of 1977 and 1978," Working Paper #31-89 (1989), Rodney White Center, Wharton School, University of Pennsylvania.

Business Failure Record, Dun & Bradstreet Corp., New York (1988).

Casey C., V.E. McGee and C.P. Stickney, "Discriminating Between Reorganized and Liquidated Firms in Bankruptcy," *Accounting Review*, April 1986, 249–262.

Cheung, Rayner and Joseph C. Bencivenga, "Original Issue High Yield Bonds: Total Returns and Historical Default Experience 1977–1988," Working Paper, Drexel Burnham Lambert, 1989.

Clark, T.A. and M. Weinstein, "The Behavior of the Common Stock of Bankrupt Firms," *The Journal of Finance*, vol. 38, No. 2, May 1983, 489–504.

Denis, Debra K. and John J. McConnell, "Corporate Mergers and Security Returns," *Journal of Financial Economics*, 16 (1986), 143–187.

Douglass, Scott and Douglas Lucas, "Historical Default Rates of Corporate Bond Issuers 1970–1988," *Moody's*, Structured Finance, July 1989.

Eberhart, Allan and Tel Moore and Rod Roenfeldt, "Security Pricing and Deviations from the Absolute Priority Rule," *Journal of Finance*, December 1990.

Ederington, Louis and J. Yawitz, "The Bond Rating Process" in E. Altman, *Handbook of Financial Institutions and Markets*, 6th ed., New York: John Wiley & Sons, 1987.

First Boston, "1990–1992: The Worst Case Scenario for Defaults," November 27, 1989), *High Yield Research*.

Forsyth, Randall W., "Megadeals Batter Industrial Bonds," in *Barron's*, October 1988, 69.

Fortgang, Chaim J. and T.M. Mayer, "Trading Claims and Taking Control of Corporations In Chapter 11," 12 *Cardozo Law Review, 1, 1990, and "Development" Update, 1990.*

Franks, Julian and Walter N. Torous, "An Empiricial Investigation of U.S. Firms in Reorganizations," *Journal of Finance*, July 1989, 747–769.

Fridson, Martin S., *High Yield Bonds: Identifying Value and Assessing Risk of Speculative Grade Securities*, Chicago: Probus Publishing, 1989.

Fridson, Martin S. and Fritz Wahl, "Fallen Angels versus Original Issue High Yield Bonds," *High Performance*, Morgan Stanley & Co., October 2–8, 1986.

Gilson, Stuart and Kose John and Larry H.P. Lang, "Troubled Debt Restructurings: An Empirical Study of Private Reorganization of

Firms in Default," *Journal of Financial Economics*, December 1990.

Hickman, W. Braddock, *Corporate Bond Quality and Investors Experience*, Princeton: Princeton University Press and the National Bureau of Economic Research, 1958.

Hradsky, Gregory T. and Robert D. Long, "High Yield Losses and the Return Performance of Bankrupt Debt Issuers: 1978–1988," *Financial Analysts Journal*, July–August 1989, 38–49.

Jarrell, Gregg A., James A. Brickley and Jeffry M. Netter, "The Market For Corporate Control: The Empirical Evidence Since 1980," *Journal of Economic Perspectives*, Vol. 2, No. 1, Winter 1988, 49–68.

Jensen, Michael, Steven Kaplan and Laurie Stiglin, "The Effect of Leveraged Buyouts on Tax Revenues of the U.S. Treasury," *Tax Notes*, Vol. 42, No. 6, February 1989.

Kao, Duen-Li, "The Default Risks of U.S. High Yield Bonds," *Journal of Cash Management*, July/August 1989, 56.

King, Roger E., "1989 Bottom Fishers Guide to Distressed Corporate Bonds," *High Yield Research*. New York: Shearson Lehman Hutton, 1989.

Lehn, Kenneth and Annette B. Poulsen, "Sources of Value in Leveraged Buyouts," *Public Policy Towards Corporate Takeovers*, New Brunswick, NJ: Transactions Publishers, 1987.

Marais, L., Katherine Schipper and Abbie Smith, "Management Buyout Proposals and Corporate Claimholders: Explicit Reconstructing and Differential Wealth Effects," Working Paper, U. of Chicago, September 1987.

Marmer, Harry S., "Junk Bonds, When Fact and Opinion Collide," *Risk*, September 1989, 66–67, 84.

Moeller, S., "Chapter 11 Filings: Good News For Investors," *AAII Journal*, April 1986, 9–12.

Moody's, "Rating Guidelines for Aaa Securities Backed by Corporate Bonds," *Structured Finance*, October 1987.

Moody's, "Rating Cash Flow Transactions Backed by Corporate Debt," September 1989.

Morse, D. and W. Shaw, "Investing in Bankrupt Firms," *The Journal of Finance*, vol. 43, No. 5, December 1988, 1193–1206.

Norris, Floyd, "Keeping Track of Default Debt," *New York Times*, December 13, 1990, D10.

Queen, Maggie and Richard Roll, "Firm Mortality: Using Market Indicators to Predict Survival," *Financial Analysts Journal*, May–June 1987, 9–26.

Ramaswami, M. and S. Moeller, *Investing In Financially Distressed Firms: A Guide to Pre- and Post-Bankruptcy Opportunities*, New York: Quorum Books, 1990.

Shearson, Lehman, Hutton, "Bottom Fishers' Guide To Distressed Corporate Bonds," January 10, 1990.

Standard & Poor's, *Bond Guides*, 1978–1989.

Warga, Arthur and Ivo Welch, "Bondholder Losses in Leverage Buyouts," First Boston Working Paper Series, May 1990.

Warner, Jerold, "Bankruptcy Costs: Some Evidence," *Journal of Finance*, May 1990, 337–347.

Warner, Jerold, "Bankruptcy Costs and the Pricing of Risky Debt," *Journal of Financial Economics*, December 1977, 239–276.

Weiss, Lawrence, "Direct Costs and Violations of Priority Claims: Bankruptcy Resolution," *Journal of Financial Economics*, December 1990.

Vanderhoof, I., F. Albert, A. Tenenbein and R. Verni, "The Risk of Asset Defaults: The Report of the Committee On Valuation and Related Areas," *Society of Actuaries*, December 1989.

White, M., "Bankruptcy Costs and the New Bankruptcy Code," *The Journal of Finance*, Vol. 38, No. 2, May 1983, 477–488.

Wyss, David, Christopher Probyn and Robert de Angelis, "The Impact of Recession on High Yield Bonds," DRI/McGraw Hill, Washington, July 1989.

Appendixes

APPENDIX A

Distressed Securities Investors
(Respondents To Questionnaire)

Responding Firm	Location (City)	Contact Person
American Capital	Houston	Ellis Bigelow
American Financial	Cincinnati	David Taylor
Angelo Gordon & Co.	New York City	Elliot Hershkowitz
ATID Corporation	New York City	Michael Triguboff
B.T. Securities	New York City	Arthur Schoen
Barre & Company, Inc.	Dallas	William Eddleman
Baupost Group	Cambridge, MA	Seth Klarman
Cargill Fin. Service	Minnetonka	Einar Hafstad
Chase Manhattan Bank	New York City	Margaret Klein
Citicorp	New York City	George Skouras
Cold Spring Mgt./Lambda	New York City	Mark Feldman
Cundill Value Fund	Vancouver, BC	Peter Cundill
Dabney & Resnick	Beverly Hills	Steven Gold
Drexel Burnham Lambert	Beverly Hills	Mitch Julis*
EBF Associates	Minneapolis	David Jackson
Fidelity Management	Boston	William Pike
First Boston	New York City	V. Rossi/S. Meadows
The Foothill Group	Agoura Hills, CA	J. Nickoll/K. Sandler
Furman & Selz	New York City	Marti Murray
Gordian Group	New York City	Patricia Caldwell
Gruss & Company	New York City	John Paulson
Halcyon Partners	New York City	Chris Mackey
Heller Financial	Chicago	Erwin Marks
Joseph, Littlejohn, & Levy Fund	New York City	Paul Levy
Lancer Industries	New York City	Paul Levy
M.D. Sass & Company	New York City	M.D. Sass/J. Rubin
Magten Asset Mgt.	New York City	Talton Embry
Massachusettes Financial	Boston	Robert Manning
Merrill Lynch	New York City	R. Siegler**/R. Curszmar
Morgens, Waterfall, Vintiadis	New York City	Bruce Waterfall
Mutual Series Fund	Short Hills, NJ	P. Langerman/M. Price
Neptune Partners	New York City	Francisco Garcia
Oppenheimer & Co. (Horizon)	New York City	J. Bauer
Paine Webber & Co.	New York City	Sidney Friedman
Perry Partners	New York City	Richard Perry
Progressive Partners	New York City	Steven B. Jones
Progressive United	Carmel, IN	William Fry

*Now with Canyon Partners, Los Angeles.
**Now with Ladenburg, Thalmann & Co., Inc. (NYC).

APPENDIX A *(continued)*

Prudential Bache Sec.	New York City	Ralph Hellmold
Prudential Bache	New York City	William Jacobs
Reiger, Robinson & Harrington	New York City	George Reiger
R.D. Smith & Company	New York City	J. Bennett/M. Singer
Rodman & Renshaw	Chicago	Jim Spirison
Saber Associates	New York City	Jeffrey Halis
Salomon Brothers	New York City	Charles Masson
Seidler/Amdec Sec.	Los Angeles	Chriss Street
61 Assoc./Spring & Co.	New York City	Richard Spring
Stonehill Investors	New York City	Neale X. Trangucci
T. Rowe Price	Baltimore	D. Breazzano/H. Styles*
Trust Co. of the West	Los Angeles	Bruce Karsh
Vasilou & Company	New York City	Basil Vasilou
W.R. Family Associates	New York City	Ross Haberman
Weiss, Peck & Greer	New York City	Mary Bechmann
Whitman, Hefferman, Rhein	New York City	M. Whitman/J. Mueller

Others Not Included as Respondents

Loews Corp.	New York City	Hillel Weinberger
Pacholder Associates	Cincinnati	Asher Pacholder
Waterstreet Recovery Fund, I (Goldman Sachs)	New York City	Michael Salovaara
Canyon Partners	Los Angeles	M. Julis/D. Negrea
Whippoorwill, Inc.	New York	S. Greenhaus/S. Warner
S. Zell	Chicago	S. Zell

*Now with Fidelity Managment, Boston, MA.

APPENDIX B

Distressed Firm Investing Questionnaire

1. Does your firm actively pursue analysis _____ and investment _____ in distressed firm securities? These include securities of firms operating under Chapter 11, whose debt is in default, or whose debt is selling at deep discount prices from par value (based on problems).   Yes _____   No _____

2. For how long has your firm been investing in distressed securities? _____ years.

3. (a) How much capital have you dedicated to investing in distressed securities? $ _____ million.
   (b) How much additional capital are you prepared to invest in those securities should attractive opportunities arise? $ _____ (approximate).
   (c) How much money is being managed by your entire firm? $ _____.

4. Do you have plans in the next two years to raise additional capital for this area, and if so how much?
           Yes _____   ($ _____ million) No _____

5. (a) Does your firm specialize in equity _____, secured debt _____, unsecured debt _____, or all _____ types of distressed securities?
   (b) Do you traditionally invest in debt (_____%) or equity (_____%)?

6. Does your firm invest in privately-held paper of distressed firms?
           Yes _____   No _____

7. Does your firm provide new capital in distressed situations, e.g., debtor-in-possession financing? Yes _____   No _____

8. What are the target _____ and/or minimum _____ *annual* returns that your firm is looking for from investing in the distressed securities markets?

9. Do you expect the supply of distressed listed *marketable* securities to grow from its present level of about $15 billion?
           Yes _____   No _____

10. With the increase in demand for distressed securities, are you optimistic _____, pessimistic _____, or neutral _____ about the future prospects for earning excess returns?

11. Is your firm a pasive _____ and/or active _____ investor in distressed securities, i.e., do you on occasion take positions to actively impact the management _____, the reorganization plan _____, the exchange offer _____, or other _____ aspects of the situation?

12. Are there any other types of investments in distressed securities that your firm undertakes? Use space below.

_____

_____

_____

_____

_____

_____

_____

_____

_____

_____

_____

13. Please use the space below to add any other comments on this subject that you feel are important.

_____

_____

_____

_____

_____

_____

_____

Name of firm: _____

Name of special division or group: _____

Name of respondent: _____

APPENDIX C

Broker/Dealer Bankruptcy Analysts
Current Troubled Company Research

Company	Analyst(s)	Firm	City
Lomas Corporation	William J. Eddleman	Barre & Company, Inc.	Dallas
	T.K. Duggan, Andrew J. Herenstein	Delaware Bay Company	NY
	Craig Davis	R.D. Smith Company, Inc.	NY
	Marie Baker	Oppenheimer	NY
	Paul Debban	Seidler Amdec	LA
Integrated Resources	Leigh Walzer	R.D. Smith Company, Inc.	NY
	Martin J. Whitman, Joe Colquhoun, Robert C. Ruocco	Whitman, Hefferman, Rhein & Co.	NY
	Marie Baker	Oppenheimer	NY
	Paul Debban	Seidler Amdec	LA
LTV	T.K. Duggan, Andrew J. Herenstein	Delaware Bay Company	NY
	Craig Davis	R.D. Smith Company, Inc.	NY
	Janice Stanton	Oppenheimer	NY
	Chriss W. Street	Seidler Amdec	LA
Revco	Stephen Levitan	Oppenheimer	NY
	T.K. Duggan, Andrew J. Herenstein	Delaware Bay Company	NY
	Kaye Handley	R.D. Smith Company, Inc.	NY
	Chriss W. Street	Seidler Amdec	LA
Southmark	Stephen Levitan	Oppenheimer	NY
	Craig Davis/Kaye Handley	R.D. Smith Company, Inc.	NY
	T.K. Duggan, Andrew J. Herenstein	Delaware Bay Company	NY
	Paul Debban	Seidler Amdec	LA
Zapata Corporation	William J. Eddleman	Barre & Company, Inc.	Dallas
	Kevin McCabe	R.D. Smith Company, Inc.	NY
	Martin J. Whitman, Joe Colquhoun, Robert C. Ruocco	Whitman, Hefferman, Rhein & Co.	NY
	David Schwartz	Oppenheimer	NY
Eastern Airlines	T.K. Duggan, Andrew J. Herenstein	Delaware Bay Company	NY

APPENDIX C *(continued)*

	Leigh Walzer	R.D. Smith Company, Inc.	NY
	Janice Stanton	Oppenheimer	NY
ICH	William J. Eddleman	Barre & Company	Dallas
	Craig Davis	R.D. Smith Company, Inc.	NY
	Martin J. Whitman, Joe Colquhoun, Robert C. Ruocco	Whitman, Hefferman, Rhein & Co.	NY
Public Service of New Hampshire	T.K. Duggan, Andrew J. Herenstein	Delaware Bay Company	NY
	Jim Bennett, Stephen Unterhalter	R.D. Smith Company, Inc.	NY
	David Schwartz	Oppenheimer	NY
SCI TV	James McNabb	Oppenheimer	NY
	Craig Davis	R.D. Smith Company, Inc.	NY
	Martin J. Whitman, Joe Colquhoun, Robert C. Ruocco	Whitman, Hefferman, Rhein & Co.	NY
Southland Corporation	David Schwartz	Oppenheimer	NY
	William J. Eddleman	Barre & Company, Inc.	Dallas
	Craig Davis	R.D. Smith Company, Inc.	NY
Allegheny International	James McNabb	Oppenheimer	NY
	Kevin McCabe	R.D. Smith Company, Inc.	NY
Dart Drug	Janice Stanton	Oppenheimer	NY
	Kaye Handley	R.D. Smith Company, Inc.	NY
Resorts International	Janice Stanton	Oppenheimer	NY
	Kaye Handley	R.D. Smith Company, Inc.	NY
Seaman Furniture Co.	David Schwartz	Oppenheimer	NY
	Martin J. Whitman, Joe Colquhoun, Robert C. Ruocco	Whitman, Hefferman, Rhein & Co.	NY

Source: *Turnarounds & Workout,* November 1, 1989.

UPDATE OF APPENDIX C *(continued)*

Firm	City	Analyst(s)	Companies
Barre & Company	Dallas	William Eddleman	Circle K Federated Department Stores Morningstar Foods, Inc. Southland Corporation
Delaware Bay Company	NY	T.K. Duggan AndrewHerenstein	Harcourt Brace Jovonovitch M Corp. Resorts International Southland Corporation Trump (Taj Mahal) Western Union
Oppenheimer	NY	Marie Baker Mark Kaufman Steve Levitan David Schwartz Janice Stanton Jamie Zimmerman	Ames Department Stores Circle K Farley, Inc. Greyhound Hillsborough Holdings Interco JPS Textile National Gypsum Traycorp, Inc. Trump (Castle, Taj Resorts)
Seidler Amdec	LA	Chriss Street Paul Debban	Ames Department Stores Federated/Allied Hillsborough Holdings Maxicare Southland Corporation Wheeling Pittsburgh
R.D. Smith Company	NY	Jim Bennett Craig Davis Kevin McCabe Leigh Walzer Stephen Unterhalter	Ames Department Stores Community Newspapers Federated/Allied Greyhound Penn Rod Rexeen Trump issues
Whitman, Hefferman, Rhein & Co.	NY	Joe Colquhoun Robert C. Ruocco Martin J. Whitman	Bank of New England General Redevelopment Home Insurance (Preferred) Southland Southmark Westar Mining (Class A Preferred)

Source: *Turnarounds & Workouts*, May 15, 1990

APPENDIX D

Troubled Company Restructuring Groups

Rank	Name of Firm	Total Consolodated Capital ($millions)	Senior Officer	Representative Clients
1.	Merrill Lynch & Co.	8,767.5	Nathan Thorne, Mgn, Dir. Restructuring Group	Care Enterprises Inc. TPA of American Inc.
2.	Shearson Lehman Hutton	8,157.0	James Harris, William Forster Mgn. Dirs., Fin. Restructuring Grp.	LTV, Southmark, Sharon Steel
3.	Salomon Brothers Holding Co.	4,440.0	Charles M. Masson, VP Financial Restructuring	Resorts International, PSNH (Creditors)
4.	Goldman, Sachs & Co.	2,771.0	Mikael Salovara, Partner Barry S. Volpert, Workout Rest.	Eastern (Creditors) LJ Hooker (Creditors)
5.	Morgan Stanley & Co.	2,413.2	Karen Vechtel Mgn. Dir. Corporate Reorg.	Would not disclose
6.	Drexel Burnham Lambert	2,143.0	Leon Black, John Sorte Executive VP's	Tiger International Mattel
7.	First Boston Corp.	1,864.0	Tony Dub, Jim Mahaer Co-heads: Investment Banking	PSNH Storage Technologies
8.	Prudential-Bache Securities	1,497.8	Ralph Hellmold, Mgn. Dir. Financial Restructuring	Lomas, (Creditors) Santa Barbara S.&L.
9.	Paine Webber Group	1,464.0	Elizabeth Lambert, Managing Director	Kaiser Aluminum
10.	Integrated Resources	1,435.5	Frank Savage Sen. Exec. VP	Network of Broker-Dealers
11.	Bear, Stearns & Co.	1,413.4	Daniel A. Celentano Mgn. Dir. Fin. Restructuring Grp.	Southmark (unsecured) Lone Star Steel (unsecured)
12.	Dean Witter Reynolds	1,343.0	Edison Buchanon, Managing Director	Southmark, ATT Creditor in Eastern
13.	Smith Barney, Harris Upham & Co.	973.0	Nicholas Sakellariadis, Managing Director	Eastern (debtor)
14.	Donaldson, Lufkin & Jenrette	950.0	Norman H. Brown, Jr. Mgn. Dir. Fin. Restructuring Grp.	Republic Health, Coleco, Qintex

APPENDIX D *(continued)*

15.	Kidder, Peabody & Co.	800.0	Gordon Paris, Mgn. Dir., Lane Genatowski, Wm Smith, Sen. VP	Pan Am, Data Point
16.	Allen & Co.	405.7	Jim Quinn Chief Financial Officer	Would not disclose
17.	J.P. Morgan Securities	404.0	Pamela Wilson VP	Interco
18.	Shelby Cullom Davis & Co.	394.0	Would not disclose	Would not disclose
19.	Charles Schwab & Co.	360.0	NA	NA; discount brokerage firm
20.	Nomura Securities International	322.0	Mark Zeidman VP	Unavailable

Source: Institutional Investor (November 1989), reprinted in *Turnarounds & Workouts,* January 15, 1990.

APPENDIX E

Corporate Bond Defaults, 1970–1990

Default Date	Company	Bond Issue	Outstanding Amount (SMM)	Issue Date	Original Rating
1970					
Feb-70	Chicago, Mil, St. Paul RR	cv 4.5s, '44	31.10	Mar-45	C1+
Feb-70	Roberts, Co.		5.03		
Mar-70	Boston & Maine RR	1st TT 6s, '67	48.30	Aug-65	CC
Mar-70	Boston & Maine RR	inc A 4.5s, '70	18.80	Jan-45	C1
May-70	Farrington Mnfg	cv 5.5s, '70	3.80	Aug-60	NR
Jun-70	Airlift Intl	cv 6.5s, '86	1.00	Dec-66	CCC
Jun-70	Airlift Intl	cv 5.75s, '87	18.00	Dec-67	CCC
Jul-70	Visual Electronics	cv 5.25s, '82	1.71	Oct-67	NR
Aug-70	Fairfield Technology	cv	2.00		
Oct-70	Computer Application	cv 5.5s, '87	3.60	Jul-67	CCC
Oct-70	Computer Application	cv 5.875s, '88	7.70	Jul-68	CCC
Nov-70	Elcor Chemical	cv 5.5s, '87	12.50	Dec-67	B
Dec-70	Ozark Airlines	cv 5.25s, '86	7.20	Jul-66	CCC
Dec-70	Ozark Airlines	cv 6.75s, '88	15.00	Dec-67	CCC
Dec-70	Viatron Computer	cv 6.25s, '89	25.00	Dec-69	CCC
Jun-70	NY & Putnam	1st mtge 4s, '93	1.58	1894	
Jun-70	Pennsylvania RR	gen D 4.25s, '84	43.60	Jan-31	
Jun-70	Pennsylvania RR	gen E 4.25s, '84	36.30	Jan-34	
Jun-70	Pennsylvania RR	gen F 3.125s, '85	46.00	Jan-45	A
Jun-70	Phila, Balt & Wash RR	gen B 5s, '74	10.00	1924	
Jun-70	Phila, Balt & Wash RR	gen C 4.5s, '77	11.30	1931	
Jun-70	Pitt, Cinn, Chi & StL RR	gen B 5s, '75	26.00	1925	
Jun-70	Pitt, Cinn, Chi & StL RR	gen E 3.375s, '75	17.80	Oct-44	A
Jun-70	Pitt, Young & Ashtabula	gen C 5s, '74	1.20	1924	
Jun-70	Pitt, Young & Ashtabula	1st gen D 4.5s, '77	1.48	1931	
Jun-70	United NJ RR & Canal	1st 4.5s, '79	6.02	Jan-51	A
Jun-70	West Shore RR	1st mtge 4s	33.00	1886	CCC
Jun-70	Kanawha & Ml Ry	1st mtge 4s, '90	1.54	1890	
Jun-70	Lake Shore & Ml S.Ry	1st mtge 3.5s, '97	43.30	1897	
Jun-70	Mohawk & Malone Ry	1st mtge 4s, '91	1.55	1892	
Jun-70	Mohawk & Malone Ry	cons mtge 3.5s, '00	3.07	1902	
Jun-70	NJ Junction RR	1st mtge 4s, '86	1.18	1887	
Jun-70	NY Central RR	con mtge A 4s, '98	63.00	1916	
Jun-70	NY Central RR	ref & imp 4.5s, '13	92.90	1914	
Jun-70	NY Central RR	ref & imp 5s, '13	64.00	1922	
Jun-70	NY Central RR	coll tr 6s, '80	20.20	May-55	NR
Jun-70	NY Central RR	coll tr 5.75s, '80			
Jun-70	NY Central RR	coll tr 6s, '90	8.60	Jul-65	B

APPENDIX E *(continued)*

Jun-70	NY Central & Hudson River	mtge 3.5s, '97	76.10	1916	
Jun-70	NY Central & Hudson River	lake shore coll tr 3.5s, '98	17.20	1898	
Jun-70	NY Central & Hudson River	mi cent coll tr 3.5s, '98	15.60	1898	
Jun-70	NY Connecting RR	1st mtge 2.875s, '75	17.80	Oct-45	A1
Jun-70	NY & Harlem RR	1st mtge 3.5s, '00	2.87	1900	
Jun-70	NY & Harlem RR	ref A&B 4s, '43	7.82	Nov-43	A
Jun-70	NY New Haven & Hart	1st ref 4s, '07	76.80	1947	
Jun-70	NY New Haven & Hart	gen cv inc 4.5s, '22	52.80	1947	
Jun-70	NY New Haven & Hart	harlem river 1st A 4.25s, '73	6.65	Jan-53	B1+
Jul-70	Lehigh Valley RR	gen con A fxd 4s, '03	4.93	Jun-49	
Jul-70	Lehigh Valley RR	con 4.5s, '89	1.99	Jun-49	
Jul-70	Lehigh Valley RR	gen con B fxd 4.5s, '03	2.05	Jun-49	
Jul-70	Lehigh Valley RR	gen con C fxd 5s, '03	1.72	Jun-49	
Jul-70	Lehigh Valley RR	gen con D in 4s, '03	10.50	Jun-49	
Jul-70	Lehigh Valley RR	gen con E inc 4.5s, '03	4.49	Jun-49	
Jul-70	Lehigh Valley RR	gen con F inc 5s, '03	3.48	Jun-49	

1971

Mar-71	Mohawk Airlines	cv deb 6s, '93	8.00	Jan-68	B
Jun-71	King Resources	cv deb 5.5s, '88	24.40	Sep-68	B
Jul-71	Waltham Industries	cv	8.00		
Oct-71	Great Markwestern	cv	2.50		
Nov-71	Reading Railroad	1st & ref 3.125s, '95	56.50	Jun-45	B1+

1972

Feb-72	FAS Intl	cv	16.34	Jan-69	B
Aug-72	American Export Ind	cv deb 5.25s, '93	60.00	Jul-68	BB
Nov-72	Harvard Ind				
Jun-72	Erie RR & Subsid	1st con F 3.125s, '90	32.80	Apr-45	A
Jun-72	Erie RR & subsid	1st con G 3.125s, '00	38.70	Apr-45	A
Jun-72	Erie RR & subsid	gen cv inc A 4.5s, '15	43.50	Jan-41	C1
Jun-72	Erie RR & subsid	inc 5s, '20	26.60	May-55	NR

APPENDIX E *(continued)*

Jun-72	Erie RR & subsid	ny l&w 1st ref C 5s, '73	5.02	Apr-45	B1
Jun-72	Erie RR & subsid	ny l&w div 5s, '93	2.28	Apr-45	C1+
Jun-72	Erie RR & subsid	penn div ref CT A 5s, '85	2.30	Jun-50	NR
Jun-72	Erie RR & subsid	1 of nj div 1st A 4s, '93	6.27	Jun-45	C1
Jun-72	Erie RR & subsid	1 of nj 1st inc B 4s, '93	2.02	Jun-45	C1+
Jun-72	Erie RR & subsid	morris & essex div CT 4.6s, '42	9.57	Jan-46	C1+
Jun-72	Erie RR & subsid	uc & sv div 1st 3.5s, '92	2.19	Jan-46	C1+
Jun-72	Erie RR & subsid	oswego & syra div 1st 4.6s, '93	0.82	Jan-46	NR
Jun-72	Erie RR & subsid	1st 5s, '82	12.00		

1973

Jan-73	DCA Development	cv deb 6s, '88	3.80	Jul-68	CCC
Mar-73	Sherwood Leasing	cv	12.90		
Mar-73	Esgro Inc	cv	5.84		
Apr-73	Equity Funding of America	cv deb 5.5s, '91	38.50	Dec-71	B
Apr-73	Equity Funding of America	sf deb 9.5s, '90	22.00	Jun-70	BB
May-73	Arian's Dept Store	cv deb 6s, '94	15.00	Nov-69	BB
Jun-73	Lyntex Corp	cv 6s, '89	13.80	Mar-69	B
Jul-73	U.S. Financial Services	cv 5.5s, '91	35.00	Apr-71	NR
Sep-73	Arden Mayfair	sub inc deb 6s, '14	21.90	Jun-64	NR
Sep-73	Ann Arbor Mich RR	1st mtge 4s, '95	5.17	1895	C1+
Oct-73	Parkview-GEM	cv 5.75s, '79	2.60	Jan-64	B

1974

Feb-74	Westgate-California				
Mar-74	Boothe Computer	cv 5.75s, '88	17.90	Aug-68	CCC
Apr-74	Electraspace	cv 5.5s, '83	9.99	Nov-68	B
May-74	Interstate Dept Stores	cv deb 4.625s, '81	0.44	Jul-61	BB
May-74	Interstate Dept Stores	cv deb 4s, '92	20.00	Aug-67	BB
Jun-74	Wolf Corp	sub deb 7.2s, '76	3.53	Jun-61	
Aug-74	Omega-Alpha Corp	sub deb 6.5s, '88	25.00	Jul-71	B
Jul-74	Bohack Corp	cv 6s, '93	3.69	Jun-69	NR
	National Bella Hess	cv 6s, '84	3.70		

1975

Jan-75	Fidelity Mortgage Inv	cv 7.75s, '85	2.75	Dec-70	NR
Feb-75	Daylin Inc	deb 8.35s, '97	25.00	Apr-72	BBB

APPENDIX E *(continued)*

Mar-75	Chicago, RI & Pac RR	1st mtg 2.875s, '80	32.70	Jun-50	A
Mar-75	Chicago, RI & Pac RR	1st mtg 5.5s, '83	14.80	Mar-58	A
Mar-75	Chicago, RI & Pac RR	inc deb 4.5s, '95	50.30	Apr-55	B1+
Mar-75	Gray mfng	cv 5.25s, '82	2.38	Sep-67	B
May-75	Hallcraft Homes	cv deb 5.75s, '96	15.00	Sep-71	NR
Jul-75	National Telephone	cv	2.50		
Oct-75	Grant, W.T.	deb 4.75s, '87	24.00	Jan-62	A
Oct-75	Grant, W.T.	cv deb 4s, '90	0.83	Jun-65	BBB
Oct-75	Grant, W.T.	dv deb 4.75s, '96	92.50	May-71	BBB
Nov-75	GAC Property Credit	sr deb 12s, '75	35.60	Jun-70	BBB
Nov-75	GAC Property Credit	sr deb 11s, '77	43.70	Aug-71	BBB

1976

Jan-76	Optical Scanning	cv deb 8s, '95	5.42	Dec-70	CCC
Mar-76	Continental Mtge Investors	cv 6.25s, '90	36.00	Feb-70	BBB
May-76	Sanitas Service	cv 9s, '90	8.21	Sep-70	CCC
Jun-76	Permaneer Corp	cv sr deb 7s, '91	5.43	Oct-71	CCC
Jun-76	Permaneer Corp	cv 5.25s, '89	7.74	Feb-69	B
Aug-76	Colwell Mortgage & Trust	sr sub nt 8.20s, '80	25.00	Mar-73	NR
Sep-76	Duplan Corp	cv deb 5.5s, '94	21.20	Feb-69	BB
Oct-76	Treco Inc		4.51		

1977

Feb-77	Wlyly Corp	cv 7.25s, '95	19.60	Mar-70	B
Feb-77	Justice Mortgage				
Mar-77	Great American M&T				
May-77	Grolier Incorporated	sf deb 9.5s, '91	30.00	May-71	BBB
May-77	Grolier Incorporated	cv 4.25s, '87	23.90	Aug-67	BB
Jul-77	United Merchants & Mnfg	deb 9.5s, '95	48.50	Jun-70	BBB
Jul-77	United Merchants & Mnfg	cv 4s, '90	19.50	Oct-65	BB
Jul-77	Guardian Mtge Investors	sr sub nt 7.5s, '79	25.00	Dec-72	NR
Jul-77	Guardian Mtge Investors	sub dep 6.75s, '86	8.61	Jul-71	NR
Jul-77	Guardian Mtge Investors	cv 8s, '85	0.21	Mar-70	NR
Aug-77	First Mtge Inv	sr deb 9s, '78	8.50	Nov-70	A
Aug-77	First Mtge Inv	sr deb A 8.25s, '77	20.30	Jun-71	A
Sep-77	Tri-South Mtge	sr sub deb 7.75s, '80	24.30	Feb-73	NR
Dec-77	Chic, Mil, St. Paul & Pac RR	1st A 4s, '94	48.70	Jul-44	A
Dec-77	Chic, Mil, St. Paul & Pac RR	gen inc A 4.5s, '19	24.70	Jul-44	BB
Dec-77	Chic, Mil, St. Paul & Pac RR	inc deb A 5s, '55	55.60	Sep-55	C1+

APPENDIX E *(continued)*

Dec-77	Chic, Mil, St. Paul & Pac RR	cv 4.5s, '44	31.10	Mar-45	C1+

1978

Mar-78	Frigitemp Corp	cv sub deb 9s, '91	5.00	Jul-76	B
Mar-78	Commonwealth Oil	cv sub deb 4.5s, '92	17.90	Dec-68	BBB
May-78	Chase Manhattan M&R	sr nt 7.5s, '83	36.70	May-71	NR
May-78	Chase Manhattan M&R	sub nt 7.5s, '83	41.20	Feb-73	NR
May-78	Chase Manhattan M&R	cv 6.75s, '90	0.53	Jun-70	NR
May-78	Chase Manhattan M&R	cv 6.5s, '96	11.00	May-71	NR
May-78	Chase Manhattan M&R	cv 11.625s, '97	19.50	Sep-77	NR
Oct-78	Food Fair Corp	sf deb 8.375s, '96	30.30	May-71	BBB
Oct-78	Food Fair Corp	sub deb 4s, '79	11.10	Apr-59	B1
Nov-78	Allied Supermarkets	cv 5.75s, '87	17.00	Dec-68	BB

1979

Apr-79	American Reserve	cv sub deb 6s, '90	7.60	Apr-70	NR
Apr-79	Allied Artists	cv 8.75s, '90	3.10	Jun-70	NR
Oct-79	Inforex	sub sf deb 10.625s, '98	20.00	May-78	B

1980

Jan-80	Dasa Corp	cv 6s, '87	2.55	Apr-75	CCC
Apr-80	Penn-Dixie Indus	cv 5s, '82	9.00	Oct-67	B
Jul-80	Itel Corp	deb 6.75s, '89	14.10	May-69	B
Jul-80	Itel Corp	sf deb 10.5s, '98	75.00	Dec-78	BBB-
Jul-80	Itel Corp	sub deb 9.625s, '98	90.80	Apr-78	BB-
Sep-80	White Motor	deb 7.25s, '93	8.69	Mar-68	A
Sep-80	White Motor	cv sub deb 5.25s, '93	6.75	Mar-68	BBB
Sep-80	White Motor	sf deb 12s, '99	4.42	Dec-79	NR
Sep-80	White Motor	sub of deb 11s, '99	10.20	Dec-79	NR
Oct-80	Combustion Equip		Oct-80	Combustion Equip	

1981

Feb-81	Seatrain Lines	cv 6s, '94	50.00	Dec-69	B
Oct-81	FSC Corp	sr sf deb 15.75s, '95	7.00	Aug-80	B
Oct-81	FSC Corp	cv sub deb 12.875s, '94	2.61	Jul-79	CCC
Dec-81	America Comm				

1982

APPENDIX E *(continued)*

Jan-82	Morton Shoes	sr sf deb 12.75s, '96	11.50	Feb-79	B
Feb-82	South Atlantic	sub deb 6.75s, '82	16.90	1972	
Feb-82	Rusco	cv	6.19	Feb-69	B
Feb-82	Lionel Corp	sub sf deb 10.625s, '99	15.00	Jul-79	B
Feb-82	Mego International	sub of deb 12.875s, '94	14.10	Feb-79	B
Mar-82	California Life Corp	sf deb 11s, '98	20.00	Mar-78	BB
Apr-82	Gambles Credit	sr nt 9.375s, '86	60.00	Aug-76	A
Apr-82	Standard Packaging/Saxon	sub deb 6s, '90		1960	
Apr-82	Standard Packaging/Saxon	cv sub deb 5.25s, '90			
Apr-82	Spector Industries	cv sub deb 6.375s, '88	3.00	May-68	B
Apr-82	AM International	sub deb 9.5s, '95		1967	
Jul-82	Nucorp Energy	cv 9.25s, '01	50.00	Apr-81	NR/B-
Jul-82	Nucorp Energy	cv 19.75s, '01	60.00	Sep-81	B+
Aug-82	Johns-Manville	sf deb 7.85s, '04	75.00	Jan-74	AA
Aug-82	Johns-Manville	nt 9.7s, '85	100.00	May-79	AA
May-82	Braniff Airways	sr sf deb 9.125s, '97	49.90	Dec-77	BBB-
May-82	Braniff Airways	loan ctf 11.125s, '87	8.76	Jul-71	BB
May-82	Braniff Airways	sr nt 10s, '86	50.00	Jul-76	BB
May-82	Braniff Airways	sub deb 5.75s, '86	25.00	Dec-66	B
Sep-82	Shelter Resources	cv 15.5s, '00	11.00	Jul-80	B
Oct-82	Revere Copper & Brass	cv 5.5s, '92	41.30	Dec-67	BB
Nov-82	TelCom Corp	sub sf deb 13.375s, '99	25.00	Oct-79	B
Dec-82	Amarex	sub sf deb 13.75s, '00	30.00	Jul-80	B
Apr-82	Wickes	sf deb 6s, '92	5.54	May-67	A
Apr-82	Wickes	sf deb 8.875s, '94	35.00	Jul-77	BBB
Apr-82	Wickes	sf deb 7.875s, '98	47.70	Apr-73	BBB
Apr-82	Wickes	sf deb 10.25s, '04	60.00	Jul-79	BBB
Apr-82	Wickes	nt 8.25s, '84	15.00	Jul-77	BBB
Apr-82	Wickes	cv sub deb 5.125s, '94	11.70	Apr-69	BB
Apr-82	Wickes	cv sub deb 9s, '99	19.10	Aug-74	BB
1983					
Feb-83	Regency Investors	cv sub deb 7.5s, '86	17.20	Dec-71	
Mar-83	Marion Corp	cv deb 9s, '95	20.00	Oct-80	
Apr-83	Texas General Resources	sub nt 11.25s, '86	30.00	Oct-81	NR
Apr-83	Wilson Foods	sf deb 9.5s, '84	9.39	Jan-74	BBB
Apr-83	Wilson Foods	sf deb 8.375s, '97	16.70	Jun-72	BBB

APPENDIX E *(continued)*

Apr-83	Wilson Foods	sf deb 7.875s, '97	21.00	Mar-72	BBB
May-83	MGF Oil	sub sf deb 14.5s, '01	75.00	May-81	B
Jun-83	Flight Transportation	sf deb 11.25s, '95	25.00	Jun-82	B-
Jul-83	Hardwicke Cors	sub sf deb 14s, '94	6.00	Jul-79	CCC
Aug-83	Pioneer Texas	cv 6.75s, '85	4.50	Apr-73	B
Aug-83	Phoenix Steel	cv sub sf deb 6s, '87	4.85	Sep-67	CCC
Sep-83	Altec Corp	sub sf deb 6.75s, '88	7.84	May-68	
Sep-83	Baldwin (D.H.) *cp	sr deb '94			
Sep-83	Baldwin United	sub sf deb 10s, '09	16.20	Jun-79	NR
Sep-83	Continental Airlines	cv sub deb 3.5s, '92	25.40	May-67	BB
Sep-83	Peninsula Resources	cv sub deb 12s, '95	15.00	Dec-80	B
Sep-83	Texas Intl	sub sf deb 10.875s, '98	19.10	Apr-78	B
Sep-83	Texas Intl Finance NV	cv sub deb 7.5s, '93			
Sep-83	Texas Intl Capital NV	U.S. fl rt nt '86		Mar-79	
Oct-83	Anglo Energy Inc	gtd sub sf deb 11.875s, '98	17.50	Jul-78	B

1984

Mar-84	Pizza Time Theater	cv sub deb 8.25s, '08	50.00	May-83	CCC
Apr-84	Charter Company	sub sf deb 10.625s, '98	25.00	Sep-78	B
Apr-84	Charter Company	sub sf deb 14.75s, '02	60.00	Oct-82	B-
Apr-84	Emons	eqp tr cert, ser 111.45s, '94	27.30	Apr-79	B
May-84	Page Petroleum	cv sub deb 10s, '00	5.44	Apr-80	NR
Jul-84	Land Resources	cb sub deb 9.5s, '89	10.00	Jun-78	NR
Jul-84	Tomlinson Oil	cont int cs deb '95	12.60	Jul-83	CCC
Oct-84	Documation Inc	sr sub sf deb 11.5s, '98	11.60	May-78	B
Oct-84	Documation Inc	sr sub sf deb 12s, '99	16.30	May-79	B
Oct-84	Kenai Corp	sub sf deb 10.5s, '98	27.50	Aug-78	B
Oct-84	Storage Technology	nt 11.625s, '93	100.00	May-83	BBB
Oct-84	Storage Technology	cv sub deb 9s, '01	83.30	May-81	BB-
Oct-84	Transcontinental Energy	sub sf deb 12.878s, '98	5.44	Jun-78	B
Dec-84	North American Car	eqp tr cert 8.1s, '92	17.30	Sep-72	BBB

APPENDIX E *(continued)*

Dec-84	North American Car	sub deb 9.25s, '92	9.82	Nov-72	B
Dec-84	North American Car	eqp tr ctf 10.5s, '92	19.70	Jun-74	B

1985

Jan-85	American Quasar	sub sf deb 14s, '93	65.00	May-83	NR
Feb-85	Oak Industries	cv sub deb 10.5s, '02	100.00	Jan-82	BB-
Mar-85	Peninsula Resources	cv sub sf deb 12s, '95	7.13	Dec-80	B
Mar-85	Peninsula Resources	exch offer ser A&B v/r nt	7.80	Nov-83	NR
Apr-85	Hunt International Resources	sub sf deb 9.875s, 04	31.40	Feb-78	NR
Apr-85	Oxoco Inc	sub sf deb 15.75s, '93	25.00	Oct-82	CCC
May-85	Oxoco Inc	sr sub ex v/r nt, '89	40.00	Oct-84	B-
Jun-85	Punta Gorda Isles	cv sub deb 6s	15.00	May-72	NR
Jun-85	Sharon Steel	sub sf deb 14.25s, '99	60.00	Oct-79	BB
Aug-85	Beker Industries	sec sub sf deb 15.875s, '08	65.00	Jul-83	CCC
Aug-85	Buttes Gas & Oil	sr sub deb 16.5s, '94	35.00	Oct-84	CCC
Aug-85	Buttes Gas & Oil	sub sf deb 10.25s, '97	70.00	Aug-77	B
Aug-85	Global Marine	sr sub sf deb 12.375s, '98	25.00	Jul-78	B
Aug-85	Global Marine	cv 13s, '03	123.00	Feb-83	B-
Aug-85	Global Marine	sr sub sf deb 16s, '01	100.00	Sep-81	B+
Aug-85	Global Marine	sr sub sf deb 16.125s, '02	150.00	Mar-82	B+
Aug-85	Tacoma Boatbuilding	cv sub deb 10.75s, '01	13.10	Aug-81	B-
Sep-85	Macrodyne Industries	sr sub cv nt 10.875s	9.02	Nov-84	NR
Sep-85	Macrodyne Industries	cv sub deb 12.5s, '95	3.34	Oct-80	B
Oct-85	Brock Hotel	sub deb 12s, 93	44.50		
Nov-85	Eisinore Corp	sub sf deb 14s, '97	25.00	Jan-80	B
Nov-85	Eisinore Finance	sr mtg bonds 15.5s, '99	115.00	Nov-84	B+
Nov-85	Pettibone	cv sub deb 4.625s, '87	20.00	Aug-67	BB
Nov-85	Pettibone	sub sf deb 12.375s, '00	20.00	Sep-80	B
Dec-85	Delmed Insurance	sr cv sub deb 10.5s, '97	6.32	Nov-84	NR

APPENDIX E *(continued)*

Dec-85	Delmed Insurance	cv sub deb 10.5s, '02	7.88	Nov-82	CCC
Dec-85	Mission Insurance	sf deb 9s, '02	21.10	Dec-77	A-

1986

Jan-86	Argo Petroleum	sub sf deb 16.5s, '02	25.00	Jan-82	B-
Jan-86	ICO Inc	sr sub deb 13.5s, '94	30.00	Jan-84	CCC
Jan-86	Texscan	cv sub deb 8.5s, '03	40.00	Jun-83	B
Feb-86	Savin Corp	sub sf deb 14s, '00	40.00	Aug-80	B
Feb-86	Savin Corp	sub sf deb 11.375s, '98	58.70	Oct-78	B
Mar-86	Kenai Corporation	sr sub deb 11.5s, '89	23.90	Dec-84	NR
Mar-86	Kenai Corporation	sr sub deb 12.5s, '90	25.50	Dec-84	NR
Mar-86	Smith International	sf deb 9.85s, '04	75.00	May-79	A
Mar-86	Twole Manufacturing	cv 9.5s, '04	25.00	Oct-80	B
Apr-86	Crystal Oil	sub sf deb 12.625s, '01	26.30	Jun-82	B-
Apr-86	Crystal Oil	sub sf deb 13.75s, '00	12.40	Jul-80	B
Apr-86	Crystal Oil	sr sub sf deb 14.875s, '98	16.70	Dec-83	B-
Apr-86	Crystal Oil	sub sf deb 12.625s, '90	10.20	Jun-78	B
Apr-86	Crystal Oil	sr sub sc nt 15s, '95	125.00	Oct-85	CCC
Apr-86	Western Co NA	sub sf deb 10.7s, '98	18.30	Apr-78	B
Apr-86	Western Co NA	sub sf deb 10.875s, '97	15.50	Sep-77	B
May-86	Na-Churs Plant Food	sub deb 16s, '01	20.00	Aug-81	B-
Jun-86	American Adventure	sr sub nt 14.25s, '92			
Jun-86	American Adventure	cv sub deb 10s, '98	10.80		
Jun-86	Damson Oil	sub deb 12s, '03	40.00	May-83	B-
Jun-86	Damson Oil	zero cpn sub nt ser C	8.75	Aug-82	NR
Jun-86	Damson Oil	zero cpn sub nt ser D	2.80	Aug-82	NR
Jun-86	Damson Oil	sub deb 13.2s, '00	20.00	Aug-80	B
Jun-86	Diglicon Inc	cv sub deb 10.5s, '01	25.70		
Jun-86	Digicon Inc	sr sub nt 12.875s, '93	35.00	Jul-83	B

APPENDIX E *(continued)*

Jun-86	Digicon Finance NV	cv sub deb 8.5s, '95	18.00		
Jun-86	Ideal Basic Industries	sf deb 9.25s, '00	21.10	Jun-75	
Jul-86	ICO Inc	sr sub deb 13.5s, '94	30.00		
Jul-86	Jones & Laughlin	1st N 9.75s, '96	42.30	Sep-76	BBB
Jul-86	Jones & Laughlin	1st G 8s, '98	20.90	May-73	BBB
Jul-86	Jones & Laughlin	1st F 9.875s, '95	22.20	Apr-70	BB
Jul-86	Jones & Laughlin	sub sf deb 6.75s, '94	10.30	May-69	B
Jul-86	Jones & Laughlin	1st E 5s, '91	18.80	Feb-66	A
Jul-86	Jones & Laughlin Ind	sub sf deb 6.5s, '88	21.20		CCC
Jul-86	Jones & Laughlin Ind	sub deb 6.75s, '94	27.90	Jul-69	CCC
Jul-86	LTV Corp	sf deb 13.875s, '02	150.00	Dec-82	BB-
Jul-86	LTV Corp	sub nt 11.5s, '97	55.80	Dec-85	CCC
Jul-86	LTV Corp	sub nt 7.875s, '98	55.70	Dec-85	CCC
Jul-86	LTV Corp	sr nt 8.75s, '98	94.70	Oct-85	NR
Jul-86	LTV Corp	sub sf 14s, '04	133.00	Aug-84	BB-
Jul-86	LTV Corp	sub ex nt 9.5s, '95	100.00	Aug-84	CCC
Jul-86	LTV Corp	sf deb 9.25s, '97	54.30	Mar-77	B-
Jul-86	LTV Corp	sub sf deb 5s, '88	181.00	Jan-68	CCC
Jul-86	LTV Corp	sub sf deb 11s, '07	65.10	Jul-77	CCC
Jul-86	LTV Intl NV	cv 5s, '88	19.40		
Jul-86	Lykes	sub deb 7.5s, '94	28.30		
Jul-86	Lykes	sub sf 11s, '00	25.00	Jan-75	NR
Jul-86	Lykes	7.5s, '94	206.00	May-69	CCC
Jul-86	McLean Ind	sub deb 12s, '03	118.00	Aug-83	B-
Jul-86	McLean Ind	sub nt 14.25s, '94	125.00	Sep-84	B-
Jul-86	Republic	sf deb 4.375s, '85	9.84		
Jul-86	Republic	sf deb 8.9s, '95	56.80	Nov-70	A
Jul-86	Republic	sub sf deb 12.125s, '03	193.00	May-83	B
Jul-86	Republic	o/s eb 11.5s, '88	98.50	Jul-80	
Jul-86	Texas American Oil	sub sf deb 12s, '99	25.00	Aug-79	B+
Jul-86	Vought Corporation	sub sf deb 6.75s, '88	17.60		
Jul-86	Youngstown Sheet & Tubing	1st K 9.875s, '91	39.40	Jun-76	BBB
Jul-86	Youngstown Sheet & Tubing	1st J 10.5s, '00	24.00	Jul-70	A
Jul-86	Youngstown Sheet & Tubing	1st H 4.5s, '90	19.30	Nov-60	AA
Aug-86	Petro-Lewis	sub sf deb 12.25s, '98	24.00	Jul-78	B
Aug-86	Petro-Lewis	sr sub sf deb 12.625s, '03	34.00	Aug-81	B+
Aug-86	Frontier Air Lines	sub deb 5s, '87	5.27		

APPENDIX E *(continued)*

Aug-86	Frontier Air Lines	csd 6s, '92	3.82		
Aug-86	Frontier Holdings Inc	csd 10s, '07	22.50		
Aug-86	Petro-Lewis	sr sub nt 11.5s, '93	22.10	Feb-83	B
	Mission Insurance Group	nt 11.875s, '93	21.10	Jan-83	A
Sep-86	Zapata Corp	sub sf deb 10.25s, '97	41.50	Apr-77	B
Sep-86	Petro-Lewis	sr sub nt 15.25s, '92	103.00	Jun-85	CCC
Sep-86	Petro-Lewis	ext sub nt, '93	95.70	Jun-85	CCC
Oct-86	La Barge Inc	sub deb 14.5s, '93	20.00	Oct-83	B-
Oct-86	Page Petroleum	sr sub cv nt 11s, '89			
Oct-86	Page Petroleum	cv sub deb 10s, '00			
Nov-86	Wedtech	sr sub nt 14s, '96	75.00		
	Wedtech	cv 13s, '04	40.00		

1987*

Jan-87	Moran Energy	sub sf deb 11.5sa, '98	14.90	Jan-78	B
Jan-87	Westworld Comm Health	14.375s, '95	35.00		
Jan-87	Westworld Comm Health	14.375s, '00	30.00		
Jan-87	Petro-Lewis	fl rt sub deb 13s, '00	24.40	Jun-80	B
Jan-87	Petro-Lewis	sr sub nt 11.5s, '93	22.20	Sep-83	B
Mar-87	Spendthrift Farms	sr sub 12.5s, '94	30.00	Dec-84	NR
Apr-87	Getty Oil Intl NV	gtd euront 14s, '89	125.00	Apr-82	AAA
Apr-87	Michigan General	sr sub deb 10.75s, '98	110.00	Dec-83	CCC
Apr-87	Penril Corp	sr sub nt 10.875s, '93	18.00	Mar-83	B-
Apr-87	Texaco Cap Inc	nt 9s, '88	300.00	Nov-86	B
Apr-87	Texaco Cap Inc	gtd nt 13.625s, '94	500.00	Jul-84	AA-
Apr-87	Texaco Cap Inc	ext nt 13.25s, '99	500.00	Jun-84	AA-
Apr-87	Texaco Cap Inc	gtd nt 13s, '91	500.00	Aug-84	AA-
Apr-87	Texaco Cap Inc	gtd euront 11.25s, '95	250.00	Apr-85	A+
Apr-87	Texaco Cap Inc	nt 11s, '89	300.00	Aug-86	B
Apr-87	Texaco Cap Inc	gtd euront 10s, '95	300.00	Jul-85	A+
Apr-87	Texaco Cap Inc	gtd ext nt 11.25s, '00	300.00	Feb-85	A+
Apr-87	Texaco Cap Inc	ext nt 10.75s, '00	500.00	Ma6-84	AA
Apr-87	Texaco Cap Inc	gtd euront 10s, '90	250.00	Aug-85	A+
Apr-87	Texaco Cap NV	gtd euront 12.875s, '92	300.00	Aug-84	AA-
Apr-87	Texaco Cap NV	gtd euront 9.75s, '90	150.00	Apr-83	AA
Apr-87	Texaco Cap NV	gtd euront 10.5s, '93	200.00	Nov-83	AA

APPENDIX E *(continued)*

Apr-87	Texaco Cap NV	gtd euront 13.5s, '89	200.00	Jul-84	AA-
Apr-87	Texaco Cap NV	gtd euront 12.875s, '87	300.00	Aug-84	AA-
Apr-87	Texaco Cap NV	gtd euront 10.5s, '90	200.00	Nov-83	AA
Apr-87	Texaco Inc	deb 7.75s, '01	135.00	May-71	AAA
Apr-87	Texaco Inc	deb 8.5s, '06	160.00	Mar-76	AAA
Apr-87	Texaco Inc	deb 8.875s, '05	223.00	May-75	AAA
Apr-87	Texaco Inc	deb 5.75s, '97	76.00	Jul-67	AAA
May-87	MacLeod Stedman	mtg nt 15.5s, '91	30.00	Oct-84	B3
Jun-87	Amer Healthcare Mgt	sub deb 15s, '04	80.00	Dec-84	B
Jun-87	Todd Shipyards	sr sub nt 14s, '96	75.00	Aug-86	B-
Jun-87	Allis Chalmers	deb 6.1s, '90	5.90	May-65	BBB
Jul-87	Republic Health	sub deb 13s, '03	50.00	Jul-83	NR
Jul-87	Republic Health	sr deb 15s, '05	47.75	Dec-84	NR
Jul-87	Dart Drug Stores	sr sub deb 12.7s, '01	160.00	May-86	
Jul-87	Cardis Corp	sr sub deb 12.5s, '97	25.00	Jun-85	
Sep-87	Radice Corp	sub sf deb 14.625s, '04	35.00	Jan-84	B-
Sep-87	Condec Corp	sub deb 14.875s, '00	24.20	Oct-80	B
Oct-87	Republic Health	sub deb 13.5s, '04	100.00	Feb-84	NR
Oct-87	Pub Serv New Hamp	deb 14.375s, '91	100.00	Feb-83	B+
Oct-87	Pub Serv New Hamp	deb 15.75s, '88	75.00	Sep-82	BB-
Oct-87	Pub Serv New Hamp	deb 15s, '03	100.00	Jan-83	B+
Oct-87	Pub Serv New Hamp	deb 17.5s, '04	425.00	Jan-84	CCC
Oct-87	Condec Corp	sub deb 10s, '97	11.10	Mar-77	B
Nov-87	Western Union Telegraph	sf deb 7.9s, '97	38.20	Mar-72	BBB
Dec-87	Chas. P. Young Co	sr sub deb13.125s, '98	50.00	Nov-86	

1988*

Jan-88	Pub Serv New Hamp	1st M 4.625s, '92	20.90	Jan-62	
Jan-88	Pub Serv New Hamp	1st N 6.125s, '96	15.10	Jan-66	B
Jan-88	Pub Serv New Hamp	1st O 6.25s, '97	13.50	Jan-67	B
Jan-88	Pub Serv New Hamp	1st P 7.125s, '98	13.50	Jan-68	B
Jan-88	Pub Serv New Hamp	1st Q 9s, '00	18.30	Jan-70	B
Jan-88	Pub Serv New Hamp	1st R 7.625s, '02	18.40	Jan-72	B
Jan-88	Pub Serv New Hamp	1st S 9s, '04	18.70	Jan-74	B
Jan-88	Pub Serv New Hamp	1st V 9.125s, '06	14.30	Jan-76	B
Jan-88	Pub Serv New Hamp	gen ref B 12s, '99	60.00	Jan-79	B
Jan-88	Pub Serv New Hamp	gen ref C 14.5s, '00	30.00	Jan-80	B
Jan-88	Pub Serv New Hamp	gen ref D 17s, '90	23.00	Jan-80	B

APPENDIX E *(continued)*

Jan-88	Pub Serv New Hamp	gen ref E 18s, '89	50.00	Jan-82	B
Jan-88	Pub Serv New Hamp	3rd mtg A 13.75s, '96	225.00	Jan-86	B
Feb-88	Hamilton Technology Inc	sr sub deb 12.5s, '99	81.00	Jan-84	CCC
Feb-88	General Defense Corp	sub deb 13s, '95	57.50	Jan-85	CCC
Feb-88	General Defense Corp	sr sub deb 14.5s, '03	30.00	Jan-83	CCC
Feb-88	Care Enterprises Inc	sr sub nt 16s, '94	16.00	Jan-84	CCC
Feb-88	Alleghany International	sf deb 9s, '95	12.90	Jan-70	B
Feb-88	Alleghany International	sub deb 9s, '89	11.90	Jan-77	CCC
Feb-88	Alleghany International	sub deb 10.75s, '99	66.50	Jan-79	CCC
Feb-88	Alleghany International	sub deb 10.4s, '02	38.70	Jan-84	CCC
Feb-88	Alleghany Ludlum Ind	deb 9s, '95	13.00		B
Feb-88	Chemetron Corp	deb 9s, '94	19.00	Jan-69	CCC
Feb-88	Chemetron Corp	nt 8.735s, '97	88.15		CCC
Feb-88	Chemetron Corp	mtg rev bonds 7s, '94	88.15		CCC
Feb-88	Sunbeam Corp	deb 5.5s, '92	17.80	Jan-67	B
Feb-88	Sunbeam Corp	rev bonds 6.375s, '91	88.15		B
Feb-88	Sunbeam Corp	rev bonds 6.5s, '94	88.15		B
Feb-88	Anglo Energy Inc	2nd inc nt 15s, '93	82.00		CCC
Mar-88	Basix Corp	sub deb 11.625s, '03	20.00	Jan-83	CCC
Apr-88	Robert Bruce Ind	sub deb 16.5s, '97	17.30	Jan-85	CCC
Apr-88	Coleco Industries	sub deb 11.125s, '01	167.00	Jan-86	B
Apr-88	Coleco Industries	sub deb 14.375s, '02	60.50	Jan-82	B
Apr-88	First City Banc Texas	nt 13.25s, '92	50.00	Jan-82	B
Apr-88	First City Banc Texas	var rt sub nt 7.188s, '96	100.00		B
May-88	General Homes Corp	sub nt 15.5s, '95	50.00	Jan-85	B
May-88	General Homes Corp	sub nt 12.75s, '98	90.00	Jan-86	B
May-88	Cannon Group Inc	sub deb 8.875s, '01	80.50		B
May-88	Cannon Group Inc	sr sub deb 12.875s, '01	127.00	Jan-86	B
May-88	Cannon Group Inc	sr sub nt 12.375s, '94	60.09	Jan-84	B
May-88	Pope Evans & Robbins	sub deb 13.5s, '02	35.00	Jan-82	CCC
May-88	IFRB Corp	deb 9.75s, '99	26.00	Jan-74	B
May-88	IFRB Corp	nt 12.75s, '89	100.00	Jan-82	B
May-88	Interfirst Texas Finance NV	fl rt nt 6.75s	100.00	Jan-84	B
Jun-88	De Laurentiis Ent Group	sr sub nt 12.5s, '01	65.00	Jan-86	B
Jun-88	First RepublicBank Corp	deb 9.375s, '01	65.00	Jan-76	BBB
Jun-88	First RepublicBank Corp	fl rt nt 7.35s, '04	75.00	Jan-79	BBB

APPENDIX E *(continued)*

Jun-88	First RepublicBank Corp	nt 11.25s, '89	100.00	Jan-82	BBB
Jun-88	Revco	nt 12.15s, '95	50.00	Jan-85	B
Jun-88	Revco	sf 11.75s, '15	125.00	Jan-85	B
Jun-88	Revco	sr sub nt 13.125s, '94	400.00	Jan-86	B
Jun-88	Revco	sub nt 13.3s, '96	210.00	Jan-86	B
Jul-88	Clabir	sf sub deb 15.875s, '97	20.00	Jan-82	NR
Jul-88	Clabir	sub deb 14.5s, '04	14.60	Jan-84	CCC
Jul-88	ALC Communications	sub deb 10.875s, '95		Jan-84	
Aug-88	Geothermal Resources Intl	sub nt 13s, '91	17.00	Jan-84	B
Aug-88	Geothermal Resources Intl	sub nt 13.75s, '96	31.60	Jan-86	B
Sep-88	Financial Corp of America	sub sf deb 11.875s, '98	25.00	Jan-78	B
Sep-88	Financial Corp of America	sub deb 6s, '10	6.61	Jan-62	CCC
Sep-88	Texas American Bancshares	nt 15.5s, '92	50.00	Jan-82	BB
Oct-88	HealthCare USA	sr sub deb 10.875s, '98	20.00	Jan-83	
Oct-88	MCorp	sf deb 9.375s, '01	29.00	Jan-76	
Oct-88	MCorp	fl rt nt 7.9s, '99	35.00	Jan-79	
Oct-88	MCorp	nt 11.5s, '89	50.00	Jan-82	
Oct-88	MCorp	nt 10.625s, '93	25.00	Jan-83	
Oct-88	Maxicare Health Plans	sr sub nt 11.75s, '96	125.00	Jan-86	

1989*

Jan-89	Columbia S & L of Colo	sub nt 15.875s, '94	40.00	Nov-84	NR/NR
Jan-89	First Texas Savings Assn	var rt sub deb 11.99s, '91	65.00	Jun-84	NR/NR
	Commonwealth S & L Florida	sr sub deb 8s	18.00	Nov-85	NR/NR
Jan-89	Erty Industries	sub dep 12.5s	14.32	Dec-78	B2/B
Jan-89	Healthcare USA	sr dub deb 10.875s	20.00	Jul-83	Bd/B-
	Financial Corp of America	sr sub deb 11.875s	23.12	Jul-78	NR/BB
Feb-89	Financial Trustco Cap	sr sub deb 13.95s	60.00	Oct-85	B2/B+
Feb-89	Financial Trustco Cap	sub dep 15.875s	50.00	Oct-89	B2/B
Mar-89	Eastern Air Lines	2nd sec eqt ctf 17.25s,	200.00	Mar-81	NR/NR
Mar-89	Eastern Air Lines	sec eqt ctf A 17.5s	34.46	Jun-81	B3/CCC
Mar-89	Eastern Air Lines	sec eqt ctf B 17.5s	27.74	Jun-81	B3/CCC
Mar-89	Eastern Air Lines	3rd sec eqt ctf 13.75s	99.00	Nov-86	NR/NR
Mar-89	Eastern Air Lines	2nd sec eqt ctf 12.75s	192.83	Nov-86	NR/NR

APPENDIX E *(continued)*

Mar-89	Eastern Air Lines	1st sec eqt ctf 11.75s	189.93	Nov-86	NR/NR
Apr-89	American Continental	sr sub nt 14.75s	10.95	Apr-85	B3/NR
Apr-89	American Continental	nt 12s	25.80	Apr-89	NR/NR
Apr-89	American Continental	nt 10.75s	31.05	Aug-83	NR/NR
Jun-89	Gibralter Financial Cap	fl rt sub nt 12s	12.50	Nov-84	Ba3/B-
Jun-89	Gibralter Financial Cap	sr sub nt 13.875s	99.50	Dec-86	NR/NR
Jun-89	Benjamin Franklin Svngs	sr sub deb 15.375s	32.10	Dec-85	NR/NR
Jun-89	Integrated Resources	sr sub nt 13.125s	125.00	Jul-85	Ba2/ BBB-
Jun-89	Integrated Resources	nt 11.125s	57.50	May-87	Ba1/ BBB
Jun-89	Integrated Resources	sr sub nt 10.75s	299.00	Apr-96	Ba3/ BBB-
Jun-89	Integrated Resources	sr sub nt 12.25s	100.00	Aug-88	Ba3/ BBB-
Jun-89	Integrated Resources	nt 10s	104.00	May-87	Ba1/ BBB
Jun-89	Integrated Resources	sr sub nt 8.625s	63.35	Apr-87	B1/B+
Jun-89	Integrated Resources	nt 10.75s	50.00	May-87	Ba1/ BBB
Jun-89	Western S & L	sub cap nt 15.625s	115.00	Jun-85	NR/NR
Jul-89	San Antonio Savings	sr sub nt 14.75s	24.00	Jan-86	NR/NR
Jul-89	Southmark	nt 15.25s	58.00	May-84	B2/B+
Jul-89	Southmark	sr sub nt 13.25s	269.00	Jan-86	B1/BB-
Jul-89	Southmark	sr nt 11.5s	117.00	Oct-86	Ba3/ BB+
Jul-89	Southmark	sr nt 10.875s	125.00	Oct-86	Ba3/ BB+
Jul-89	Southmark	sr nt 11.875s	136.00	Oct-86	Ba3/ BB+
Jul-89	Southmark	sub nt 8.92s	39.00	May-84	B2/B+
Jul-89	AP Industries	sub dep 12.375s	95.00	Jun-86	B3/ CCC
Aug-89	Simplicity Hldngs	sr sub nt 14.5s	61.00		NR/NR
Aug-89	SCI Television	PIK 15.5s	249.00	Oct-87	B-
Aug-89	SCI Television	sub deb 16.5s	100.00	Oct-87	CCC+
Aug-89	SCI Television	PIK 17.5s	128.00	Oct-87	CCC+
Aug-89	Dart Drug	incr rt deb	106.00		B-
Aug-89	Dart Drug	sf deb 12.7s	28.60	May-86	B-
Aug-89	Zapata	sf deb 10.25s	41.50	Mar-77	B
Aug-89	Zapata	sf deb 10.875s	36.10		B
Aug-89	Seaman's Furniture	jr sub deb PIK 15s	85.15		C
Aug-89	Griffin Resorts	1st mtg nt 13.875s	200.00	Nov-88	B
Aug-89	Griffin Resorts	sr sec reset nt 13.5s	125.00	Nov-88	B
Aug-89	Resorts Intl Financing	sub deb 16.625s	200.00	Aug-84	B+
Aug-89	Resorts International	sub of deb 10s	95.10		BB
Aug-89	Resorts International	sub of deb 10s	75.00	Aug-79	BB

APPENDIX E *(continued)*

Aug-89	Resorts International	sub of deb 11.375s	230.00	May-83	BBB+
Aug-89	Service Control Corporation	sr sub deb 14s	100.00	Jul-88	CCC
Sep-89	Lomas Financial Corp	fl rt nt 10s, '89	60.00	1986	A
Sep-89	Lomas Financial Corp	fl rt nt 10s, '89	40.00	1986	A
Sep-89	Lomas Financial Corp	fl rt nt 10s, '98	45.90	1983	A
Sep-89	Lomas Financial Corp	sub nt 10.75s, '93	200.00	1988	BBB
Sep-89	Lomas Financial Corp	sub nt 11.375s, '95	175.00	1988	BBB
Sep-89	G-Acquisitions Corp	sub deb 13.375s	45.00		NR
Sep-89	American Building Co	sr extended nt 12s	19.00		NR
Sep-89	American Building Co	sr sub deb 13.375s	22.50		NR
Sep-89	Alpine Group	sr sub deb 13.5s	46.70		NR
Sep-89	Gibralter Financial Corp	sr sub deb 13.875s	99.50		NR
Sep-89	Leaseway Transportation	sub deb 13.25s	193.00		NR
Sep-89	AP Industries	sub dep 12.375s	88.00		NR
Sep-89	Fin Corp of Santa Barbara	sub deb 13.375s			NR
Sep-89	Fin Corp of Santa Barbara	sub deb 9s			NR
Sep-89	Quintex Entertainment	sr sec nt 12s	30.00		NR
Dec-89	Geothermal Resources	sub nt 13s, '91	15.00		NR
Dec-89	Geothermal Resources	sub deb 13.75s, '96	31.60		NR
Dec-89	U.S. Pipe, Jim W. Homes,	ser B sr extd rst int 14.625s	176.00	Jan-88	Ba3/NR
Dec-89	and Jim W. Resources	ser C sr extd rst int 14.5s	5.00	Jan-88	Ba3/NR
Dec-89	U.S. Pipe, Jim W. Homes	ser sub extd rst PIK nt 16.625s	444.00	Jan-88	B1/NR
Dec-89	U.S. Pipe, Jim W. Homes	sub nt 17s, '96	350.00	Jan-88	B2/NR
Dec-89	Jim Walter	sub nt 13.125s, '93	50.00	Jan-83	Ba2/BB-
Dec-89	Jim Walter	sub deb 13.75s, '03	100.00	Jan-83	Ba2/BB-
Dec-89	Jim Walter	sub deb 10.875s, '08	79.00	Apr-83	Ba2/BB-

*Convertibles excluded.

APPENDIX E *(continued)*

1990 (as of December 1, 1990)

Default/ Exchange Date	Company	Bond Issue	Out'g Amount ($mil)	Coupon (%)
Jan-90	(D) Linter Textiles	sr sub deb '00	200.00	13.750
Jan-90	(D) ALC Communications	sr sub deb '94	60.00	11.875
Jan-90	(D) Allied Stores	sr nts '92	200.00	10.500
Jan-90	(D) Allied Stores	nts '92	175.00	6.000
Jan-90	(D) Allied Stores	sr sub deb '97	700.00	11.500
Jan-90	(D) Federated Dept Stores	sf deb '95	27.50	8.375
Jan-90	(D) Federated Dept Stores	sf deb '02	42.50	7.125
Jan-90	(D) Federated Dept Stores	sf deb '10	200.00	10.250
Jan-90	(D) Federated Dept Stores	sf deb '13	100.00	10.625
Jan-90	(D) Federated Dept Stores	sf deb '16	100.00	9.500
Jan-90	(D) Federated Dept Stores	nts '92	200.00	9.375
Jan-90	(D) Federated Dept Stores	nts '96	200.00	7.875
Jan-90	(D) Federated Dept Stores	sr sub deb '00	500.00	16.000
Jan-90	(D) Federated Dept Stores	sub disc deb '04	583.00	0.000
Jan-90	(D) Service Control	sr sub deb '98	100.00	14.000
Jan-90	(D) Digicon	sr sub deb '94	12.00	12.000
Feb-90	(D) T G X Corp	sub deb '94	59.00	15.750
Feb-90	(D) Leaseway Transportation	sub deb '02	192.50	13.250
Feb-90	(E) Univision	sr sub disc nts '98	145.00	0.000
Feb-90	(E) Univision	sub deb '99	105.00	13.375
Mar-90	(D) Doskocil	sr sub deb '99	50.00	14.500
Mar-90	(D) Doskocil	sub notes '93	35.00	8.500
Mar-90	(D) CenTrust (Savings)	sub deb '2000	150.00	15.875
Mar-90	(D) Imperial Corp Amer	deb '97	100.00	12.400
Mar-90	(D) Community Newspapers Inc.	sr sub rst nts '97	125.00	12.000
Mar-90	(D) Community Newspapers Inc.	sub disc deb '97	114.00	0.000
Apr-90	(D) General Development	sub deb '05	175.00	12.625
Apr-90	(D) General Development	sr sub nts '95	126.00	12.875
Apr-90	(D) Ames Dept Stores	sr sub reset nts '99	200.00	13.000
Apr-90	(D) Circle K	sr sub deb '97	125.00	12.750
Jun-90	(D) Circle K	jr sub deb '97	71.90	13.000
Apr-90	(D) Motor Wheel Corp	sr sub nts '97	115.00	11.375
Apr-90	(D) Divi Hotels	sr debs '98	60.00	14.500
Apr-90	(D) Divi Hotels	sub nts '96	50.00	12.750
May-90	(E) Insilco	sr sub nts '99	270.00	15.000
May-90	(E) Insilco	sub disc nts '01	218.00	0.000
May-90	(D) Service America Corp	sub disc deb '99	131.70	0.000
May-90	(D) Greyhound Lines	sr nts '95	150.00	13.000
May-90	(D) Greyhound Lines	sr sub nts '97	75.00	12.500
Jun-90	(D) S.E. Nichols	1st sr sub deb '99	19.20	14.875
Jun-90	(D) S.E. Nichols	sr sub deb '00	10.00	15.000

APPENDIX E *(continued)*

Jun-90	(D) Salant Corp	sr sub ext rst nts '95	75.00	13.375
Jun-90	(D) Salant Corp	sr sub deb	28.40	13.250
Jun-90	(D) United Merchants & Mfrs	sub deb '00	116.00	13.750
Jun-90	(D) United Merchants & Mfrs	sub deb '04	55.00	15.000
Jun-90	(E) International Controls	sr sub deb '01	148.00	12.750
Jun-90	(E) International Controls	sub disc deb '06	206.00	0.000
Jul-90	(D) Starcraft	sr sub nts '98	25.00	16.500
Jul-90	(D) Edgell Communications	sr sub deb '00	100.00	14.000
Jul-90	(D) Southland Corp	sr ext rst nts '95	541.00	14.500
Jul-90	(D) Southland Corp	jr sub disc deb '07	71.00	0.000
Jul-90	(D) Southland Corp	sr sub disc nts '97	402.00	0.000
Jul-90	(D) Southland Corp	sub deb '02	500.00	16.750
Jul-90	(D) Southland Corp	sr sub nts '97	350.00	15.750
Jul-90	(D) Interco	sub disc deb '03	386.00	0.000
Jul-90	(D) Interco	sr sub deb '00	405.00	13.750
Jul-90	(D) Interco	jr PIK sub deb '03	237.00	0.000
Jul-90	(D) Western Union Corp	sr sec rst nts '92	500.00	19.250
Jul-90	(D) Western Union Corp	sub deb '97	14.50	10.750
Jul-90	(D) Western Union Tel	SF deb '92	7.96	5.000
Jul-90	(D) Western Union Tel	SF deb '96	8.06	8.450
Jul-90	(D) Western Union Tel	SF deb '97	5.02	7.900
Jul-90	(D) Western Union Tel	SF deb '98	7.70	8.100
Jul-90	(D) Western Union Tel	SF deb '08	30.00	13.250
Jul-90	(D) Western Union Tel	nts '91	32.80	16.000
Jul-90	(D) Western Union Tel	nts '94	6.33	13.625
Aug-90	(E) LVI Group	sr sub nts '98	36.80	13.500
Aug-90	(D) Gillett Holdings	sr sub deb '98	250.00	12.625
Aug-90	(D) Gillett Holdings	sub deb '99	170.00	13.875
Aug-90	(D) Gillett Holdings	sr nts ser A '92	75.00	0.000
Aug-90	(D) Gillett Holdings	sr nts ser B '93	66.00	0.000
Aug-90	(D) Gillett Holdings	sr nts ser C '94	58.00	0.000
Aug-90	(D) Gillett Holdings	sr nts ser D '92	72.50	0.000
Aug-90	(D) Gillett Holdings	sr nts ser E '94	84.40	0.000
Aug-90	(D) Forum Group	sr sub nts '93	17.50	10.000
Sep-90	(D) Tracor Inc	sr sub nt '98	230.00	14.000
Sep-90	(D) Tracor Inc	sub disc deb '00	228.00	0.000
Sep-90	(D) Weintraub Entertainment		81.00	13.000
Sep-90	(D) Darling-Delaware	sr sub nts '99	175.00	14.000
Sep-90	(D) Black Box Inc	incr rt nts	110.00	
Oct-90	(D) Aancor (Nat Gypsum)	sen deb '01	176.00	14.500
Oct-90	(D) Aancor (Nat Gypsum)	sub disc deb '04	573.00	0.000
Oct-90	(D) Aancor (Nat Gypsum)	pr sr sub nts '97	293.00	11.375
Oct-90	(D) Fairfield Communities	sr sub nts '92	46.00	
Oct-90	(D) Fairfield Communities	sub SF deb '97	26.00	
Oct-90	(D) Forstmann Textiles Inc	sr sub nts '99	100.00	14.750
Nov-90	(DE) Trump Taj Mahal Funding	1st A '98	675.00	14.000
Nov-90	(D) Harvard Industries	sr sub deb '98	200.00	14.500
Nov-90	(D) Days Inn of America	sr sub nts '93	744.00	11.250

APPENDIX E *(continued)*

Nov-90	(D) Bally's Grand, Inc	1st mtg nts '96	320.00	11.500
Nov-90	(D) Goldriver Finance Corp	1st 13.875 '97	118	13.875
Dec-90	(D) Continental Airlines	1st eq ctfs '92	99.00	10.000
Dec-90	(D) Continental Airlines	2nd eq ctfs '95	66.00	11.000
Dec-90	(D) Continental Airlines	3rd eq ctfs '99	18.00	11.375
Dec-90	(D) Continental Airlines	eq ctfs '95	87.00	11.750
Dec-90	(D) Continental Airlines	eq trust ctfs '99	58.00	12.500
Dec-90	(D) Continental Airlines	eq trust ctfs '96	104.00	12.125
Dec-90	(D) Continental Airlines	eq trust ctfs '95	13.00	14.000
Dec-90	(D) Continental Airlines	eq trust ctfs '99	7.50	14.750
Dec-90	(D) Continental Airlines	sr FTR SF nts '96	38.00	
Dec-90	(D) Continental Airlines	eq trust ctfs '96	12.00	14.375
Dec-90	(D) Continental Airlines	nts '01	113.00	10.000
Dec-90	(D) Continental Airlines	nts '06	38.00	10.500
Dec-90	(D) Continental Airlines	sr nts '97	171.00	11.500
Dec-90	(D) Continental Airlines	sub deb '96	12.00	11.000
Dec-90	(D) Continental Air Holding	sr nts '92	66.00	15.750
Dec-90	(D) Continental Air Holding	sr ext rt nts '90	28.00	14.375
Dec-90	(D) Continental Air Holding	sr nts '93	53.00	14.250
Dec-90	(D) Continental Air Holding	sr nts '95	41.00	14.900

APPENDIX F

Companies in Chapter 11 Reorganization and in Default*
Whose Securities Were Traded as of June 1, 1990

1	After Six	46	Darling-Delaware Co, Inc
2	ALC Communications	47	Dart Drug Stores
3	Allegheny Beverage	48	Delmed Inc
4	Allegheny International	49	Digicon Inc.
5	Allied Stores	50	Divi Hotel NV
6	Alpine Group	51	Doskocil
7	AmBrit Inc	52	Eastern Air Lines
8	American Capital	53	Eckerd (Jack) Corp
9	American Century Corp	54	ECL Industries
10	American Continental	55	Equitec Financial Group
11	American Healthcare Management	56	Fairfield Acceptance
12	American Healthcare Management	57	Farley Inc
13	Ames Dept Stores	58	Federated Dept. Stores
14	Ampex Group	59	First Republic Bank
15	Amphenol Corp	60	Forum Group
16	Anacomp	61	General Development
17	AP Industries	62	General Homes
18	APL Corp	63	Geothermal Res Intl.
19	Argo Petroleum	64	Global Marine
20	Aris Corp	65	Greyhound Lines, Inc
21	Associated Inns Resorts	66	Griffin Resorts
22	Bank of New England	67	Gulf Mobile & Ohio
23	Basix Corp	68	G-Acquisition
24	Bay Financial	69	Halmi (Robert) Inc
25	Blair (John) & Co	70	Health Resources Cp. Amer.
26	Bond Brewing	71	Healthcare International
27	Calton Inc	72	Hunt Intl. Resources
28	Care Enterprises	73	Ideal Basic Industries
29	CBT Corp	74	IFRB Corporation
30	CenTrust (Savings)	75	Imperial Corp Amer
31	Charter Medical Corp	76	Ingersoll Newspapers
32	Chemetron Corp.	77	Integrated Resources
33	Cherokee Group	78	Intelogic Trace
34	Circle Express	79	Int'l Controls
35	Circle K	80	Jim Walter
36	Clabir Corp.	81	Jones & Laughlin Ind
37	Coleco Industries	82	JPS Textile Group
38	Consolidated Oil & Gas	83	Kane Industries
39	Continental Health Affil	84	Kay Jewelers, Inc

APPENDIX F *(continued)*

40 Continental Homes Hldgs
41 Continental Info Systems
42 Crowthers Mc Call
43 Curtis Industries
44 Daisy Systems
45 Damson Oil
91 LTV Corp.
92 Lykes Corp.
94 MCorp
95 Miramar Marine
96 Mission Insurance Group
97 Missouri Pacific RR
98 Monon R.R.
99 Moran Energy
100 Morningstar Food
101 MS/Essex Holdings
102 M.D.C. Holdings
103 NBI Inc.
104 New American Shoe
105 Nichols (S.E)
106 Northern Pacific
107 NVF Co
108 Oak Industries
109 Olympic Broadcasting
110 PALCO Acquisition Co
111 PCPI Funding
112 Penril Corp
113 Ply-Gem Industries
114 Polycast Technology
115 Public Service NH
116 Publicker Industries
117 Qintex Entertainment
118 Rapid-American Corp
119 Raytec
120 Republic Steel Corp.
121 Resorts International
122 Resorts Intl Financing
123 Revco
124 ROPS Textiles, Inc.
125 Saint Louis-San Fran Ry

85 Koch (R.N.), Inc
86 Koor Industries
87 K-H Corp
88 Leaseway Transportation
89 Leisure Technology
90 Lomas Financial Corp.
126 Savin Corp.
127 SCI Holdings
128 SCI Television
129 Service Control
130 Sharon Steel
131 Sheller-Globe Corp
132 Simplicity Holdings
133 Southland Corp
134 Southmark Corp.
135 SPI Holding Group
136 Sterling Banc
137 Sunbeam Corp.
138 Swan Brewery
139 Telecom Corp
140 Texas Amer. Banc.
141 Texas International
142 Thackeray Corp.
143 Thousand Trails
144 Todd Shipyards
145 Tracor Inc
146 Tridex
147 Unimax Holdings
148 Union Valley Corp
149 United Merch & Mfrs
150 Univision
151 URS Corp
152 US Home Corp
153 Vought Corp.
154 Western Union Corp
155 Western Union Telegraph
156 Westwood Group
157 Wheeling Pittsburgh Steel
158 Youngstown Sheet & Tube
159 Zapata Corp.

*Includes coupon bonds of distressed companies trading flat.

APPENDIX G

Trade Debt Purchasers
Active Buyers of Troubled Company Trade Debt

Amroc Investments
(212)418-6050
New York
Officers: Mark Lasry, Managing Partner; Phillip Schaefer, Managing Partner
Current Bids: Eastern Airlines, LTV, Revco
Cowen & Company
(212)495-6000
New York
Group/Division: Corporate Reorganization Finance
Officers: Steven Selbst, Senior VP, Director of Corporate Reorganization Finance; Na
Tavakoli, Senior VP
Current Bids: Allegheny International (Sunbeam), Coleco, Eastern Airlines, LTV, Rev
Wheeling Pittsburgh
Oppenheimer
(212)667-7000
New York
Group/Division: Oppenheimer High Yield
Officer: Jon Bauer, Senior VP
Current Bids: Allegheny International, Eastern Airlines, Lomas, LTV, Revco, Southma
Wheeling Pittsburgh
T. Rowe Price
(301)547-2000
Baltimore
Group/Division: T. Rowe Price Recovery Fund
Officers: David Breazzano, President; Herbert Stiles, VP
Current Bids: Would not disclose.
Seidler Amdec
(213)489-2260
Los Angeles
Group/Division: Reorganized Finance Group
Officers: Paul D. Debban, Managing Director; Chriss Street, Managing Director
Current Bids: Allegheny International, Eastern Airlines, Ideal Basic, LTV, Revco, Sou
mark, Wheeling Pittsburgh
R.D. Smith
(212)952-8100
New York
Group/Division: Smith Factors, Inc.
Officer: Joseph Alia, Manager of Special Projects
Current Bids: Eastern Airlines, LTV, Revco, Wheeling Pittsburgh

Source: *Turnarounds & Workouts,* December 15, 1989.

APPENDIX H

Securities Comprising
The Defaulted Debt Index
(In Order of Appearance, 1986-1990)

COMPANY	BOND	AMT. OUT ($mil)
Hunt Intl. Resources	Sub SF DEB 9.875 '04	31.400
Oxoco Inc.	Sr. Sub v/r NT 10.89 '89	25.000
Oxoco Inc.	Sub SF DEB 15.75 '92	40.000
Sharon Steel	Sub SF DEB 14.25 '99	60.000
Beker Industries	Sec. Sub SF DEB 15.875 '03	65.000
Buttes Gas & Oil	Sr. Sub DEB 16.50 '94	35.000
Buttes Gas & Oil	Sub SF DEB 10.25 '97	70.000
Global Marine Inc.	Sr. Sub SF DEB 12.375 '98	25.000
Global Marine Inc.	Sr. Sub SF DEB 16 '01	100.000
Global Marine Inc.	Sr. Sub SF DEB 16.125 '02	150.000
Elsinore Corp.	Sub SF DEB 14 '97	25.000
Elsinore Finance	Sr. Mtg. 15.50 '99	115.000
Pettibone Corp.	Sub SF DEB 12.375 '00	20.000
Mission Insurance Group	SF DEB 9 '02	21.100
Charter Co.	Sub SF DEB 10.625 '98	46.100
Charter Co.	Sub SF DEB 14.75 '02	60.000
Emons Inds. Inc.	Eq. Tr. CTFS. Ser 11.45 '94	22.900
Storage Technology	NTS 11.625 '93	100.000
North American Car Corp.	Eq. Tr. 8.10 '92	17.300
North American Car Corp.	Eq. Tr. 10.50 '94	19.700
North American Car Corp.	Sub SF DEB 9.25 '92	9.820
Anglo Co. Inc.	Gtd. Sub SF DEB 11.875 '98	17.500
Baldwin United Corp.	Sub SF DEB 10.00 '09	16.200
Argo Petroleum	Sub SF DEB 16.50 '02	25.000
Savin Corp.	Sub SF DEB 11.375 '98	4.650
Savin Corp.	Sub SF DEB 14 '00	4.110
Kenai Corp.	Sr. Sub DEB 11.5 '89	23.900
Kenai Corp.	Sr. Sub DEB 12.5 '90	25.500
Smith International	SF DEB 9.85 '04	75.000
Crystal Oil	Sr. Sub SF DEB 14.875 '98	16.400
Crystal Oil	Sr. Sub Sec NTS 15 '95	125.000
Crystal Oil	Sub SF DEB 12.675 '90	7.720
Crystal Oil	Sub SF DEB 13.75 '00	12.700
Crystal Oil	Sub SF DEB 12.675 '01	26.300
Western Co. NA	Sub SF DEB 10.875 '97	12.800
Western Co. NA	Sub SF DEB 10.70 '98	18.200
Digicon Inc.	Sr. Sub NTS 12.875 '93	35.000
Damson Oil	Sub SF DEB 13.20 '00	20.000
Damson Oil	Sub SF DEB 12 '03	40.000
Damson Oil	Sub Nt C Zero Cpn '86	8.750

APPENDIX H *(continued)*

Ideal Basic Industries	SF DEB 9.25 '00	21.100
LTV Corp.	SF DEB 9.25 '97	26.700
LTV Corp.	SF DEB 13.875 '02	36.000
LTV Corp.	SF DEB 14 '04	133.000
LTV Corp.	Sub SF DEB 5 '88	131.000
LTV Corp.	Sub SF DEB 11 '07	62.000
LTV Corp.	SubEx v/r Nt 9.5 '95	100.000
LTV Corp.	Sr v/r Nt 8.75 '98	94.700
LTV Corp.	Sub v/r Nt 11.5 '97	50.800
LTV Corp.	Sub v/r Nt 7.875 '98	55.700
McLean Inds.	Sub Deb 12 '03	118.000
McLean Inds.	Sub Nts 14.25 '94	125.000
Republic Steel Corp.	SF DEB 8.9 '95	49.900
Republic Steel Corp.	Sub SF DEB 12.125 '03	193.000
Texas American Oil	Sub SF DEB 12 '99	25.000
Jones & Laughlin Steel	1st E 5 '91	18.800
Jones & Laughlin Steel	1st F 9.875 '95	2.200
Jones & Laughlin Steel	1st G 8 '98	20.900
Jones & Laughlin Steel	1st N 9.75 '96	42.300
Jones & Laughlin Steel	Sub SF DEB 6.75 '94	10.300
Yongstown Sheet & Tube	1st H 4.5 '90	15.700
Youngstown Sheet & Tube	1st J 10.5 '00	20.900
Youngstown Sheet & Tube	1st K 9.875 '91	32.200
Lykes Corp.	Sub DEB 7.5 '94	94.600
Lykes Corp.	Sub SF DEB 11 '00	25.000
Vought Corp.	Sub SF DEB 6.75 '88	17.600
ICO Inc.	Sr. Sub DEB 13.5 '94	30.000
Petro-Lewis Corp.	Sr. Sub Nts. 11.5 '93	22.100
Petro-Lewis Corp.	Sr. Sub SF DEB 12.625 '03	65.000
Petro-Lewis Corp.	Sub SF DEB 12.25 '98	24.000
Petro-Lewis Corp.	Extd Sub Nts. 13.75 '93	27.000
Petro-Lewis Corp.	Sr. Sub Nts. 15.25 '92	106.000
Zapata Corp.	Sub SF DEB 10.25 '97	41.500
LaBarge Inc.	Sub DEB 14.5 '93	20.000
Wedtech Corp.	Sr. Sub Nts. 14 '96	75.000
Moran Energy	Sub SF DEB 11.5 '98	14.900
Spendthrift Farm	Sr. Sub DEB 12.5 '94	30.000
Michigan General	Sr. Sub DEB 10.75 '98	110.000
Penril Corp.	Sr. Sub Nts. 10.875 '93	18.000
Texaco Inc.	SF DEB 5.75 '97	76.000
Texaco Inc.	SF DEB 7.75 '01	135.000
Texaco Inc.	SF DEB 7.875 '05	298.000
Texaco Inc.	SF DEB 8.5 '06	298.000
Texaco Capital	Extd Nt 13.25 '87	500.000
Texaco Capital	Extd Nt 10.75 '88	500.000
Texaco Capital	Extd Nt 11.25 '89	300.000
Texaco Capital	Nts 9 '88	300.000
Texaco Capital	Nts 11 '89	300.000

APPENDIX H *(continued)*

Texaco Capital	Nts 13 '91	500.000
Texaco Capital	Nts 13.625 '94	500.000
Amer. Healthcare Mgmt.	Sub Nt '04 15 '94	80.000
Todd Shipyards	Sr. Sub Nts 14 '96	75.000
Allis-Chalmers Corp.	SF DEB 6.10 '90	5.900
Republic Health	Sr. Sub DEB 15 '05	50.000
Republic Health	Sr. SF DEB 13 '03	50.000
Republic Health	Sr. SF DEB 13.5 '04	100.000
Radice Corp.	Sub SF DEB 14.625 '04	35.000
Condec Corp.	Sub SF DEB 10 '97	10.800
Condec Corp.	Sub SF DEB 14.875 '00	22.900
Public Service NH	DEB 14.375 '91	100.000
Public Service NH	DEB 15.75 '88	75.000
Public Service NH	DEB 15.0 '03	100.000
Public Service NH	DEB 17.5 '04	425.000
Western Union Telegraph	SF DEB 7.90 '97	38.200
Public Service NH	1st M 4.625 '92	20.900
Public Service NH	1st N 6.125 '96	15.100
Public Service NH	1st O 6.25 '97	13.500
Public Service NH	1st P 7.125 '98	13.500
Public Service NH	1st Q 9.0 '00	18.300
Public Service NH	1st R 7.625 '02	18.400
Public Service NH	1st S 9.0 '04	18.700
Public Service NH	1stV 9.125 '06	14.300
Public Service NH	GenRefB 12 '99	60.000
Public Service NH	GenRefC 14.5 '00	30.000
Public Service NH	GenRefD 17.0 '90	23.000
Public Service NH	GenRefE 18.0 '89	50.000
Hamilton Technology	Sr. Sub DEB 12.5 '99	70.000
General Defense Corp.	Sr. Sub DEB 13 '95	57.500
General Defense Corp.	Sr. Sub DEB 14.5 '03	30.000
Care Engerprises	Sr. Sub Nts 16.0 '94	16.000
Allegheny International	SF DEB 9 '95	12.900
Allegheny International	Sub SF DEB 9 '89	11.900
Allegheny International	Sub SF DEB 10.75 '99	66.500
Allegheny International	Sub SF DEB 10.40 '02	38.700
Chemetron Corp.	SF DEB 9.0 '94	17.200
Sunbeam Corp.	SF DEB 5.5 '92	17.800
Basix Corp.	Sub DEB 11.625 '03	20.000
Coleco Industries	Sub SF DEB 11.125 '01	167.000
Coleco Industries	Sub SF DEB 14.375 '02	60.500
General Homes	Sub Nts 15.5 '95	50.000
General Homes	Sub Nts 12.75s'98	100.000
Cannon Group Inc.	Sr. Sub DEB 12.875 '01	110.000
Pope, Evans & Robbins	Sub SF DEB 13.5 '02	35.000
IFRB Corporation	SF DEB 9.75 '99	26.000
IFRB Corporation	Nts 12.75 '89	100.000
De Laurentiis Entmt	Sr Sub Nts 12.5 '01	65.000

APPENDIX H *(continued)*

First Republic Bank	SF DEB 9.375 '01	65.000
First Republic Bank	Nts 11.25 '89	100.000
First Republic Bank	F/R Nts 7.35 '04	75.000
Revco	SF DEB 11.75 '15	125.000
Revco	Nts 11.125 '95	50.000
Clabir Corp.	Sub DEB 14.5 '04	15.000
Geothermal Res Intl.	Sub Nts 13 '91	17.000
Geothermal Res Intl.	Sub Nts 13.75 '96	31.600
Financial Corp. America	Sr. Sub SF DEB 11.875 '98	25.000
Financial Corp. America	Inc DEB A 6 '10	6.610
Financial Corp. America	SF DEB 6 '88	5.330
Texas Amer. Bankshares	Nts 15.5 '92	50.000
Healthcare USA	Sr. Sub DEB 10.875 '98	20.000
MCorp	SF DEB 9.375 '01	29.000
MCorp	F/R Nt 7.9 '99	35.000
MCorp	Nts 11.5 '89	50.000
MCorp	Nts 11.5 '92	49.000
MCorp	Nts 10.625 '93	25.000
Maxicare Health Plans	Sr. Sub Nts 11.75 '96	125.000
Eastern Air Lines	Sec Eq Ctf A 17.5 '98	39.000
Eastern Air Lines	Sec Eq Ctf B 17.5 '97	41.900
Eastern Air Lines	1st Pr Sec Eq Ctf 11.75 '93	200.000
Eastern Air Lines	2nd Pr Sec Eq Ctf 12.75 '96	200.000
Eastern Air Lines	3rd Pr Sec Eq Ctf 13.74 '01	100.000
American Continental	Sr. Nts 10.75 '90	125.000
American Continental	Sr. Sub Nts 14.75 '95	11.000
Integrated Resources	Sr. Nts 10 '90	104.000
Integrated Resources	Sr. Nts 10.75 '92	50.000
Integrated Resources	Sr. Nts 11.125 '94	57.500
Integrated Resources	Sr. Sub DEB 8.625 '97	85.000
Integrated Resources	Sr. Sub Nts 13.125 '95	125.000
Integrated Resources	Sr. Sub Nts 10.75 '96	297.000
Integrated Resources	Sr. Sub Nts 12.25 '98	100.000
Southmark Corp.	Sr. Nts 10.875 '89	125.000
Southmark Corp.	Sr. Nts 11.5 '91	140.000
Southmark Corp.	Sr. Nts 11.875 '93	150.000
Southmark Corp.	Sr. Sub Nts 13.25 '94	341.000
Southmark Corp.	Sub Nt 15.25 '91	65.700
AP Industries	Sub DEB 12.375 '01	95.000
SCI Television	Sr. Extd Nts. 15.5 '90	200.000
SCI Television	Sr. Sub DEB 16.5 '97	100.000
SCI Television	Sub DEB 17.5 '99	100.000
Dart Drug Stores	Incr Rt F/R DEB 6.0 '92	106.000
Dart Drug Stores	SF DEB 12.70 '01	28.600
Griffin Resorts	1st Mtg Nts 13.875 '98	200.000
Griffin Resorts	Sr. Sec Reset Nts 13.5s'95	125.000
Resorts Intl Financing	Sub DEB 16.625 '04	200.000
Resorts International	Sub SF DEB 10 '98	95.100

APPENDIX H *(continued)*

Resorts International	Sub SF DEB 10 '99	75.000
Resorts International	Sub SF DEB 11.375 '13	230.000
Service Control Corp.	Sr. Sub V/R DEB 14 '00	100.000
Lomas Financial Corp.	F/R Nts '89	60.000
Lomas Financial Corp.	F/R Nts '89	40.000
Lomas Financial Corp.	F/R Nts '98	45.900
Lomas Financial Corp.	Sub Nts 10.75 '93	200.000
Lomas Financial Corp.	Sub Nts 11.375 '95	175.000
Alpine Group	Sr. Sub DEB 13.5 '96	43.700
Leaseway Transportation	Sub DEB 13.25 '02	193.000
Allied Stores	Sr. Nts '92	200.00
Allied Stores	Nts '92	175.00
Allied Stores	Sr Sub Deb '97	700.00
Federated Dept. Stores	SF Deb '95	12.50
Federated Dept. Stores	SF Deb '02	32.50
Federated Dept. Stores	SF Deb '10	39.70
Federated Dept. Stores	SF Deb '13	13.90
Federated Dept. Stores	SF Deb '16	100.00
Federated Dept. Stores	Nts '92	200.00
Federated Dept. Stores	Nts '96	200.00
Federated Dept. Stores	Sr Sub Deb '00	500.00
Federated Dept. Stores	Sub Disc Deb '04	329.00
Miramar Marine	Sr Sub Reset Nts '98	125.00
Univision	Sr Sub Disc Nts '98 '0's	138.00
Univision	Sub Deb '99	105.00
Doskocil	Sr Sub Deb '99	57.50
Doskocil	Sub Notes '93	35.00
CenTrust (Savings)	Sub Deb '2000	150.00
CenTrust (Savings)	Flt Rate Note	100.00
Imperial Corp Amer	Deb '97	80.50
Service Control	Snr Sub Deb '98	100.00
General Development	Sub Deb '05	175.00
General Development	Sr Sub Nts '95	126.00
Ames Dept Stores	Sr Sub Reset Nts '99	200.00
Ames Dept Stores	Sub SF Deb '95	1.91
Circle K	Sr Sub Deb '97	125.00
Circle K	Jr Sub Deb '97	71.90
Linter Textiles	Sr Sub Deb '00	200.00
Motor Wheel Corporate	Sr Sub Nts '97	100.00
Greyhound Lines, Inc.	Sr Nts '95	150.000
Total Amount Outstanding		20,132,800

APPENDIX I

Investment Banking Boutiques
Firms Providing Financial Advisory Services to Troubled Companies

Chilmark Partners
Chicago, IL
Officer: David M. Schulte, Manager Partner
Recent Debtor Clients and Officers Involved in Deals:

Revco:	Joel S. Friedland, David J. Rosen
Ideal Basic:	David M. Schulte, Joel S. Friedland, David W. Anderson
Horsham D.S.:	John C. Haeckel, David J. Rosen

Gordian Group
New York, NY
Officers: Henry Owlsley, Patricia Caldwell
Recent Debtor Clients and Officers Involved in Deals:

Liquor Barn:	Henry Owlsley
Thortec International:	Henry Owlsley
Dest Corporation:	Henry Owlsley
Domain Technology:	Henry Owlsley

HLHZ Capital Corporation
Los Angeles, CA
Officers: Jeff Warbalowsky (LA), Irwin Gold (LA), Don Smith (NY), Rick Bail (Chicago), Jim Cigelski (San Francisco)
Recent Debtor Clients and Officers Involved in Deals:

Care Enterprises:	Jeff Warbalowsky, Irwin Gold
Allegheny International:	Don Smith
Aca Joe:	Jim Cigelski, Jeff Warbalowsky

Japonica Partners
New York, NY
Officer: Michael G. Lederman
Recent Debtor Clients and Officers Involved in Deals:

Allegheny International:	Michael G. Lederman
C&W:	Paul B. Kazarian

McFarland Dewey & Company
New York, NY
Officers: Alan R. McFarland, Thomas Dewey, Benjamin W. McCleary, Thomas Bryson, John Finnerty
Recent Debtor Clients and Officers Involved in Deals:
The Firm was recently formed. Prior debtor clients handled by the McFarland Dewey officers include: Dome Petroleum and Charter Co.

Seidler Amdec Securities Group
Los Angeles, CA
Officers: Paul D. Debban, Chriss W. Street
Recent Debtor Clients and Officers Involved in Deals:

APPENDIX I *(continued)*

LTV: Paul D. Debban, Chriss W. Street
Revco: Paul D. Debban, Chriss W. Street
Maxicare: Paul D. Debban, Chriss W. Street
Lomas: Paul D. Debban, Chriss W. Street

Whitman, Hefferman and Rhein

New York, NY

Officers: Martin J. Whitman, James O. Hefferman, C. Kirk Rhein, Jr.
Recent Debtor Clients and Officers Involved in Deals:
Circle Express: James P. Hefferman
Hauserman: John Mueler
Neloors Industries: James P. Hefferman

APPENDIX J

The Largest Bankruptcy Law Firms

| Firm | Bankruptcy Attys | | Partners | Clients |
	Total	Part-ners		
Weil, Gotshal & Manges New York	100	25	Harvey R. Miller	Texaco (debtor) G.E. Credit Corp. Prudential Insurance Co.
Skadden, Arps, Slate, Meagher & Flom New York	66	12	Michael L. Cook Blaine V. Fogg	A.H. Robins (debtor) N.Y. Life (in Kaiser Steel) First Fidelity Bank
Latham & Watkins Los Angeles	55	12	Robert J. Rosenberg Michael S. Lurey Ronald W. Hanson	Citicorp First National Bank of Chicago AmeriTrust Co.
Gendel, Raskoff, Shapiro & Quittner Los Angeles	39	17	Bernard Shapiro Arnold M. Quittner Herbert Katz	Wickes Inc. (debtor) Baldwin-United (creditors committee) Smith International (creditors committee)
Sheinfeld, Maley & Kay Houston	31	17	Myron M. Sheinfeld Robert C. Maley, Jr. Joel P. Kay	Buttes Oil & Gas Co. (debtor) First Interstate Bank of Dallas Global Marine (creditors committee)
Sidley & Austin Chicago	36	15	H. Bruce Bernstein A. Bruce Schimberg J. Ronald Trost	Smith International (debtor) Brooks Fashions (creditors committee) Citicorp
Stroock & Stroock & Lavan New York	38	15	Lawrence M. Handelsman Ronald L. Leibow Scott L. Baena	LTV (creditors committee) Wheeling-Pittsburgh (creditors committee) R.D. Smith & Co.
Murphy, Weir & Butler	34	17	Patrick A. Murphy William J. A. Weir	G.E. Credit Corp. Bank of America

APPENDIX J *(continued)*

San Francisco			Penn Ayers Butler	The First National Bank of Chicago
Stutman, Treister & Glatt Los Angeles	30	20	Herman L. Glatt	Pennzoil (in Texaco) Storage Technology (debtor) Public Service of New Hampshire (debtor)
Buchalter, Nemer, Fields & Younger Los Angeles	31	9	Ronald E. Gordon Stephen F. Biegenzahn Robert E. Izmirian	Bank of America TreeSweet Products Co. (debtor) Mossian Ins.
Danning, Gill, Gould, Diamond & Spector Los Angeles	29	10	David A. Gill David Gould Steven M. Spector	Bank of America Oasis Petroleum (Ch. 11 trustee) Attorneys Office Management (debtor)
Jones, Day, Reavis & Pogue Cleveland	35	11	David G. Heiman Marc S. Kirschner Henry L. Gompf	Allied Federated Resorts Int'l. Manufacturers Hanover/CIT Group
Hertzberg, Jacob and Weingarten Detroit	21	12	Stuart E. Hertzberg Barbara Rom	Wickes (creditors committee) Wilson Foods (creditors committee) American Monitor (creditors committee)
Sulmeyer, Kupetz, Baumann & Rothman Los Angeles	21	9	Irving Sulmeyer Arnold L. Kupetz Richard G. Baumann	Knudsen (debtor) Transamerica G.E. Credit Corp.
Zalkin, Rodin & Goodman New York (21)	21	10	Henry Lewis Goodman Richard S. Toder Robert H. Scheibe	
Shea & Gould New York	16	5	Herman Bursky Lonn Trost	Manufacturers Hanover/CIT Group Carey Transportation (debtor) Intrepid Sea Museum (debtor)
Mayer, Brown & Platt Chicago	18	9	Milton L. Fisher J. Robert Stoll Harold L. Kaplan	Continental Bank Canadian Imperial Bank of Commerce FDIC
Streich, Lang, Weeks & Cardon	26	5	John Dawson Susan Boswell	M&R Investment Co. G.E. Pension Trust

APPENDIX J *(continued)*

Phoenix				First Interstate Bank of Arizona
Winston & Strawn Chicago	18	8	Gerald F. Munitz Lewis S. Rosenbloom Norman H. Nachman	Pettibone Corp. (debtor) Kroh Brothers Development (debtor) Continental Illinois
Daris Polk & Wardell New York	25	8	Stephen H. Case Donald Bernstein	Lomas LTV Manville
Fullbright & Jaworski Houston	31	8	John L. King Evelyn H. Blery	Travelers Ins. Crystal Oil Bank of America
Sheinfeld, Maley & Kay Houston	31	17	Myron M. Sheinfeld Joel P. Kay	Battes Oil & Gas National Bank of Canada Global Marine (creditors)
Mayer, Brown & Platt Chicago	30	13	Milton Fisher J. Robert Stoll Harold Kaplan	Bank of Nova Scotia Continental Bank FDIC
Sheppard, Mullin, Richter & Hampton Los Angeles	30	10	Merrill Francis Joel Ohlgren Prentice O'Leary	Sec. Pacific N.B. Wells Fargo Bank CIT Group

Source: Turnarounds & Workouts, March 15, 1988 (updated Feb. 1, 1990).

APPENDIX K

Bankruptcy Tax Specialists in the Largest Law Firms

Firm	Home Office	# of Bankruptcy Specialists (from 2/1/90 ranking)	Tax Partners
Blank, Rome, Comisky & McCauley	Philadelphia	31	Edwin A. Easton (Philadelphia; Harry T. Lamb (Philadelphia)
Buchalter, Nemer, Fields & Younger	Los Angeles	31	Philip J. Wolman (LA)
Danning, Gill, Gould, Diamond & Spector	Los Angeles	29	Unavailable
Davis Polk & Wardwell	New York	35	Car Ferguson (NY); Michael Rollyson (DC); Sam Dimon (DC); Richard Fabbro (NY); Leslie Hoffman (NY)
Duane, Morris & Hecksher	Philadelphia	25	Sheldon M. Bonovitz (Philadelphia)
Fulbright & Jaworski	Houston	31	William Caudill (Houston); Robert H. Wellen (DC)
Gendel, Raskoff, Shapiro & Quittner	Los Angeles	39	Outside Firms
Jones, Day, Reavis & Pogue	Cleveland	35	John L. Sterling (Cleveland); Carl Jenks (Cleveland); Barry Cass (NY); Dan Kusnetz (NY)
Laiham & Watkins	Los Angeles	55	Irvin Salem (NY); John Clair (LA); Steven Bowen (Chicago)
Mayer, Brown & Platt	Chicago	30	Timothy C. Sherck (Chicago); Fred M. Ackerson (Chicago)
Milbank, Tweed, Hadley & McCloy	New York	38	Robert A. Jacobs (NY); Simon Friedman (NY); Susan Halpern (NY); Lewis Karvist (NY)
Murphy, Weir & Butler	San Francisco	34	Outside Firms
Pepper, Hamilton & Scheetz	Philadelphia	23	Michael E. Freeland (Philadelphia); Lisa B. Petkun (Philadelphia)
Shea & Gould	New York	16	Richard Halperin (NY); Steven Mastbaum (NY)
Sheinfeld, Maley & Kay	Houston	31	George R. Nelson (Houston)
Sheppard, Mullin, Richter & Hampton	New York	30	Michael Fernhoff (LA); Robert Joe Hull (LA); John R. Bonn (SD)
Sidley & Austin	Los Angeles	36	Robert J. Frei (Chicago); John P. Simon (Chicago)

APPENDIX K *(continued)*

Shearman & Sterling	Chicago	60	Robert A. Bergquist (NY); Thomas J. Carlson (NY)
Streich, Lang, Weeks & Cardon	Phoenix	26	Fred Witt (Phoenix); David Weiss (Phoenix)
Strook & Strook & Lavan	New York	38	Charles Hochman (NY); Jeffrey Uffner (NY); Micah Bloomfield (NY); Gerald Mehlnem (LA)
Slutman, Triester & Glatt	Los Angeles	30	Kenneth Klee (LA)
Weil, Gotshal & Manges	New York	91	Gordon Henderson (NY); Martin Pollack (NY); Stuart Goldring (NY); Paul Asofsky (Houston)

Source: *Turnarounds & Workouts*, March 1, 1990, p. 7.

APPENDIX L

Bankruptcy Tax Specialists in the Largest Accounting Firms

Name of Firm	# of Bankruptcy Specialists Firm-Wide	Tax Partners In Firm	City
Arthur Andersen & Co.	Would not disclose	Paul Sheahen	NY
		John O'Neill	NY
BDO/Seidman	Would not disclose	Would not disclose	NY
Coopers & Lybrand	25 partners, 200 staff	Jack Crestol	NY
Deloitte & Touche	20 Partners	Howard Sniderman	Pittsburgh
		Molly Gallagher	Pittsburgh
		John Price	LA
		Richard Boysen	Dallas
Ernst & Young	100	Richard Reichler	NY
		Jacob Blank	NY
		Ken Malek	Chicago
Grant Thornton	No bankruptcy group	Thomas Bottiglieri	NY
Laventhol & Horwath	16	Michael Costello	NY
Kenneth Leventhal & Co.	8	Jerry Josezef	NY
		Steven Schaeffer	NY
McGladrey & Pullen	Would not disclose	Dennis Craven	Iowa City
		Diane McNulty	Mason City
		Linda Klemme	Sterling, CO
			Dallas
Pannell Kerr Forster	15-17	J. James Jenkins	LA
		Bruce Baltin	San Francisco
		Patrick Quek	
KPMG Peat Marwick	28	Gilbert Bloom	Washington, DC
		Paul Govert	Chicago
		Don Mason	Fort Worth
Price Waterhouse	9 Partners, 15 staff	Dominic DiNapoli	NY
Spicer & Oppenheim	12	Jack Solomon	NY
		Murray Schwartzberg	NY

Source: *Turnarounds & Workouts*, March 15, 1990, p. 7.

APPENDIX M

Bankruptcy Departments of the National Accounting Firms

Firm	Total	Partners Bankruptcy	Bankruptcy Partners in Charge	Representative Clients
Arthur Andersen Chicago	2405	8	Barry M. Monheit/ New York	debtor in Revco
			Tom Allison/Chicago	debtor in Greyhound unsecureds in Federated
BDO/Seidman Grand Rapids, MI	1600		Jack Weisbaum/ New York	
			Gerald D'Amato/ New York	
			William Lenhart/ New York	
Coopers & Lybrand New York	1270	25	Seymour Jones/ New York	unsecureds in Revco
			Joseph Giordano/ New York	unsecureds in Allis-Chalmers unsecureds in Kaiser Steel
Deloitte & Touche New York	1700	15	Daniel Gruber/ New York	unsecured in LTV debtor in Amdura debtor in Gen'l Dev. Corp.
Ernst & Young New York	2200	20	Warren Petraglia/ New York	LTV
			Kevin J. McDermott/ New York	Integrated Resources Ames Department Stores
Grant Thornton New York	330	"Not Determin- able"	Dom Esposito/ New York	"Less than one percent of our business"
			Thomas Bottiglieri/ New York	
Laventhol & Horwath Philadelphia	435	25	Stuart A. Gollin/ New York	debtor in Wedtech unsecureds in Zenith Lab unsecureds in Bretano's
Kenneth Leventhal & Co.	70	31	Kenneth Leventhal/ Los Angeles	Donald Trump

APPENDIX M *(continued)*

Los Angeles			Stan Ross/ Los Angeles	NVD
			Terry Gilbert/Los Angeles	
McGladrey & Pullen Des Moines, IA	375	5	Alan W. Anderson /Bloomington, MN	"Works primarily with creditors on
			Darwin M. Voltin/ Bloomington, MN	a very confidential basis"
Pannell Kerr Forster New York	130	17	Jim Jenkins/Dallas	declined
			Edward Nickels/Boston	
			Kenneth Guidry/ Houston	
KPMG Peat Marwick New York	1933		Robert Swartz/ New York	unsecureds in Todd Shipyard
			Dennis J. Taura/ New York	debtor in U.S. Lines
			Martha W. Flynn/ New York	unsecureds in Smith Int'l
Price Waterhouse New York	870	9	Peter J. Gibbons/Philadelphia	equity holders in LTV
			Dominic Dinapoli/ New York	unsecureds in Heck's
			Donald Thomas/Dallas	
Spicer & Oppenheim New York	97	12	Richard Holmes/Dallas	unsecureds in LTV
			Bernard Augen/ New York	unsec. in Chas. A. Stevens
				unsecureds in Salant

Firms are listed in alphabetical order. Source: T & W database/research and
Turnarounds & Workouts, September 15, 1990, p. 7.

APPENDIX N

The Asset Recovery Units of the Largest U.S. Commercial Banks

Rank	Bank	Assets ($Billion)*	Senior Officer/Department	Non-Performing Portfolios Domestic ($Million)**
1.	Citibank NA New York	154.4	Nancy Teachout, VP Recovery Management	5,906
2.	Chase Manhattan Bank NA New York	82.5	Jeffrey Sell, Senior VP Special Loan Administration	3,453
3.	Bank of America NT&SA San Francisco	81.3	Frank Somers, Senior VP Special Assets	3,250
4.	Morgan Guaranty Trust Co. New York	67.0	Albert B. Gordon, VP Special Loan Department	1,651
5.	Manufacturers Hanover Trust Co. New York	59.4	John B. Belisle, Senior VP Special Loan Group	2,655
6.	Chemical Bank New York	59.3	Lavillon M. Martyr, VP Asset Management	2,055
7.	Bankers Trust Co. New York	54.4	A. Whitman Marshand, Senior VP Special Loan Department	1,218
8.	Security Pacific National Bank Los Angeles	44.4	Sherman White, Exec. VP Special Assets Department	1,373
9.	Wells Fargo Bank NA San Francisco	41.3	P. Steven Dobel, Senior VP Loan Adjustment/Special Situations	1,137
10.	First National Bank Chicago	35.4	Michael Kohn, VP Commercial Asset Management Harold Pletcher, VP Real Estate Asset Management	850
11.	Continental Illinois Nat'l Bank & Trust Co. Chicago	31.8	Daniel W. Persinger, Senior VP Special Asset Administration	763
12.	First National Bank Boston	25.1	Dennis J. Duckett, Division Executive Asset Recovery	862
13.	Bank of New York New York	21.1	Robert Gardella, Senior VP Credit Division	421

APPENDIX N *(continued)*

14.	Mellon Bank NA Pittsburgh	21.0	Richard H. Daniel, Vice Chairman Credit Recovery	825
15.	Marine Midland Bank NA Buffalo, NY	20.9	Gary Fowler, VP and District Manager Asset Based Lending Department	791
16.	Irving Trust Co. New York	20.4	John Baldwin, VP Special Asset Recovery	449
17.	First Interstate Bank of California Los Angeles	19.6	Sal Abeyta Jr., VP Special Credits	473
18.	First Republic Bank Dallas NA Dallas	19.4	James R. Erwin, President Special Asset Bank	2,970
19.	Republic National Bank New York	18.8	Ralph E. Spiegel, Senior VP Credit Department	94
20.	First Bank NA Minneapolis	17.8	Richard L. Shepley, Executive VP Credit Policy	504
21.	First Union National Bank Charlotte	16.1	Joseph M. Mayhew, VP Credit Standards	48
22.	NCNB National Bank of North Carolina Charlotte	16.0	Fred J. Figge, Executive VP Credit Policy	144
23.	Pittsburgh National Bank Pittsburgh	15.7	Robert J. Miller, VP Special Loan Administration	272
24.	National Bank of Detroit Detroit	14.8	Gerald L. Harvey, First VP Risk Assets Group	46
25.	Bank of New England NA Boston	13.3	Stephen D. Steinour, Senior VP Controlled Loans	281

*as of 12/31/87; source: *American Banker and Turnarounds & Workouts*, December, 1, 1988, p. 7.
**as of 3/31/88; source: Sheshunoff Information Services.

APPENDIX O

Nation's Largest Commercial/Industrial Auctioneers
Firms With More Than $20 Million in Auction Sales for the Year Ending December
31, 1989

Rank	Name of Firm	Commercial/ Industrial Sales Volume for the 1989 Calendar Year	Contact	Recent Representative Clients
1.	Ritchie Brothers Brighton, CO	$500 million	Brian Wannop	Unavailable
2.	Miller and Miller Fort Worth, TX	$125 million	William M. Miller	Haliburton Exxon FDIC
3.	First Team Auction Americus, GA	$117 million	Grant Stepp	Bechtel Caterpillar Dealers Southern Co.
4.	Hudson and Marshall Macon, GA	$95 million	Tom Webb	FDIC Mineral Land Co. SBA
4.	Norman Levy Associates Southfield, MI	$95 million	Lew Nucian	AT&T UNISYS Chrysler
5.	Taylor and Martin Freemont, NE	$80 million	Haines Hill	"Too numerous to mention"
6.	Superior Auctioneers San Antonio, TX	$65.8 million	Daniel Kruse	Continental Illinois Bank FDIC First Interstate Bank of TX
7.	Continental Plants Chicago, IL	$60 million	Cary Goldberg	International Telephone and Telegraph Inland Steel Armco Steel
8.	Max Rouse and Sons Beverly Hills, CA	$57.4 million	Harold Rouse	Kaiser Steel Weyerhauser Sunbelt Mining
9.	Vilsmeier Auction Co., Inc. Montgomeryville, PA	$50 million	Walter Vilsmeier	Glasgow, Inc. Pennsylvania Power and Light Niagra Mohawk Power Corp.

APPENDIX O *(continued)*

10.	Blackmon Auctions Little Rock AR	$42 million	Thomas Blackmon	Southwestern Bell International Paper Company Union Pacific Railroad
11.	Ross-Dove Co. San Mateo, CA	$41 million	Ross Dove	Unavailable
12.	Albin Auctioneers Lincoln, NE	$40 million	Rick Albin	FDIC Norwest Leasing Weaver Construction
13.	Plant and Machinery, Inc. Houston, TX	$39 million	Ronald Moore	General Motors USX Corp. Armco, Inc.
14.	Kaufman-Lasman Associates Chicago, IL	$35 million	Joseph Milek	Freddie Mac Trans Ohio S&L First City Bancorporation of Texas
15.	Michael Fox Auctioneers Baltimore, MD	$34 million	William Fox	Proctor & Gamble Black and Decker General Electric
16.	Nelson International Auctioneers Dallas, TX	$21.4 million	James Short	Chase Manhattan Leasing Company Peabody Coal Company The CIT Group, Industrial Financing
17.	Industrial Plants Corporation Northbrook, IL	$20 million	Daniel Herz	Black & Webster, Inc. So Good Potato Chip Co. Weaver Corp.
17.	Rene Bates Auctioneers McKinney, TX	$20 million	Rene Bates Susan Bates	City of Dallas Arkansas Power and Light Corp. City of Mobile, AL

Source: *Turnarounds & Workouts*, May 1, 1990

APPENDIX P

Regional and Local Bankruptcy Accounting Firms

Name of Firm	Bankruptcy Partners	Total Partners	Contact
Bederson & Company (West Orange, CA)	2	6	Edward P. Bond
Canby Maloney & Co. (Framingham, MA)	0	4	Anthony Anchukaitis
Cohen & Rogozinski (Allentown, PA)	1	4	Howard S. Cohen
Concannon Gallagher Miller & Co. (Allentown, PA)	0	14	Robert M. Caster
Finn Wishengrad Warnke Gayton (Wellesley Hills, MA)	3	3	Joseph F. Finn Jr.
Gerald T. Reilly & Company (Milton, MA)	4	6	Anthony P. Smeriglio
Goldstein Golub Kessler & Co. (New York, New York)	2	28	Ronald F. Ries
Jay Alix & Associates (Southfield, MI)	6	6	Jay Alix
Kafoury Armstrong & Company (Reno, NV)	1	22	Leroy R. Bergstrom
Kaplan & Swicker (Encino, CA)	1	1	Arthur R. Swicker
Litzler Segner Wolfe (Dallas, TX)	3	3	John H. Litzler
Lowry & Co. (San Antonio, TX)	1	3	James Zacaggni
Mauldin & Jenkins (Albany, NY)	1	19	William W. Kidd
Miller Newlin & Co. (Houston, TX)	2	8	John A. Miller
Miller Tate & Co. (Philadelphia, PA)	3	3	George L. Miller
Mortenson Fleming Grizzeti (Cranford, NJ)	3	15	H. Charles Hess
Moss Adams (San Francisco, CA)	2	68	Gene E. Harrison
Padgett Stratemann & Co. (San Antonio, TX)	2	9	D. Frank Bohman
Philip Rootberg & Co. (Chicago, IL)	1	14	Scott Peltz

APPENDIX P *(continued)*

Sol Schwartz & Associates (San Antonio, TX)	1	3	Sol Schwartz
Stephen I Soble & Co. (New York, New York)	3	5	Stephen I. Soble
Sugarman & Co. (San Francisco, CA)	3	5	Randy Sugarman
Toback & Co. (Phoenix, AZ)	2	13	Timothy J. Gay
Tsakopulos Brown & Co. (San Antonio, TX)	1	3	Jim Tsakopulos
Zolfo Cooper & Co. (New York, New York)	3	3	Frank Zolfo

Source: T & W database and *Turnarounds & Workouts,* October 2, 1990.

APPENDIX Q

Nation's Largest Crisis Management Firms

Yr. Founded	Company	Contact	City
1981	Jay Alix & Associates	Jay Alix	Southfield, MI
	Alvarez & Marsal	Antonio Alvarez	New York, NY
1969	Argus Management	David J. Ferrari	Natick, MA
1978	Bahr International	C. Charles Bahr	Dallas, TX
1981	Buccino & Associates	Gerald P. Buccino	Chicago, IL
1982	Bunker Hill Associates, Inc.	Michael Fowler	Houston, TX
1984	The Caslin Group	Michael Caslin III	Tiverton, RI
1973	Claymore International	William A. Jeffreys	New York, NY
1974	Conway & Youngman	Carl Youngman	Wilmington, MA
1982	Conway MacKenzie & Dunleavy	Van Conway	Birmingham, MI
1976	Development Specialists Inc.	William A. Brandt Jr.	Chicago, IL
1986	The Finley Group	Tim Finley	Dallas, TX
1985	Glass & Associates	Kenneth Glass	Canton, OH
1972	Grisanti, Galef & Goldress	Jerry Goldress	Los Angeles, CA
1983	Kibel Green	Harvey Kibel	Los Angeles, CA
1980	Kurt Salmon & Associates	David Linch	Atlanta, GA
1983	The LEK Partnership	James Lawrence	Boston, MA
1977	Locke Venture Management	E.L. Walsh	Lake Forest, IL
1981	Management Partners	Robert Jenkins	Atherton, CA
1980	Morris-Anderson & Associates	Daniel Morris	Glenview, IL
1975	Nightingale & Associates Inc.	William J. Nightingale	New Canaan, CT
1970	The Palmieri Company	John Koskinen	Washington, DC
1986	R.G. Quintero & Co.	Ronald Quintero	New York, NY
1989	Sigoloff & Associates	Sanford Sigoloff	Santa Monica, CA
1982	Sternco, Inc.	Douglas E. Coy	Minneapolis, MN
1981	Walquist & Associates	Ron Walquist	Portland, OR

Firms with six or more project managers are listed above in alphabetical order. Data compiled from *T&W* industry-wide survey. Some firms which did not return the survey may not appear on the list.

Source: *Turnarounds & Workouts,* August 15, 1990.

APPENDIX R

Canadian Bankruptcy Professionals
Who's Who in the Major Banks and Accounting Firms

Firm	Canadian Bankruptcy Professionals	Senior Officer Insolvency Group	Recent Representative Clients
Arthur Andersen Toronto, Ontario	32 partners, 55 managers	Melvin C. Zwaig, Partner, Financial Reorganization	
Coopers and Lybrand Toronto, Ontario	150 partners	Robert Lowe, President	
Deloitte and Touche Toronto, Ontario	150 partners professionals	Jim Morrison, President	Bank of Nova Scotia Royal Bank of Canada Toronto Dominion Bank
Ernst and Young Toronto, Ontario	130 partners	Harold Stevens, President	Air Toronto Canada Leasing (receivership) Oddessy International
Peat Marwick Thorne Toronto, Ontario	300 partners, professionals	Gary Colter, Chairman	
Price Waterhouse Toronto, Ontario	22 partners	Garth McGirr, President	Canadian Commercial Bank Massey Combine Pension Plan

Bank	Senior Officer Commercial Loan Workouts	Senior Officer Real Estate Workouts
The Bank of Montreal Toronto, Ontario	John Graham, VP, Commercial Banking	J.W. Stoddert, Sr. Account Mgr., Real Estate
The Bank of Nova Scotia Toronto, Ontario	E.D. Macnevin, Sr. VP, Commercial Credit	R.W. Hale-Sanders, Sr. VP, Real Estate
Canadian Imperial Bank of Commerce Toronto, Ontario	Paul Farrar, Sr. VP, Special Loans Div.	Paul Farrar, Sr. VP, Special Loans
National Bank of Canada Toronto, Ontario	Ian Cook, Sr. Manager, Commercial Lending	Jim Dysart, VP, Real Estate
The Royal Bank of Canada Toronto, Ontario/ Montreal, Quebec	Terry McDermid, Sr. Exec. VP, Special Loans	Terry McDermid, Sr. Exec. VP, Special Loans

APPENDIX R *(continued)*

Toronto Dominion Bank Toronto, Ontario	Chris Griffin, Accountant Manager, Commercial Banking	Ronald Ruest, Sr. VP, Real Estate

Source:*Turnarounds & Workouts*, June 1, 1990.

APPENDIX S

Bankruptcy Lending Departments of Major Financial Institutions
Debtor-In-Possession Financiers
Sources of Funds in Excess of $10 million

Capital Research Partners *(Westport, CT)*
Name of Bankruptcy Lending Group: Capital Research Partners
Group Officers and titles: Thomas A. Romero (Managing Partner)
Types of Loans Offered: Debtor in Possession, Equity, Senior Debt

Chemical Bank *(New York)*
Name of Bankruptcy Lending Group: Restructuring/Reorganization Group
(within Corporate Finance)
Group Officer and title: Darla Moore (Managing Director)
Type of Loans Offered: Debtor in Possession Financing, Reorganization Plan Financing,
Buyout Financing

CIT Group/Business Credit Inc. (subsidiary of Manufacturers Hanover Trust, Inc.)
(New York)
Name of Bankruptcy Lending Group: Financial Restructuring Group
Group Officers and titles: Mitchell Drucker (VP), Victor Russo (VP), David Weinstein (VP)
Types of Loans Offered: Turnaround Financing, Exchange Offer Financing, Confirmation
Financing, Debtor in Possession Financing

Citicorp *(New York)*
Name of Bankruptcy Lending Group: Restructuring Group
Group Officers and titles: Ann Lane (VP-Debt Head), Bruce Cantania (VP), Michael D.
Browne (VP)
Types of Loans Officered: Debtor in Possession Facilities

Congress Financial *(New York)*
Group Officer and title: Robert Steckel (VP)
Types of Loans Offered: Debtor in Possession: Leveraged Buyout, Debt Restructuring (all
asset-based)

Foothill Capital *(Los Angeles)*
Name of Bankruptcy Lending Group: Foothill Capital Corp.
Group Officers and titles: Peter E. Schaub (President), Scott R. Piehl (VP, Mkt. Mgr.)
Types of Loans Offered: Debtor in Possession, Revolving Credit, Secured Loans

J.P. Morgan *(New York)*
Name of Bankruptcy Lending Group: Restructuring Group
Group Officers and Titles: Robert Kiss (VP), Pamela Wilson (VP)
Types of Loans Offered: Debtor in Possession, Recapitalization, Debt and Equity

Mellon Bank *(Pittsburgh)*
Name of Bankruptcy Lending Group: Special Assets Department
Group Officer: Lou Zircher (Sr. VP)
Types of Loans Offered: Debtor in Possession

APPENDIX S *(continued)*

National Westminster Bank *(New York)*
Name of Bankruptcy Lending Group: National Westminster USA Credit Corporation
Group Officers and titles: Louis Rubin (President)
Types of Loans Offered|: Debtor in Possession, Re-leverage buyout, Restructuring

Source: Turnaround & Workouts, December 1, 1990.

Index

Printed in the United States
84803LV00003B/49-66/A